Living Wisely and Well in the Evening of Life

ALSO BY DUNCAN S. FERGUSON

Biblical Hermeneutics: An Introduction

Making the Bible Your Book: Content and Interpretation

Lovescapes: Mapping the Geography of Love

The Radical Teachings of Jesus: A Teacher Full of Grace and Truth

The Radical Invitation of Jesus: How Accepting the Invitation of Jesus Can Lead to Living Faith and Fulfilling Life for Today

New Age Spirituality: An Assessment (as editor)

Called to Teach: The Vocation of the Presbyterian Educator
with William J. Weston

Mindful Spirituality: The Intentional Cultivation of the Spiritual Life: A Book of Daily Readings

Traces of Transcendence: The Heart of the Spiritual Quest

The Teachers of Spiritual Wisdom: Gaining Perspective on Life's Perplexing Questions with Mary Petrina Boyd and Jamal Rahman

Living Wisely and Well in the Evening of Life

Foundations for Flourishing: A Spiritual Perspective

DUNCAN S. FERGUSON

WIPF & STOCK · Eugene, Oregon

LIVING WISELY AND WELL IN THE EVENING OF LIFE
Foundations for Flourishing

Copyright © 2024 Duncan S. Ferguson. All rights reserved. Except for brief quotations in critical publications or reviews, no part of this book may be reproduced in any manner without prior written permission from the publisher. Write: Permissions, Wipf and Stock Publishers, 199 W. 8th Ave., Suite 3, Eugene, OR 97401.

Wipf & Stock
An Imprint of Wipf and Stock Publishers
199 W. 8th Ave., Suite 3
Eugene, OR 97401

www.wipfandstock.com

PAPERBACK ISBN: 979-8-3852-0908-8
HARDCOVER ISBN: 979-8-3852-0909-5
EBOOK ISBN: 979-8-3852-0910-1

03/25/24

The Bible quotations are taken from the New Revised Standard Version published by Thomas Nelson Publishers, Nashville, TN, 1989.

With special gratitude to Dr. Susan Marie Smith who gave wise counsel for the content and character of the book.

"In the evening of life, we will be judged by love alone."
St. John of the Cross

Contents

	Introduction	ix
1	Living Wisely and Well	1
2	A Way Forward	17

SECTION ONE | MAINTAINING A THOUGHTFUL AND CREDIBLE FAITH IN THE MATURE YEARS

3	Faith as the Dedicated and Continuing Quest for Truth	37
4	Faith as the Deep and Abiding Trust in Divine Wisdom	54
5	Faith as the On-Going Commitment to the Divine Mission	71

SECTION TWO | SUSTAINING HOPE ACROSS THE YEARS

6	Hope as the Attitude and Spirit of Gratitude	91
7	Hope as the Quest for Justice and Peace	108
8	Hope as Living a Joyful Life in God's Presence	123

SECTION THREE | PRACTICING LOVE IN THE EVENING OF LIFE

9	The Love that Cares and Is Compassionate	145
10	The Love of Others and the Community of Faith	161
11	The Love that Seeks Justice and Healing for All Who Suffer	178
12	Conclusion: A Still More Excellent Way	197
	Bibliography	209

Introduction

> "And the Word became flesh and lived among us. . .full of grace and truth."
>
> (JOHN 1:14)

ACROSS THE YEARS OF service in the church and in institutions of higher education, I have often been asked to reflect upon and speak about how the life and teaching of Jesus might inform and guide those who face the task of living with dignity and purpose in their settings and in the larger context of a world in crisis. I have done so in a variety of ways and roles, some as one serving in a pastoral role in local congregations and even more in my years of service in higher education as a professor and administrator where the reflections took a slightly different turn. The church and the academy have different cultures and each one invited carefully nuanced reflections on how the one "full of grace and truth" might guide people of faith to live in a world filled with severe challenges.[1] As time passed, I was often invited to provide guidance for those who were facing the challenges of living wisely and well in the "evening of life." How was it possible to flourish in this phase of life? I decided to explore in some depth some possible answers to this question.

---

1. See my recent article in the Princeton Theological Seminary journal, "How Then Shall We Live?," 18–28.

CHAPTER ONE

Living Wisely and Well

> "So, all the generations from Abraham to David are fourteen generations, and from David to the deportation to Babylon, fourteen generations, and from the deportation to Babylon to the Messiah, fourteen generations."
>
> (MATTHEW 1:17)

BECAUSE OF THE CHALLENGE of this current writing project and my current age, I have been doing a great deal of self-reflection on the contours and dimensions of living wisely and well in the evening of life. As I look back and trace the various pathways that guided me into the present, I find myself profoundly grateful for all of the blessings that have come my way, although there has been an equal number of challenges. This process is full of memories, some gratifying and others full of questions and some sadness. I find that I have a mixture of emotions with some full of joy and yet other emotions that reveal some lingering pain and regret. Just recently, I was contacted about the decline of a person who had been very dear to me in my university years as a student and in my early career. We went our separate ways, now over fifty years ago. Although there was no consistent communication across the years, I still cared deeply about her and hoped that her evening years would be happy and joyful. But that was not the way it was to be. Not long ago, I was contacted by her sister and informed that my friend was slipping toward dementia and had severe and debilitating arthritis. Of course, as I reflected on the sister's call, I remembered those early years with that person, hiking in the great Northwest, swimming and water skiing on beautiful lakes, and discovering new dimensions of life during the university and seminary student years and early professional life. The age range between twenty-one and thirty-one were relatively good years for me in many ways, although there was an edge of sadness.

Following the call, I did visit my friend who had moved to a nearby city, and she revealed her fears about her current state. She looked at me and expressed regrets that she did not find a life mate who gave her love and support across the years, implying that I might have been the one who could have given her this comfort. Her illnesses had made her much smaller than when I had known her as a close friend. She was full of pain, a bit forgetful, and sad. In just a few weeks after our conversation, she passed away. I thought of my health and happiness, my deep gratitude for all that I have, and, my own life mate with whom I have shared deep love and support across the years. When I compare the joy in my own life with my friend in those earlier years, I feel sad at the disparity. I grieved when I learned that this one for whom I cared had slipped into eternity. Her evening of life was difficult and full of pain. I could only hope in my grief that there might be more for her in the beyond.

I have pondered at length on the several dimensions of my feelings about and my understanding of this evening phase of life. I write out of the deep experiences of joy and sadness, the study of this phase of life in current literature, and what I observe in my daily interactions and conversations with people who are in their sunset years. I have learned that there are several ways of understanding this period of life. Initially, I want to underline that these years are indeed a different phase of life,[1] although I have been careful not to make the descriptive category of stages of life an absolute and consistent pattern that is universal for all of humankind. The research suggests that there is great diversity in describing age-related patterns or stages, and I will use a variety of terms as they are appropriate to the context of my writing. I will reference historical and cultural influences that shape human development as well.

I have struggled some with categories and inclusive terms to use for the patterns and modes of being in this phase, calling it "the evening

---

1. I have reviewed the work of the developmental psychologists currently working and writing as well as those of an earlier foundational period such as Sigmund Freud, Carl Jung, Carol Gilligan, Lawrence Kohlberg, and Jean Piaget, each informing us about stages of development. James Fowler and Erik Erikson have been especially helpful in their work stages of life and faith development. I value this understanding. There are also study centers researching this phase of life, such as the Stanford center with the title of Distinguished Careers Center.

of life," wanting the language to be accurate, relatively inclusive, and describe a foundational way of "having it together" in order to flourish in the sunset years. Another term, often used to describe this phase of life, is the "golden years"; I am a bit cautious about using this term to describe these years because it is a bit vague and these years may not always be golden. Even the term, mature years, although suggesting the aging process, may not describe those in this phase of life who are not fully mature in the developmental process, but have reached retirement age.

There are developmental phases in our lives, and also a generational context that has influenced our identity. There are names given to generations such as the Greatest Generation (b. 1901–24) suggested by Tom Brokaw, an NBC newscaster. It was this generation, which faced all the challenges of the Second World War, which did so with great wisdom, courage, and persistence. Other generations have also received a label, and they include the Silent Generation (b. 1925–45), the Baby Boomers (b. 1946–64), Gen X (1965—79), Millennials (b. 1980–94), Z (1995–2012) and now Alpha (2013–25). The generations about which I am primarily concerned in this writing are the Silent Generation and the Baby Boomers.

Those in the Silent Generation have been characterized by their willingness to accept the realities of a harsh and challenging world, their country's place in that world, and their immediate and challenging circumstances living in the context of a struggling economy in the Great Depression. It was a condition that was still present in their early adult years. They also lived through the shock and challenge of a world war. Given these circumstances, it is remarkable that they are characterized not by complaint and discouragement, but by their willingness to make changes that will improve their lives and the lives of others in their respective settings. They have also been called traditionalists, eager to preserve the best expressions of democratic government and the ways in our society, which have enabled and even empowered them to live a life with a good measure of personal joy and in a context where there is opportunity for meaningful work and social justice. Other descriptions of this generation suggest that they tend to be conformist, have a strong work ethic, and while sometimes critical of their surroundings, they are not inclined to make waves and tend to seek peaceful solutions in disagreements about political issues and social change. Recent developments in the political life of the United States have been deeply troubling for most of this generation. Their partial resistance to social change includes those with both conservative and progressive outlooks, although the conservative side of this generation has had more trouble dealing with rapid social change, the shifts in the character of the American population, the changing roles for women, and concerns about sexual identity.

The Baby Boomers have little memory of and only a limited grasp of the self-sacrificing pain of World War II, although they may have heard stories from their parents and read about this era. They have a slightly different outlook than those who preceded them. They were inclined to take for granted the relative peace and even the unjust social conditions in the 1950s. They addressed the challenges of their era bravely, seeking to live with a good measure of contentment and acceptance of their era's values and challenges. One carry-over from World War II for the Baby Boomers was their awareness that they could not easily retreat into a protected and isolated context. They became keenly aware that they lived in and were influenced by a global context. Their nation's engagement in the Korean War and the conflicts with the Soviet Union reminded them that the United States was not separate from the rest of the world.

The 1960s brought change to nearly all the generations, and Baby Boomers in particular felt free in the 1960s to rebel against traditional expectations. Many did not enter into careers, but lived in communes and alternative households, some taking years to "find themselves." The confusing and disturbing Vietnam conflict, the draft, and the tragedies of this war in Asia merged with the experience of protest into a mixture that forced them to deal with the harsh realities of global conflict. Influenced by the work of the United Nations and their financial linkages in a world economy, they joined with others in the quest for peace and justice, nationally and globally.

Baby Boomers learned how to earn money and pursued financial security with energy. In addition to seeking financial security, many in this generation took up the mantle of service to build a better society and to care for the planet, now showing symptoms of the neglect of generations of exploitation. Many in this generation became aware that the privileges they had come to expect from their childhood were in fact not sustainable. Yet many in this generation still felt entitled; narcissism grew and entered into the mix with the pursuit of wealth as almost an incurable disease. Many Baby Boomers are presently not sure how to bring their lives to a satisfying close. They are not fully prepared to cope with, relate to, and live in a world they cannot control. The challenge for this generation, given the mixture of the pursuit of wealth and the call to care for the disenfranchised, has been immense.

THE SILENT GENERATION AND THE BABY BOOMERS: CURRENT REALITIES

As I have studied those who are living in the sunset years in the United States, the Silent Generation and to some extent, the Baby Boomers, I have discovered there is great diversity, often dependent on family, cultural heritage, education, careers, wealth, health, location, religious orientation or lack of it, and several other factors. I sensed a great need to understand these generations of people in that they are the heart of our topic for this book, and I share their experience. It was necessary and wise to learn as much about them as possible.[2] What follows is a modest summary of what I have learned, and as I go along, I will add more to this brief description.

In 2019, the population of those over 65 was 54.1 million, and it is projected that by 2040 that this population will be 21.1 percent of the population of the United States. It is a sizable group, as big in population as many countries. Nearly one in four older adults in 2019 were members of an ethnic minority population, again an important statistic in that the minority populations do have more than their fair share of social problems. In 2019, the median income of older persons was $27,398 with men having a higher income than women. The average income of those in this generation who owned a home was $36,200. This range of income suggests that there may be many in this group who have housing and even medical needs that are not easily addressed. In 2020, 9.8 million Americans 65+ were in the labor force. In 2019, 4.9 million people lived below the poverty line. In 2020, 89 percent of Americans 65+ had completed high school.[3]

The particular challenges and values of these generations vary depending on social class, education, levels of income, and cultural heritage as well as the specific conditions of their early life. The lists below of the

---

2. As I am part of these generations, and to some extent able to identify with the values and challenges of these groupings, I do not sense that I am stereotypical of those in these generations. I have discovered in several conversations that people in these generations want to preserve their distinctiveness. There is strong desire to find a way of life that supports individual choice and the preservation of one's distinctive identity.

3. "2020 Profile of Older Americans."

values and challenges provide some perspective on how these generations of people are managing the evening of life, although each individual and family grouping have distinctive features. Each life story is remarkably idiosyncratic.[4] The first list speaks to the domains of life, and how one's environment plays a substantial role in the challenges one faces and the values one draws upon in order to make sense of life and find a pathway that sustains them.

AREAS OF CHALLENGE

In this study, I have been able to identify domains of life in which there are common challenges, although with alternative ways of meeting these challenges. These challenges include:

1. The management of finances, with an eye to having sufficient income to support themselves through the remainder of their lives.
2. The ways of sustaining good health, with a concern about the cost of drugs and finding good and affordable health care.
3. The well-being of all of the family members, especially those in the family who are aging and those just beginning life.
4. How to find the best place to live, given affordability and the resources needed for a comfortable life.
5. Exploring ways to meet inner needs, such as feeling peaceful and being free from excessive worry and anxiety; it has not been easy for many in these generations to know how to find healthy ways of coping with the demands of life.
6. Cultivating and sustaining a sense of self-worth, feeling accepted, and being affirmed.
7. Dealing with somewhat negative feelings about the changing of one's body and appearance as well as concern about diminishing mental abilities.
8. Searching for ways of increasing the level of gratification and fulfillment in daily activities. For example, many of those with whom we spoke wanted to improve their computer skills and master the skills

---

4. I have consulted several lists and arranged for conversations with people at this point in life. Each person with whom I have spoken has a slightly different set of values and concerns.

of the digital age. In addition, because of the dramatic social changes in their environment, they wanted more contact with persons in a different generation or from a different racial and ethnic background.

9. Sustaining an appropriate level of self-confidence, given the changes that occur with aging.

10. Continuing the nurture of a spiritual center, or seeking a spiritual center if this dimension of life was not a part of the earlier years.

In summary, it is important to note that the Silent Generation and the Baby Boomers use different ways of understanding the way these challenges are addressed depending where one is in the financial, social, and education realms. It is clear that there is a developmental process, and that the environment and setting in which one lives shapes perception, values, needs, and the capacity to cope.

SUSTAINING VALUES AND CHOICES

As mentioned, the ways of coping with these challenges in the evening of life will vary greatly depending upon one's heritage, culture, context, levels of education and income, and social class.[5] As a way of grasping these differences, I will speak first about the needs of those who are middle to upper middle class, reasonably well-educated, and with a good income and family support system. I will then briefly describe those who have fewer resources with which to cope and do not have the range of skills required to adequately navigate the complex social and economic structure in our society.

For this group of upper middle class and well-educated people with reasonably good jobs, the list of challenges is almost identical with the challenges that I have faced. I will describe this range of challenges in a first-person voice, drawing upon my experiences. I will share a comparable list from conversations with people in the evening of life who live in poverty, have less income, and in some cases are minority persons. This group has a different level of education, less income, and in some cases a different cultural heritage. There was the possibility of a comparison with the life of the extremely wealthy, knowing that there would be quite

---

5. This subject, of course, has many components, and our goal is not to do a comprehensive study of social class behaviors, but to stress the need to understand in a general way how those from different parts of the population address their challenges and shape their lives.

different characteristics. In the conversations with people in this level of our society, I learned about several "class differences," but thought this comparison with the wealthy was another book in itself, and that it might take us away from underlining the need to understand and serve those who have more immediate and pronounced needs.

A PERSONAL PERSPECTIVE

As a white, upper middle class, and well-educated person, I sense the following needs and challenges and note that they are somewhat representative of the middle to upper middle-class population.

1. I need financial security as I age, and it appears that my wife and I have sufficient funds for the present and for the rest of our lives. Yet it is still a concern.
2. I need good health in order to sustain my way of life, and I am concerned about the health of the members of my family who have health concerns. Fortunately, we are all reasonably healthy and have access to good health care providers, with a medical doctor in the immediate family, and a disciplined program to stay healthy.
3. I want to preserve the family's common values and essential identity, and so I will encourage our son and his family to have similar values and goals. I will be only slightly concerned and yet accepting if they have different values and an alternative life style. I also accept and endorse their choice to live in a different part of the country.
4. I need to live, and do live, in a setting that is convenient in terms of my daily needs. This setting has natural beauty, access to recreation, easy shopping, community cultural events, and good institutions of higher education.
5. I am grateful for government programs such as Social Security and Medicare. While I do not want to be overly dependent on government support, I still have some fear about the possible reduction of support from these programs.
6. I am self-reliant and willing to do volunteer work to help those who live on the edge.
7. I do have a desire to feel worthwhile, appreciated, acknowledged, and taken seriously. I want to be respected, and I sense that these

needs are met through good friendships and settings in which I volunteer to serve.

8. I also have a desire to feel well-liked and, even with the changes in my body as I age, I still want to be relatively attractive to others.

9. I value moments of quiet in settings where I can experience a good measure of joy and peace, with limited worry, anxiety, and fear. It is one of the gifts of retirement.

10. I want to be reassured and confident that all the details of approaching death are taken care of, including wills, arrangements for the final days, and a planned approach to a funeral or memorial service. I want my wife to also be reassured and to know that she will have adequate resources to live out the remainder of her life without worry, and that our son will be supportive of all the arrangements we have made.

11. I want to be spiritually grounded and centered, not in the sense of having all the answers and a narrow and exclusive view of religion. I do want to know that I can be honest, trust good scholarship, and be well-informed in this domain, not judged by those with a narrow and exclusive view. When needed, I want to be forgiven, and then be at peace with nothing hidden from the family. I want to be at peace and have my family's love at the end.

A colleague, Karen Hunt, suggested putting these concerns and others in the form of questions:

1. Am I healthy? Will my physical well-being enable me to enjoy being alive and not merely tolerate another day being alive?

2. Will I sustain my mental capacity to think and remember?

3. Am I sufficient? Can I do things necessary to live each day? If not, can I get help when I need to do those daily tasks?

4. Do I have a meaningful relationship with my family and friends? Can I trust the people in my life to love me and do they trust me to love them?

5. Do I have a meaningful relationship with God? Do I trust and rely on my understanding of and faith in God?

6. Am I financially secure? Will I be able to pay my own way to the end of life?

7. Can I be of some help or use to other people? Do I have a purpose other than just staying alive?
8. Can I continue to be curious and eager to learn? Will I read, listen, discuss, watch people and events happening in the world and want to understand them?
9. Am I willing and able to cope with the technological and physical changes in the world that impact me?
10. Am I grateful for continuing life?

A CULTURAL AND GLOBAL PERSPECTIVE:

I want to move slightly away from the personal perspective and explore the cultural context and world conditions in which those in the Silent Generation and the Baby Boomers have experienced as they move through the years of adulthood. Let me illustrate with a few examples.

The values of those born toward the end of the Silent Generation and at the beginning of the Baby Boomer period have been shaped by a dramatic shift in national and global realities. A new world was being born in which they have had to find their way, and the rapid pace of change and the severity of the problems continue. It is not possible nor appropriate to provide a comprehensive description of the multitude of changes that have occurred and the severe problems that continue to be present. I want to be somewhat selective and identify a few major shifts that have had a substantial influence on these generations and were influential in shaping their identity and values.

One national and global concern that has shaped the thinking and behavior of these generations has to do with the issues of ecology. The health of the environment in which we live has become a central concern for all who dwell on the earth. We ask whether our earth home will remain a habitat that allows humans and all sentient beings to sustain a high quality of life. There are fundamental shifts in the weather, global warming, and a deteriorating environment. With overpopulation, there is the risk of whether there will be an adequate supply of food and water. Already, deep and profound shifts of the weather are occurring, and the risk of world hunger, always with us, has become even more intense.

A second major shift, and perhaps a positive one, is the changing role of women; their emancipation from traditional roles in family life, their opportunities for education, and the vast range of choice in the world of work. The clear distinctions between the roles of women and men within most countries of the world have passed, although still present in some parts of the world. Both men and women have had to adjust to this shift, but women have felt more deeply this profound sense of change in values and ways of life. For example, most women now have a good measure of freedom to choose to marry, whom to marry, and whether to have children. Many women have been able to break out of the earlier generational expectations about employment and to pursue professional careers. College education, participation is sports, and leadership in many domains of life are the norm. The choice of a career is theirs, and leadership in the world of work has changed dramatically, with women assuming roles of leadership in business and professional life.

A third fundamental shift in the world at large is the increase in the population, or we might say, the challenge of over population. The resources of certain parts of the world are not sufficient to sustain the needs of the population, nor are the governmental structures of some settings sufficiently agile and adept at serving the needs of the increased population. Lack of education, inadequate health care, and insufficient opportunities to earn a modest wage still plague many parts of the world.

An additional challenge that exists in many parts of the world, in large measure because of the lack of natural resources, is the presence of a poor economy and unstable governments. When these conditions occur, there is the inevitable increase in the range and severity of problems that include severe poverty, hunger, and disease.

I want to mention as well, as a shaping influence on all of us regardless of our generational identity, is the continual threat of violence and war. The Korean War, the war in Vietnam, the violence in Iraq, the presence of violence and war in Ukraine, and the tragedies of Gaza and Israel suggest that the human family continues to have great difficulty in resolving differences in peaceful ways. Hanging over us is the ever-present threat that one side in a conflict will resort to nuclear warfare.

FINDING A SOLUTION: COMMON VALUES

There is a matrix of interconnected factors that have shaped the outlook of these generations. We have become very aware of the crisis of the deteriorating environment and global warming, a severe threat and challenge.

Our country seems to be unable to form a collaborative government that serves the needs of the people. In many parts of the world, there continues to be war and violence. There are the terrible tragedies taking place in Ukraine and in region of Gaza. There is violence in cities and, of course, there are the frequent shootings, and we share a profound concern for the safety of our children in our schools. We must find a frame of reference, undergirded by common values, that will guide us through our current crisis. I want to suggest as a starting point that we remember the foundational words of Jesus, often called "The Golden Rule": "In everything do to others as you would have them do to you; for this is the Law and the prophets" (Matt 7:12). It would be easy to set aside this guiding principle and say it is a vague ideal and it is difficult to translate its relevance into social change and governmental policy. Yet, that is exactly what Jesus was attempting to do, linking it to "the Law and the prophets" and seeking a just and peaceful context in which to live. He saw it as a summary of the vision of Israel to form a government, one that would be rooted in justice for all and the continuing quest for peace. As he taught and functioned in a prophetic role, he spoke not just to individuals, but to those in power whose task it was to create a more just and peaceful country and world.

As we think of those in the evening of life, we are aware that there are many in our country and in the world who must struggle just to live. It was this population to which Jesus often turned as he traveled in Galilee and on down to Judah and the capitol, Jerusalem. Those with illness, victims of injustice, and those in poverty were attracted to his teaching because he cared about them and lived in solidarity with them. As we attempt to describe how we might live wisely and well in the evening of life, we need to turn our attention to how he served this segment of the population, helping them to live wisely and well.[6] By poverty, we mean those with inadequate income and who are living with cultural norms and structural social systems that limit them.[7] Poverty is present nearly everywhere and occurs in all races and countries. To understand it fully requires a comprehensive study of

---

6. There are several excellent resources that describe poverty, including the fully updated classic by Ruby K. Payne, *Framework for Understanding Poverty*. Our brief sketch is only a glance at this nearly universal phenomenon, and it is beyond the scope of our writing to undertake a full analysis. If one wants to understand poverty in the United States, the books of Matthew Desmond such as *Evicted* and *Poverty by America* are excellent.

7. As we speak about the poor, we must be careful not to use this term as a statement about a certain kind of person, but as a description of a social condition that can be changed.

employment, education, relationships, and settings that enable social mobility and have a positive vision of the future. Addressing how those in poverty might live wisely and well in the sunset of life will take us beyond the scope of this writing. Meeting their needs will require a massive effort of education, creating increased opportunities, changing social structures, and a huge financial investment by both government and private wealth. Fortunately, there are current creative and successful programs which illustrate what can be done, such as the restoration of homes and services in Detroit. As we write, we will attempt to include those who live in poverty as we describe the goals and ways of flourishing in the evening of life for the general population. We do care about those who live in poverty because we remember and follow the model of Jesus who deeply cared for these people. We will continue in our twilight years to serve others, following the example of Jesus. It is from him that we learn how to live and serve, and from his teaching that we share many common values that will guide as we seek to create a more just and humane world.

We now want to suggest the values, drawn from the life and teachings of Jesus, which we need to affirm as we seek to live in this phase of life wisely and well. We hope many of them will be present for all those engaged in the task of living in a purposeful and healthy way in the evening of life. Once again, I will speak in a personal way, and draw values from the Golden Rule.

1. Caring and compassionate *love* is our most important value, and we want to express this kind of love to family, friends, and all those whom we encounter. We especially want to extend care and compassion to those in need. There are times when we fail, but it continues to be our core ethical norm, and we say with the apostle Paul ". . . and the greatest of these is love" (1 Cor 13).

2. We want to maintain our *health* as we age, and we will need to be realistic about the impact of age on our bodies. But they are a gift and reality which we hold dear, and we will make it a priority to honor and take care of them. As we are healthy, we are better able to serve the needs of others. As we are freed from the preoccupation with self-care, we become enabled and empowered to serve the needs of others.

3. We want to be persons of *integrity and character*, honest in sensitive ways, and therefore trusted and able to care for others in loving and

healing ways. We follow Jesus in our concern to be truthful and loving in all of our relationships.

4. We want to live in a *setting* that has a good measure of social justice, quality education, natural beauty, a good climate, and cares deeply about the integrity of creation. We have the responsibility to secure these blessings and, in part, to share them and provide access to them for others.

5. We want to have a comfortable and attractive *home* in that we do spend a great deal of time at home during these retirement years. We want to use our nice surroundings for our own health and enjoyment, and then have the capacity to be able better to lend a hand in serving the needs of others.

6. We want to have sufficient *income* to buy what is needed, to attend cultural events, and travel to settings with historical significance and great beauty. Once again, we may be able to turn this blessing into a blessing for others, as we are able to share our financial resources with others in need.

7. Grateful for many government and local services, we continue to value being self-reliant with the opportunity to *study, read, and learn* in order to continue our professional interests such as writing and volunteer service, praying that what we do will improve the lives of others. Part of our values of self-reliance and commitment to service will involve staying in touch with current affairs, local, regional, and national; a goal that will expect us to be keep abreast of the digital revolution.

8. We want to have access to a *good place of worship*, to continue living in a spiritually honest way, and then have the opportunity to *serve* those who live on the edge.

9. We have a deep concern about local, regional, state, and national *governments*; we want them to serve the needs of their constituencies and not be overly influenced by political pressures and be driven by the needs for power and acclaim. We want our government officials to express and *live with integrity* in reference their spoken values. We know that it is our responsibility to hold them accountable, and as possible enter into public life as we are able, advocating peace and justice and concern for the integrity of creation.

10. In short, we want to have a pattern of life that has *peace and purpose*, yet is relatively free from worry and anxiety, and from which we can be strengthened to serve.

We represent the generations that are in the evening of life. We will not likely take on again the kinds of responsibilities that we have once had, but there are many different ways to serve, and we look to Jesus whose values we seek to emulate. He represents of model of "grace and truth" and used his life to the show compassion to all whom he met.

In short: "In the evening of life, live with a gracious attitude and the goal of service, thankful for the goodness, and even the challenges, that we have faced across the years."

Terms, Resources, and Discussion Questions

Terms

1. Phase: A period in one's life with particular characteristics and challenges.
2. The Silent Generation: Those born in the United States between 1925 and 1945, with the tendency to adjust well to difficult times, such as World War II.
3. Baby Boomers: Those born in the United States between 1946 and 1964, part of great increase in the birth rate and characterized as wanting to maximize their financial resources and be generous with their wealth.
4. Millennials: Those born between 1981 and 1996 and characterized as having a global outlook, information technology skills, and able to manage profound social change.
5. Class and cultural differences: The values and approach to life are different among those with different wealth, level of education, and cultural backgrounds, based in part on level of education and financial resources.

Resources

1. Diana Butler Bass, *Christianity After Religion: The End of Christianity and the Birth of a New Spiritual Awakening*
2. Marcus Borg, *The Heart of Christianity: Rediscovering a Life of Faith*
3. Ilia Delio, *Making All Things New: Catholicity, Cosmology, and Consciousness*
4. James Fowler, *Becoming Adult, Becoming Christian: Adult Development and Christian Faith*
5. Ruby K. Payne, *A Framework for Understanding Poverty: A Cognitive Approach*
6. Ronald Rolheiser, *The Holy Longing: The Search for Christian Spirituality*
7. Brian D. McLaren, *A New Kind of Christianity: Ten Questions that are Transforming the Faith*

Discussion Questions

1. How would you describe your family and cultural heritage? In what ways were you influenced by the presence of these outlooks?
2. How have you changed in your outlook since you left your home, and how much of your family heritage have you retained? Do you find the influence of family values to be a positive influence in your life?
3. How would you describe your outlook and commitment to the religious/spiritual life and what has been its influence on you?
4. What are the four or five ethical guidelines in your life?
5. How have these values and guidelines been an influence on you as you have matured?

CHAPTER TWO

A Way Forward

> "Again, Jesus spoke to them, saying, 'I am the light of the world. Whoever follows me will never walk in darkness, but will have the light of life.'"
>
> (JOHN 8:12)

I WRITE AS ONE deeply rooted in the Christian Way, although I am very open to other religious and secular modes of living well, nurturing the soul, and serving the needs of others. I understand the Christian perspective as a guiding foundation for life and a way of seeking to work toward a high quality of life for those who are living in the evening of life. The model for us on how to live wisely and well at any age is the life, the teaching, and values of Jesus of Nazareth and, of course, the enormous wealth of wisdom that has accumulated across the centuries of the study of Jesus. As we read about him, we learn that he was indeed younger than those of us currently in this final phase of life, yet he epitomized how to live well at any age. It was also the case that to be in the thirties in his time and place was to be thought of as fully mature and a person of experience. The lifespan in those years was much shorter. We note as well that he was in fact in the evening of life as we learn in reading his story. A horrible death was just around the corner.

He addressed the needs of those whom he encountered, and many of those with whom he served lived on the poverty edge of his setting.[1]

---

1. See Marcus Borg, *Jesus: Uncovering the Life*, 225–29, and Crossan, *Historical Jesus*. Hugh Echegaray, in his book, *Practice of Jesus*, demonstrates how Jesus was deeply dedicated to serving the poor.

His ministry was primarily with the poor, the peasant class, although he met and worked with those in all classes of society. His mode of service reflected his commitment to and inherent wisdom about meeting the needs of those whom he encountered and served. Dozens of titles were and have been given to him, including law-breaker and heretic; we will focus on his character and ministry and primarily use the titles of rabbi (teacher), prophet, and healer.[2] On occasion, we will discuss the titles of messiah, Son of God, and Christ, which almost became a last or family name for him, although it is more a reference to his identity and mission.

The Gospel of John, telling that story, says that there are guidelines in the Hebrew Bible, the Bible of Jesus, about how to live wisely and well.[3] These guidelines were summarized as the Law, with specific reference to the Torah, the first five books of the Hebrew Bible. The guidance from the Torah is specific and enlightening. It was written in a very different culture and era than ours, yet it is possible to learn a great deal from the Torah about how to live a constructive and satisfying life.[4] John, in this passage in his Gospel, adds to the Torah or Law and says that Jesus brought grace and truth, love and light. From Moses and the Torah there is the emphasis on guidance about how to live wisely day-to-day and how to be responsible in the social context of peace and justice. From Jesus we learn about grace, the unconditional love of God, and how we should affirm love as the center of our lives. We learn how loving grace is transformative and how to be made a new person by the generous grace of God. We are guided by the one who was full of light and love, who saw the truth clearly, and who demonstrated the life-changing power of love. Jesus has come, full of grace and truth, and as we follow him, we are empowered by grace (sustaining love given freely) to live wisely and to flourish.

It is necessary to study these passages and other sections of the New Testament to understand the life and teaching of Jesus; they are very enlightening, although the reader has to move into a different era of history and language for a comprehensive understanding. Not everyone can engage in such an academic study, and so I thought it wise to use several contemporary words and phrases, hoping that our English will capture

---

2. See my two books in which I use these three categories for understanding Jesus, *The Radical Teaching of Jesus* and *The Radical Invitation of Jesus* I also speak about other titles such as messiah, Son of God, and Son of Man.

3. John 1:14–18.

4. This literature, honored in the Jewish faith, has guided people with great insight and wisdom over the centuries.

the meaning of the Gospel of John and the accounts in the other Gospels as they describe the life and teaching of Jesus and invite us to follow his example.

It is essential to be keenly aware that this phase we are describing, the evening of life, is complex; trite formulas and platitudes will not help us. All too often I have heard well-meaning teachers and pastors say, "Just trust God" or "Just pray about it." I have dear friends who find these words a bit empty, and I do not think these phrases give us adequate help in dealing with the profound challenges of aging in our complex world. These simple comments and others like them, suggested to us by well-meaning pastors and teachers, have a trace of the truth in them, but they do not take us deep enough nor do they adequately unpack the subtlety of what it is we face in contemporary life. To fully understand the place of the Christian faith in the evening of life, we will need more expansion of Christian thought and practice and vivid examples and illustrations from those in the past and present who followed this pathway. For starters, I am persuaded that it may help us to understand the biblical message in a deeper way when these important concepts in the New Testament are translated into contemporary English. This translation will especially help those who are not familiar with religious language.

Initially, I will employ five English words, which I hope will begin to capture the meaning of the biblical perspective on personal responsibility and ethical behavior, and which partially summarize and describe contemporary life goals and modes of being. These five foundational modes of being have the capacity to give us a focus and orientation to life. They are: spiritual, contemplative, mindful, thoughtful, and mature. As we blend them into an integrated whole, they give us a comprehensive orientation and foundation for living wisely and well. This strategy will increase our understanding of these biblical passages and give us a frame of reference that we hope will guide us and be accurate and insightful. We will be especially conscious of how they contain the heart of the teaching of Jesus and then speak to those of us who seek to live wisely and well in the evening of life.

If there is one word that captures our understanding of the message of Jesus about living wisely and well, one that gives us our larger frame of reference, it is *spiritual*. We are writing from the perspective of an open and spacious Christianity that embraces a way of being and values the several practices inherent in Christian spirituality. This frame of reference, I hope, will give us a foundation for living wisely and well in the evening of life.[5] The goal is to describe in a helpful and life-changing way what it means to have a growing faith and trust in the unconditional love of God; a way of being that affirms that to be in relationship with God is a way to find a peaceful and joyful way of living and to flourish. Our task, then, is to begin to cultivate this relationship with God through deep and thoughtful faith and spiritual practices such as study, prayer, worship, and service. As we do, we begin to live in a spiritual way.

As we seek to live in a spiritual way, we will become more aware of the extraordinary development of the cultivation of many forms of spirituality all across the world in our time, perhaps in part a human response to the world in crisis. This has been especially common for those of us in the second half of life with a deep desire to be at peace in these years. Richard Rohr, the Franciscan priest captures this mood:

> Most of us tend to think of the second half of live as largely about getting old, dealing with health issues, and letting go of our physical life, but the whole thesis of this book is exactly the opposite. What looks like falling can largely be experienced as falling upward, into a broader and deeper world where the soul has found its fulness, is finally connected to the whole, and lives inside the Big Picture.[6]

A second word, related to living in a spiritual way, is *contemplative*, a way of being silent before and open to ultimate truth and receiving the gracious presence of the divine.[7] This way of life has characterized the life of many remarkable people who have become models for countless numbers of searchers; from Gandhi to the Dalai Lama, from Muhammad to Julian of Norwich, from St. Francis to Mother Teresa, we find life-giving patterns of contemplation.

We learn from them and others that we must undertake our search for a contemplative spirit in wise and careful ways in that religious commitment is fundamentally life-changing. It does have a risky dimension; the invitations are numerous and not all of them lead to a healthy life.

---

5. Jesus, referring to a passage in the Hebrew Bible, describes his mission: "The Spirit of the Lord is upon me, because he has anointed me to bring good news to the poor. He has sent me to proclaim release of the captives and recovery of sight to the blind, to let the oppressed go free, to proclaim the year of the Lord's favor" (Luke 4:18).

6. Rohr, *Falling Upward*, 153.

7. Again, Jesus would have been contemplative, guided, for example, by Ps 19:14: "Let the words of my mouth and the meditation of my heart be acceptable to you, O Lord, my rock and my redeemer."

Religious commitment is complex, and we have seen some conversions that are actually harmful, exclusive, tribal, restrictive, sectarian, cultic, manipulative, and controlling. We know that we must be careful and wise about using and suggesting ways that are grounded in truth, full of insightful, and nurturing, emancipating, and life-giving! The fact is that the "market" is full of questionable invitations to affirm religious beliefs and practices that may be harmful.

It follows that there is a third necessary component of living wisely and well in the sunset years. If we acknowledge that making a spiritual commitment is a powerful force touching all aspects of life and that it can be dangerous and harmful as well as nurturing and bring peace and purpose, then we must be very *mindful* in our commitment. As we learn from Buddhism, being *mindful* in our religious beliefs and practices is essential. To be mindful is to be a person whose mind is focused in the present, in each moment, free from distraction, fear, agitation, and even cautious regarding previous assumptions about the religious life. This way of life is a contrast to being mindless or shallow. Mindfulness frees us from a "monkey mind" and the chaos of thoughts and feeling that fill us with distracting noise and confusion. The practice of mindfulness makes possible the reception of great insight into the mysteries and challenges of life.[8] It also enables us to make good choices in the present as we face a multitude of options.

Nearly all of the great religions of the human family teach that an insightful grasp of the complexity of life gives one the capacity to manage life wisely and well. Mindfulness is at the heart of Buddha's teaching, undergirding the Four Noble Truths and one of the key elements in the Eightfold Path. This profound teaching urges the follower to be wise, cultivate the Buddha within, or in the Christian faith, be responsive to the guidance of the Holy Spirit. We must be appropriately attentive across each day, reminding ourselves to live in the present or, as the case may be, return to the present, especially if we are bogged down with guilt about the past and worry about the future.[9]

---

8. Following the death of Jesus, two of his disciples were walking to their home village, and one turned to the other and spoke about how it was now time to be mindful. As they spoke, they had a profound mystical experience, sensing the presence of Jesus, and understanding that this was the time to be profoundly mindful (John 24:13–35).

9. Thich Nhat Hanh, *Heart of Buddha's Teaching*, 64–65. See as well the practical book by Tessa Watt, *Mindfulness: A Practical Guide*.

There is a fourth additional and related component and practice in the evening of life, which is to be *thoughtful*, that is to be careful that our belief system is credible and to find and use contemplative practices that are healthy and nurturing.[10] We need to focus on what is true, not be led by those who are deceptive, seeking power over us or chasing our money. We are living in a time when "The Great Lie" was used to question the election of the forty-sixth president of the United States in 2020. It was the product of intentional deception; several studies showed that the election was fair and had a true outcome. This same approach of using misinformation is staying with us in our political life. Systematic deception and lying about pieces and parts of reality have become a powerful force in our culture and in many other parts of the world. There is a "do what it takes" attitude to achieve goals, even if the means of gaining power or wealth are driven by mixed motivations that are untruthful, harmful, and even violent. Our culture's values are filled with this kind of deception.[11]

Religious teaching, although not intentionally so, is occasionally filled with information and perspectives that are barely on the edge of truth. In some religious traditions, children are taught a pattern of belief that is essentially nourishing, although a case can be made that some of this teaching is not literally true. Often this happens in cultural traditions that use patterns of thought and writing dating back before the rise of science and critical historical study. To challenge some of these beliefs may evoke a strong reaction from "true believers" who are profoundly committed to an ideological theological system, one that might resist a critical historical study of the Bible or an affirmation that a scientific understanding of cosmic evolution accurately tells us how it all happened. They say it is wrong because it is not described in and goes against the accounts of the Bible. A better way of understanding the biblical stories in the Bible is to say that there are many "stories" containing long held and traditional ways of understanding. Some of them should not be presented as literal truth, but as suggestive parables pointing to an ethical

---

10. In a conversation with Jesus, a village woman meets Jesus in a setting where there was water. As they talk, Jesus is very sensitive, hears her story with profound empathy, and says: "You worship what you do not know, we worship what we know . . . but the hour is coming, and is now here, when true worshippers will worship the Father in spirit and truth . . . " (John 4: 22–23). We must be thoughtful and discerning as we seek to find the truth.

11. See, for example, the book by David Corn, *American Psychosis*, for an insightful expression of how our culture has used untruthful ways to achieve political gain.

and spiritual way of life.[12] Integrating a contemporary understanding of the world with one's religious faith is a necessary step in living wisely and well in the evening of life.

There is an additional mode of being and pattern of life that will undergird one's sense of well-being in the evening of life. It is *maturity*, that capacity to be at ease and comfortable as one finds one's way through the dangers and challenges of contemporary life. To be mature is to be able to handle threat, complexity, and frustration wisely and to challenge ignorance and dishonesty with composure and wisdom.[13] To be mature is not to lose one's balance by a harmful event, a disagreement, or the discovery of being unable to pay all of one's bills in a particular month. It is to be calm in the midst of a conflict and to advise a thoughtful and factual solution to the vast range of problems facing each of us in these troublesome times, a time filled with crisis after crisis. The mature person faces these crises in calm, wise, informed, courageous, and mindful ways.

There are other descriptive words that suggest a healthy way of living in the evening of life. We know that this list is not comprehensive in naming all the ways of being that lead to a good and peaceful life. But these five ways of being, spiritual, contemplative, mindful, thoughtful, and mature constitute a mindset that will move us toward growth and give us the capacity to flourish. In as much as they are present for us in our senior years, we will have the capacity to live with a good measure of peace, joy, purpose, and love in evening of life. Yet we are never quite fully "at home," in that contemporary life is indeed complex for all ages. Yet we believe that these ways of being do create a mindset in the evening of life that empowers us to live with integrity in such a world, indeed, to flourish in it. We must be committed to healthy norms of thinking, feeling, and behavior across the years.

The catch in this conviction, as in most advice on how to live the good life, is that it is easier to say than to do. The goal is to learn how to implement these foundational values and modes of being, making them integral to our daily walk. One part of the risk is that these values may remain in our minds exclusively as ideals, but not be fully implemented

---

12. The first two chapters of Genesis are an example of how we might understand creation in a way that honors it and invites us to be good stewards, but we know that the formation of the universe didn't happen in six days.

13. The apostle Paul, in guiding the new Christians in Corinth, says: "Brothers and sisters, do not be children in your thinking; rather be infants in evil, but in thinking be adults" (1 Cor 14:20).

and realized in day-to-day living. Our exposure to them may not sufficiently include the implementation and action dimension, but they may just remain vague ideals. In our reading and observations, we hear people describe this time of life as the years of contentment because these qualities are present, although some have acknowledged that these modes of being were not as fully present as they thought when there was a major problem or profound change in their lives. For example, some people have lost their way with the death of a spouse or the loss of financial security or even the change of the political climate in their country. Living with these conditions has increased their need for guidance and support. The hope is that they will find it with these modes of being, a comprehensive mindset taught by Jesus, knowing all too well that our culture invites us to chase many false and harmful ways. We think and then say to ourselves: "if only I had that new car, or the house on the hill with the view, or had power and control over those with whom I disagree!" But these "possessions" do not satisfy.

I want to underline that these terms, spiritual, contemplative, mindful, thoughtful, and maturity all have an action clause as well as an observational and a descriptive component. These modes of being must be understood, cultivated, and integrated into our identity, and this process takes time. We know from experience that they will not always be fully present and that people in the evening of their lives may only have a trace of the values inherent in the meaning of these words. For example, there are many senior people who have not managed to reach full maturity, and the contemplative way would be a mystery to them. Their pattern of life has not included these avenues of successful living; they struggle with the complexity and demands of life and often feel defeated. The modes of being that are spiritual and contemplative may have the limitation of describing only a small percentage of people living in the evening of their lives. The categories may seem to be too religious in tone in our secular culture and suggest the life of one who is almost exclusively committed to prayer and meditation, living in a protective retreat from real life. Yet there are many people who are mature and mindful about their judgments and pray and meditate about their life choices.[14]

As these terms are used, we know that there may be others that also point to a good and gratifying life, ones that we might integrate and combine with the five we have suggested. We suggest the cultivation of

---

14. A very helpful guide to coping with the challenges of aging is Katy Butler, *Art of Dying Well*.

these values and goals, knowing that they may not always be sufficiently inclusive and that we need to remain open to other healthy concepts and patterns as well. We have found that if undertaken with the best possible spirit or attitude, these values, with others added from our unique experience, do lead to a life filled with peace and contentment. They are a firm foundation for living wisely and well in the evening of life.[15] They will become our dearest friends if we are intentional about cultivating them. With this foundation, we engage in living with a good measure of contentment and have a peaceful soul.

Those of us in this phase of life need to continue to engage in self-exploration and introspection, read widely, remain involved in counseling relationships, go to conferences, and engage in many searching conversations about the evening years. As we do, we hope that that these terms, spiritual, contemplative, mindful, thoughtful, and mature are accurate ways of speaking about our goals in life, how we assess who we are and what we do in life, and how they describe an approach to living that enables us to flourish. Each of these terms describe a slightly different life pattern, and as they are integrated, we believe that they will guide our understanding of how best to live in the evening of life.

In addition to describing these evening years as a phase, lived wisely and well with several foundational qualities, we want also to make clear that these words suggest a healthy way of living in the hours of each day. We ask, "how will they help us live wisely and well today, this evening, and tomorrow?" Finding the answer to this question is our goal in the remainder of the book. These ways of being, integrated into our lives, give us a foundation and describe how this foundation takes shape in day-to-day life. We will emphasize that the spiritual life is foundational, complemented by the contemplative life. The spiritual life is one that is centered; our heart is in the right place. Then, as we engage in and reflect on our complex life, we discover the need to be mindful and thoughtful. We

---

15. Philo, a Jewish mystic who lived in Alexandria, Egypt, almost a contemporary of Jesus, wrote a stimulating essay entitled "On the Contemplative Life." Joan Taylor and David M. Hay wrote an excellent commentary with the name of Philo's essay; it was published in 2020. Joan Chittister, in her book, *Gift of Years: Growing Old Gracefully*, easily moves through her description of being wise in these years with these and other words and ideas. It is a complex arena. We have been especially moved and guiding by the writing of Richard Rohr, founder of the Center for Action and Contemplation in Albuquerque. His book, *Falling Upward*, is especially germane to our theme as he divides life up into two segments, the first half being the time we create a foundation with these values, and the second is the time when these values fill our lives and guide those seeking to live wisely and well.

realize that life asks us to think deeply about how our lives have unfolded, their current state, and where they might go in the few remaining years. We are mindful when we seek to be ready for the night; it will come and our eyes will close. So, with a measure of maturity, we prepare wills, make funeral arrangements, get our finances in order, and speak with special people about helping with a possible memorial service. As we get ready, we are inclined to make judgments about how well we have done, whether we have been fulfilled in our life choices, whether there have been some poor choices along the way, and how we might deal with them.

Further, these several qualities remind us to hold dear the people whom we love, family and especially children, and also other members of the family and close friends with whom we have shared life. We ask whether they are reasonably happy and content and what we might do to help them achieve a good measure of peace and joy. We visit our families, have dinner with friends, read holiday and birthday cards, make periodical phone calls, and live "electronically" with the exchange of texts and emails. We join groups that give guidance and perspective on how to manage these years, some of which are religious in character and others that have to do with common interests and needs. We watch television according to our interests and outlooks, selecting the evening news, reporting on political realities, and escaping from some worries as we watch dramas, comedies, and sports programs. Ideally, we do so thoughtfully, mindfully, and in a mature and contemplative way.

In all of this swirl, there is a human person who ponders and prays, has values, has beliefs and convictions, and expresses them in a wide variety of ways in a given day, week, or month. Often there is a deep interest in one's body, and we observe that it has changed some over the years. We are grateful for good health although we may be worried about what the doctor may have said last week. Thoughtful persons take care of their bodies, maintain healthy habits of exercise and diet, and they find their body to be beautiful and functional, although changing and declining. The contemplative and mature person is one who thinks deeply, is honest about themselves and others, and willing often to take risks to express one's needs, points of view, and values. Thoughtful persons tend to be responsive to the sick and anxious, able because of their own challenges to identify those who suffer and to interact with them in an empathic way. They tend to be creative in a given day, manifest a good measure of competence, and willing to make changes as new situations emerge. The mindful person is willing to try new approaches, open to change in attitude and spirit, keeping that which has been foundational and discarding that which has been negative and limiting. At the end of the day, the mature person tends to be as physically healthy as possible, mentally alert, spiritually tuned, and has a reasonably good self-image. These persons feel loveable and love easily and well, take good care of themselves, and can be serious or playful as a new situation unfolds. They are thoughtful, value centered, authentic, open, creative, caring, productive, and spiritual human beings.[16] They move into the evening of life with a mindful and contemplative spirit, sensing all that is around them and inside of them, nurturing the best and leaving the harmful behind. They are free to be truthful, responsible, and loving.[17]

THE SPIRITUAL CENTER

We want to underline again that this particular form of the life is enhanced with a spiritual center. This center, and from it the practices which sustain it, may come from many different religious traditions, even those that are slightly more secular and speak about reaching the Center and encountering or sensing Truth, the ground of being or ultimate reality. We honor these traditions, knowing that people use different ways of finding comfort, healing, guidance, and meaning. From a more theological perspective, we might say that God speaks many languages and guides and teaches the children of the world in a way that they can understand, and from this understanding, they can find peace and a life-giving pathway in life.

The spiritual life that I know best is the Christian way, lived without flaw by Jesus of Nazareth. We will attempt to describe and capture the heart of this way of life. Other ways toward the Center have great value as well, and we will draw from them. Yet our focus will be on the way (the Way) of Jesus, the term used by the first Christians. It is a way that is spacious and inclusive. As we look at other ways of finding peace and purpose, we will tend to use them to compare with the Christian way and illustrate more generally what are the healthy patterns of living in the evening of life.

We will develop our understanding of the Christian way in the remainder of the book, and want at this point to suggest two essential

---

16. See Virginia Satir, *Peoplemaking*, 2–3.
17. "The truth will set you free" (John 8:32).

components of the Christian way of living the spiritual life. They are foundational and will guide us. The first is to understand and make our own the central teaching of Jesus, that the kingdom of God or reign of God is present for us to claim and endorse.[18] We do prefer the word reign over kingdom in that it does not have the masculine or authoritarian connotation. Jesus taught from the model of his life and in his teaching, that the essence of the good life, one filled with peace and purpose, is to open one's mind and heart to the presence and reign of God. We emphasize that when we speak of God, we speak of that which is personal being and with whom we can have a relationship. This relationship begins by fully opening our heart, mind, and spirit to the presence of One who is Love and Light. Happiness is not found in the possession of things, control over others, gaining prestige and power, or experiencing passing and intense pleasures. Rather, deep joy and peace come when we receive the power and presence of God in our lives.

In addition, he taught that we cultivate this life by study, prayer,[19] meditation, and service, or to say it another way, we cultivate and sustain our connection with God by living a mature, thoughtful, mindful, spiritual, and contemplative life. Even Jesus left his disciples and the crowds of people who longed for his teaching and healing in order to restore his center and his gifts of love and grace.[20] So, as we speak about this way of life, we speak about a way that has an open heart and mind and sufficient discipline to remove oneself from the rush of daily life in order to engage in spiritual practices and the several dimensions of mindful and thoughtful contemplation, not the least of which is a prayerful spirit. The spiritual life about which we speak is filled with love for all and the practice of quiet meditation and prayer. We follow Jesus in the contemplative, mindful, thoughtful life as we move toward spiritual maturity.

THE VULNERABLE LIFE

We have found that there is much that is happy and joyful about these years, grounded as we are in our worldview and disciplined practices. But the reality is that we who are in the sunset of life are still vulnerable. For example, there are a number of world problems that give us cause to fear

---

18. See Mark 1:14–15.

19. See the teaching of Jesus in Matt 6:9–14, a section often called "The Lord's Prayer."

20. Matt 14:23.

and feel deep concern about the future. There is the crisis of the deteriorating environment and global warming. Many of us in this phase of life have found ways, given our income, education, and social status not to feel the immediate pinch of this global crisis. Yet we sense that it is very real, negatively impacting millions of people and getting worse.[21] There are numerous global, national, and regional efforts to address this crisis, and we often join with others in these initiatives. Yet we know that we are almost too late to turn the tide as it splashes dangerous waves on our world. We are vulnerable on this beach where we live. We live in a moment of history that requires that we be mindful about all aspects of our lives.

We know that many people, and especially leaders of nations, still think that military action or violent rebellion will help them achieve their goals. In the time of Jesus, and his follower Paul, Rome used violence and military power to secure what was called peace. Yet fear was the result. Both Jesus and Paul say that the transformation of the person and social justice bring peace. Deep down, we know that to use military violence or even local violence in order to gain power and control over others nearly always creates more problems than it solves and enormous suffering. We wonder how and why President Putin believes he will improve the lives of the Russian people by invading Ukraine, or why the invasion of Gaza by the Jewish military will change the leaders of Hamas, although we read the arguments that are part of a larger plan to restore a more peaceful context. How will violence improve the lives of the Russian people or the lives of Palestinians? It is clear that these actions of violence have had a devastating impact on the lives and well-being of millions of people and created fear in their lives. In addition, we wonder why there are shootings in schools and why a minority population might be attacked as we read about these events in the daily news.

We also wonder how the use of deception with mis- and dis-information can possibly improve the lives of the citizens of the United States. We live in the midst of a serious political divide that makes it increasingly hard for nearly all levels of the government to guide the country, states, and regions toward peace and justice for all.[22] Differences do have a place, and serious debate does refine perspectives and increases our knowledge. But to treat others with little respect and to propose actions, based on

---

21. We write at the time of the earthquakes in Turkey and Syria, and incredible and almost unbearable heat in several parts of the world. There is no peace in Ukraine, and the situation in Gaza is causing suffering beyond comprehension.

22. The coming election for President in 2024 will be filled with misinformation.

misinformation, will be harmful to them, nearly always creating more problems. The attack on the United States Capitol on January 6, 2022 is but one example.[23] Living in this kind of context is evidence that a life lived wisely and well is difficult because of our culture. Rather than fully accept our culture and its values, we need to be part of the process of creating a more just and humane nation and world and live our lives above its corrupt forms.[24]

Our vulnerability is connected with international and national problems; they touch us in many ways and are often below the surface as we plan a trip to the grocery store or have lunch with a friend. The impact may be subtle, but it is there and we are vulnerable. More frequently, it may be regional, local, and personal concerns that grab the attention of those of us who are in our mature years. I do give attention to global and national crises, and I read widely about them and feel relatively well-informed about these larger concerns. I do try to help in local ways to solve some of the problems of our troubled world. In our home, living with a mature and wise life partner, we try to give attention to the threat of global warming and attempt to live in a way that at least does not aggravate the problem. We read widely, have a basic understanding of many of the other troublesome conditions on our planet, and engage in practices and respond affirmatively to settings in which we are invited to help, to speak, teach, or perhaps write so that others may better understand. Yet our way of life may not be sufficiently designed to make a noticeable difference in creating a better world. We live with the reality of compromise.

Though comfortable, there are still times when I feel vulnerable and suspect that I am not the only one with a measure of caution and even fear in this time of history. In part, because of these haunting concerns, I attempt to live in a mature and thoughtful way, drawing upon a number of resources and relationships. I have learned from my Buddhist friends to be mindful and contemplative as I cope and make decisions.[25] Again, perhaps some personal examples may be helpful.

---

23. See the recent book by David Corn, mentioned above, *American Psychosis*, for one perspective on the deep divisions in our country.

24. Once again, see the book by Richard Rohr, *Falling Upward*, a statement about those of us in the evening of life who must be true to our most precious values and challenge the harmful values inherent in our culture.

25. Joseph Goldstein's book, *Mindfulness: A Practical Guide to Awakening* has been especially helpful. I have used the concept of mindfulness in my book, *Mindful Spirituality*.

I am in the sunset years, now in my mid-eighties; night is coming, the lights will go out, and I will miss living as I now know it. Perhaps there is an afterlife, and my Christian faith teaches us that there is, yet I don't want to let go of what I now have. I have enormous gratitude for a wonderful life partner, a mature and healthy son with a marvelous family, and live in a beautiful setting with mountains, lakes, rivers, blue skies, and a comfortable home. I enjoy the modest work I do, continuing my life-calling with some teaching, writing, and assisting others as they attempt to find their way. Yet I continue to identify with my father, who on his death bed, said with tears: "I don't want to die." I will never forget his words; I am vulnerable.

I am also vulnerable in terms of health, though very grateful for reasonably good health and the long history of staying fit that is part of the life of an "old jock." There is the occasional forgetfulness, a slowing pace on my daily walks, a few aches and pains, and less activity. I am vulnerable.

We have adequate financial resources, but I still worry some about our nation's economy and whether there will be sufficient funds for my wife who is a decade younger to live well. We have been wise and careful, and she is incredibly competent, but I still feel vulnerable about leaving her. It will be also painful to leave our son and his wonderful family.

Like most people, I do have an active inner life, engaging in all that we describe as the mindful and contemplative life. Yes, I do have the presence of joy and peace, yet there is still some anxiety that is part of life, not specifically connected to day-to-day living. As a borderline perfectionist, I have some worry about nearly every endeavor. Will I be able to do it well, say the right thing, and make a positive contribution? Will my fears, subtle feelings of inferiority, and the need to be accepted cause me to miss a beat and say or do the wrong thing? Why do I sometimes feel anxious and depressed? I am vulnerable.

I live in the world I describe above, vulnerable because of personal, local, regional, national, and global problems. I try to live in a thoughtful and mature way, practicing mindfulness and contemplation, in part because these ways of being bring so much deep inner peace and happiness and because it is fulfilling and responsible way to live. Yet, in part because of the alcoholic home in which I grew up, there is a continuing sense that all might not be in place and on track. The boy in me still asks, "Will my father come home on Friday night?" When this happens, I pause and seek the comfort of the divine presence. We need to slow down, find quiet moments, and rest in God's love.

SLOWING DOWN

After I hurry through days
of busy occasions dutifully noted
on a calendar with fast-turning pages,
I hear whispers around me,
talk of how I am slowing down

As if something's wrong with that
and I should be sorry to be my age,
mournful about the changes.

But for now, I have to say
how welcome the changes are,
that it's good sometimes
to live within a small compass,
no longer in charge of everything
more than daily necessities,

that I am learning
to be worthy of time
and robust with memory
in a sanctuary of silence
where the loves of my long life
walk the shadows with me

where we embrace,
where we sing.

Jeanne Lohmann

Terms, Resources, and Discussion Questions:

Terms

1. Spiritual: in the religious world, it is the quest to make the "spirit" or the core of human life, rooted in the desire to integrate one's life with the person, will, and way of God or ultimate reality.
2. Contemplative: to focus with continued attention, in silence, and in the religious sense to meditate on spiritual matters that form the foundation of life.

3. Mindful: to overcome the gap of the endless streams of thought and focus on an immediate goal and purpose, staying in the present and caring for the immediate tasks in front of me.
4. Thoughtful: careful, reasoned thinking, able to arrive at credible understanding of issues and what is important.
5. Mature: to reach the condition of a desired state that is at rest, calm, capable, and wise.
6. Vulnerable: a way of living at risk and being overcome by negative forces and a shared human characteristic that enables us to empathize with others and connect with them.

Books to Read and Consult

1. Katy Butler, *The Art of Dying Well: A Practical Guide to a Good End of Life*
2. Joan Chittister, *The Gift of Years: Growing Old Gracefully*
3. Duncan S. Ferguson, *Mindful Spirituality: The Intentional Cultivation of the Spiritual Life*
4. James Fowler, *Stages of Faith: The Psychology of Human Development and the Quest for Meaning*
5. Richard Goldstein, *Mindfulness: A Practical Guide to Awakening*
6. Richard Rohr, *Falling Upward*
7. Ronald Rolheiser, *Sacred Fire: A Vision for a Deeper Human and Christian Maturity*
8. Tessa Watt, *Mindfulness: A Practical Guide*

Questions for Thought and Discussion

1. What are the greatest challenges you face in the evening of life?
2. What are the primary values and beliefs that give you guidance for living in the sunset years?
3. What are the practices that sustain you and give you hope in the evening of life?

4. How are other people helpful to you as you make your way through the sunset of life?

5. What is the place of organizations and small groups as you seek to be stable in these mature years?

SECTION ONE

Maintaining a Thoughtful and Credible Faith in the Mature Years

> "I am the light of the world. Whoever follows me will never walk in darkness but will have the light of life."
>
> (JOHN 8:12)

JESUS WAS A REMARKABLE story teller, and those who listened were moved by the insight and life-changing message of his stories, often in the form of parables. In his stories and teaching, he used vivid illustrations, images, symbols, metaphors, and analogies. He often used light as metaphor for truth and encouraged his followers of the Way to see truth and to live wisely within its boundaries. Spirit, too, was a word of importance to him. The word spirit in the Greek language is one that also means wind, and he likened the presence of God to a gentle and fresh wind, always with us, gently blowing and refreshing us.

We will explore the dimensions of faith, underlining that our faith must be filled with light, that is, be grounded in the truth and expressed in thoughtful and credible ways. He also said that the Spirit would guide and empower us. The lesson for all of us is that we must place our faith in that which is true; truth alone merits our trust. There are a variety of truths, and they come to us in many ways. It may come to us like a gently blowing wind that will heal us and empower us to flourish. It may come to us as a frightening tempest, blowing us away from dangerous shoals toward the current that will lead us home. It may come to us in the profound insight of one of the parables of Jesus, inviting us to put our trust in the will and way of God. In this quest to find and affirm the truth, we must also note that there is a course of action prescribed, one that asks us to engage in the divine mission. We add the obvious; there are many temptations and invitations to place our faith in that which is unworthy and even false. At times, there is even a failure to trust fully that it is wise to place our lives in the hands of God; we may not be sure what that means and ask whether there are implications that may be too demanding. We need to know, at least in part, what it means, for example, to be invited to engage in the divine mission. What is the divine mission? There are plenty of hucksters around who want to tell you that it means, often advancing their cause. We ponder, carefully read the signals, and make a wise choice, yet still wondering if I will have to give up a way of life that I enjoy? In short, we must be careful, thoughtful, and diligent, seeking and maintaining a credible faith in the sunset years of life.

CHAPTER THREE

Faith as the Dedicated and Continuing Quest for Truth

> "Then Jesus said to the Jews who believed in him, 'If you continue in my word, you are truly my disciples; and you will know the truth, and the truth will make you free.'"
>
> (John 8:31–32)

FINDING OUR WAY

IN THE INTRODUCTION, WE maintained that in order to live life wisely and well in the evening of life, we need to have a strong foundation, one built in the earlier years of life and one upon which we can draw with confidence in our later years. Across the early formative years of building our foundation for life, we may have had the opportunity and challenge to cultivate a spiritual frame of reference and be nurtured by the spiritual practices of prayer, study, contemplation, and quiet meditation. Now, in the evening of life, there are quiet moments of contemplation in which we have a new opportunity to nurture a receptive spirit that is open to the presence of the divine. We cultivate the capacity of staying focused and living in the present. We are now mindful about our inner being and thoughtful about our life choices. Yet we still sense a measure of vulnerability, given our age and the uncertain, complex, and even dangerous context in which we live. We need to have courage and be healthy and mature in all aspects of life.

So, we draw upon the foundation we have created in order to guide us in the sunset of life. We are able to be reflective and intentional about our inner life. We have the capacity to stay the course even though we live in a threatening environment. We are keenly aware of the elusiveness of truth and sense a great need to make religious commitments based on the truth; we want to make these commitments in a way that directly faces the harsh realities of our time, taking into account the pattern of our growth and the setting in which we live. As we do so, we are grateful for all the ways we have matured and for the people who have guided us. We hope that we have a relatively firm foundation, one that empowers us to live in a healthy way in this later phase of life. We sense that over the years, with a breadth of experience and managing the challenges in a changing and dangerous world, we have cultivated a mindset and frame of reference which have the qualities of a deep spirituality, the practice of contemplation, a mindful pattern of living in the realities of the present moment, all held together by an increasing maturity and the growing ability to cope wisely with life's challenges and celebrate life's joys.

As we move through this phase of life, grateful for a life-giving foundation, we now discover that *we need to build on this foundation*. We move forward into this phase of life, wanting above all to enjoy our new reality and have a peaceful evening. We are keenly aware that the earlier foundations we built are not where we stop, but they are what we build upon and move forward from to create a functional and beautiful structure, one that will bring us great satisfaction and a sense of peace. We start from within our spiritual frame of reference, continue to be contemplative and mindful, and make thoughtful decisions built on what we hope is an advanced level of our maturity.

In this new phase of life, we go forward within this well-developed mindset and frame of reference and begin to realize that we must nurture, sustain, and perhaps change and expand it. We do not stop changing and maturing when we approach the sunset of life, and we ask ourselves how to be wise and creative and live fully in this new and challenging period of life.

I am, as I write, in this moment facing the challenges of aging. In my vulnerability, I am asking myself what patterns of living and being are nurturing and life-giving at this moment? How can I live in a creative way that brings deep gratification? How do I live fully, using all that I have learned, yet aware of all that I need, and then chart my course toward a peaceful and fulfilling existence? I turn, as was implied earlier in the Introduction, to my Christian faith and carefully reflect on my fairly advanced understanding of the life and teaching of Jesus. What are the ways he lived that I might emulate and what did he teach that will enable me to flourish in the evening of life? I turn to the Gospel accounts with serious dedication, learn and grow as I study them, and then ponder the ways that competent scholars and devout saints have understood the life and teaching of Jesus across the centuries. My life has been enriched by this careful study and reflection.

In this process, of course, I have turned to his most influential interpreter, the apostle Paul, knowing that Paul does have his detractors. They point to some passages that appear to be chauvinistic, sexist, supportive of unjust social structures, and affirm traditional patterns of life that limit the freedom of parts of the population, counseling that they stay in traditional and subservient roles. One does have to read these passages with care, but in nearly every case where there are borderline traces of sexist and patriarchal passages, thoughtful scholars maintain that these documents are not likely his writing, but were likely written later by a more conservative author, perhaps a colleague and disciple of Paul, who used the custom of the time to name a noted person as the author to give the writing more authority.[1]

There was a time near the midpoint of Paul's mission in life when he addresses our basic question about how to live life in the best possible way. He is writing to a group of new Christians in Corinth, a quite diverse and good-sized city on the coast of Greece. It was a cosmopolitan city that had few restrictions on appropriate and ethical norms of living. The new church, which he was instrumental in founding, has members asking in a variety of ways the questions we are asking. How, then, given our new faith and our changing and complex environment, should we live in order to find more efficient structures in the church and encourage the members to become more spiritual and live an ethical life? To Paul, they essentially say: "Since you left, we have had many problems, some about how we organize and who should lead in our new congregation, and even more stressing are the urgent questions about how we should live, given our new faith and the challenging setting in which we live." Paul, drawing upon his understanding of the mission of Jesus, says in his first letter to

---

1. Only seven of the thirteen writings attributed to him are clearly his writing. Ephesians, Colossians, 2 Thessalonians, 1 and 2 Timothy, and Titus are considered questionable. We value these writings, especially the theological insights in Ephesians and Colossians. Crossan and Reed, *In Search of Paul*, 105–23.

the Corinthians, at the close of chapter 13: "And now faith, hope, and love abide, but the greatest of these is love." It is these three words, faith (*pistis*), hope (*elpis*), and love (*agape*), that will give us categories for finding our way and empowering us to flourish in the evening of life.

> Now you are the body of Christ and individually members of it. And God has appointed in the church, first apostles, second prophets, third teachers, then deeds of power; then gifts of healing, forms of assistance, forms of leadership, various kinds of tongues. Are all apostles? Are all prophets? Are all teachers? Do all work miracles? Do all possess gifts of healing? Do all speak in tongues? Do all interpret? But strive for the greater gifts. And I will show you a still more excellent way (1 Cor 12:27–31).

It is this "more excellent way" on which we want to focus; it will help us better to understand how we are to live in this challenging period of life. Following his observations about order, he moves directly to the great verities of the new emerging religion, capturing the essence of the message of Jesus. The foundational norm of Christian living is selfless and unconditional love, *agape*, yet he begins with faith, and we will follow his example and order. Faith is a word that has many connotations and subtle variations, one of which suggests that faith is the process of putting one's trust and confidence in what we believe to be a good foundation for life. While not directly expressed in this way by Paul, it is clear that he understands faith as trust, and he implies that there are three primary characteristics of faith that give us a good foundation: it must be based on truth, it must be trustworthy in guiding us in healthy and ethical behavior, and it must point toward action and a way of life filled with love and the commitment to justice.

We begin with the first dimension of faith and maintain that authentic faith in the evening of life is to place our confidence and belief in a spiritual outlook and way of life that is credible; that is, as far as humanly possible, our faith must be placed in that which is true.

A THOUGHTFUL AND CREDIBLE FAITH

The first dimension of the thoughtful and credible faith, then, is that it must be based on that which is true, that is, as close as we can understand it, it must be based on reality (what is) and what has actually happened. In suggesting that this reality is rooted in a religious understanding only intensifies the urgency of the requirement of truth. Religion has certainly been a domain in which a wide assortment of beliefs about the world, about life, and about how to live have been generated. There is an incredible assortment of beliefs in the several religions of the human family. Among them are a range of beliefs and ethical norms that are different and in conflict; these many ideas and consequent practices cannot all be true, wise, and healthy.

It is important to note that many of these beliefs and practices have grown out of the human need to understand the world, even the cosmos, and nature in all of its diversity and power. It also points to how humans come together for the common good. They seek to know how to govern the association of people living in tribes, regions, and recognize the need for a government that will bring some order, justice, and peace. Humans in particular have been very creative in framing beliefs and ethical norms out of their immediate needs. So, we have a vast range of beliefs about the gods, perhaps the god of our realm, or even a more cosmic, universal, and eternal God or Spirit who might be interested in how we care for the universe and find ways to live together with a sense of peace.

As an occasional teacher of world religions, I have spent years of my career learning about this vast domain of beliefs and practices. Some are rooted in nature as those living close to nature have tried to understand its power, unpredictability, and dangers. Some are rooted in the mysteries that surround human experience, probing the depth of the human psyche, wondering how to understand the range of human feelings and answer an abundance of questions about the meaning of life. There are the ethical questions such as how to live next to another group or tribe or country that needs the resources that are abundant in our region. Some, of course, have been guided by religious leaders and teachers, given authority by the tribe or group to prescribe patterns of belief and practice. These great leaders and teachers, Moses, Buddha, Jesus, Muhammad and a few others, with both female and male identities, have been elevated to a place that suggests they speak and act with divine authority. How is it possible to discern patterns of truth in this vast array of options? Is it wise just to describe these patterns, beliefs, and religious commitments, leaving the question of ultimate truth aside and focusing more on description and historical understanding? Such an approach is one option, and I have been both enlightened by my study of the religions of the world and also learned to be fearful and cautious because so much harm has been done in the name of religion.

My goal has been to be aware of the danger of what we might call religious superstition, carefully outlining its possible risks, and then to seek those religious beliefs and practices that appear to be true to reality, have life-giving teachings, suggest healthy patterns of growth, and provide ethical norms that protect, guide, and lead to the common good. One part of this strategy has been to ask two of the most fundamental questions about this array of religious beliefs and practice. One, of course, is the question of what is true, and the related one is what is life-giving and healthy. Ideally, they will come together in a religious outlook. First, let's *underline what we mean by true*; the answer is not easy, but the following criteria may help us start a long and complex undertaking of describing the nature of truth.

The first and most obvious part of the answer is that a statement or belief is true if it describes and matches reality. Does the belief or statement describe what is, what actually happened, what is currently the case, and what might come our way if we affirm it? Our religious commitments will be severely compromised if what they say and do does not match our best understanding of reality. But to move beyond our experience and attempt to discern reality in reference to metaphysical religious beliefs is very difficult. Mathematical, logical, and scientific statements and descriptions tend to fit more easily into the question of truth. Generally, we have confidence in these statements because of a careful process of studying evidence and using logical reasoning. Yet I am told that advanced scholars in mathematics disagree with one another, not so much about 2 plus 2 equals 4, but in much more advanced calculations.

Other disciplines, in fact most of the ones in a university catalogue, also make judgments about truth. They work diligently to make sure what they describe and teach are close to the truth, although there are generally differences of opinion because an interpretation of the data is expressed in different ways. For example, most would say that it is true that Abraham Lincoln was a good president, but some scholars, perhaps on the question of slavery, might say that he did not move fast enough in making slavery a violation of the national law. Historical scholarship carefully seeks answers to these questions, and clean-cut judgments about what is true and what is false are often addressed in careful language. It is not uncommon to make a lead statement that starts with the observation that my observation is partially true and needs further study.

There is another form of truth, and there are several. I want to underline one that is very important to our inner life; it is what is often called personal truth, an encounter between two people that is authentic, or in the religious context, a way of being in a relationship with a personal God, a way that is open, honest, and life-giving, a way that truly connects with another. This is the kind of truth that speaks about being fulfilled because *the relationship* is based on authenticity, trust, and commitment. For example, I may say that I know there is a deep level of sincerity in this relationship. It sets me free and has insight and practices that heal. Religious thought and descriptions of practice often fall in this category.

Yet these same qualities are also present in the category of truth that seeks answers to metaphysical questions, especially about the existence of God. As we do ask this ontological question, we reason deeply and carefully, and also review the history of the founding (and perhaps the founder) and the development of the religion. Our judgments about truth take the form of expressions of partial truth, saying this part of the religious outlook is essentially true, and then acknowledge that there are others parts that are accepted as starting presuppositions and essentially accepted on faith.

So, nearly all religious traditions ask in some form whether their beliefs and practices are true. In order to answer this question, they have a variety of tasks, one of which is to study diligently and ask a range of inquiries. For example, there is likely the need to gain assurance that their faith is based on a correct interpretation of history, that its beliefs are framed in a logical order, and that it leads its followers to health, inner peace, ethical guidance, purpose, and maturity. When some assurance is given on these aspects of the belief system, then it is possible to say that the religion is essentially true and its teachings can be affirmed and trusted. These questions may have to do with the issue of ontological truth, others may have to do with healthy practices, and still others have to do with both historical study and cultural understanding. In the cases of the Abrahamic monotheistic religions, the questions are often historical, although the other forms of truth are certainly present. Jews, Christians, and Muslims ask whether the contemporary practice of the religion matches the beliefs, values, and aims of the original founders, with attention focusing on Moses, Jesus, and Muhammad. The question is also present in Buddhism, as followers seek to understand what Buddha said and did. A careful answer will require a very dedicated study, sifting through centuries of development, examining with care the historical documents, and then studying the current outlook and practices of the religion. In short, scholars must unpack and assess the historical formation of traditions, and it is difficult to know whether the present understanding within these traditions matches the starting point of the original founding. Do the present beliefs and practices accurately describe and reflect the original teaching and historical circumstances? Is this necessary? We must then ask whether contemporary teachers and interpreters of the faith have created their understanding of the religion out of their own prior understanding, the cultural assumptions of their time, and whether the interpretations are accurate, nurturing, and trustworthy. The hermeneutical task is to circle around historical origins to faith statements and back again to a more advanced understanding; this circling around is a necessary hermeneutical endeavor in seeking truth.[2]

The apostle Paul approaches this subject in a careful way in his letter to the Corinthian church. He says: "But we speak about God's wisdom, secret and hidden, which God decreed before the ages for our glory. None of the rulers of this age understood this; for if they had, they would not have crucified the Lord of glory" (1 Cor 2:7–8). Paul is using his current understanding and interpretation of the Jesus event and is suggesting that Jesus was not fully understood by many of his contemporaries. Paul is implying that one needs not only the basic facts, but also "the eyes of faith" to truly understand. One must stand within a faith orientation and be open to its teachings in order to get the message.

In reference to the question of God's existence, it must be admitted that God does not fit under a microscope, and that we often do create God in our own image and out of our preunderstanding. Is there really a true God, or is the idea of God generated out of our deep needs and then created in our own image? And if there is such a God, do we often describe this God out of our own cultural assumptions and in words that may make sense to us, but may be a mystery to others? For example, we often use family metaphors in order to make God personal, one with whom we can have a relationship. We call God a "person" and say "our Father" although the term Father has been called into question because it has a patriarchal bias. Is this a good way to speak about God?[3]

---

2. Philosophers and religious scholars often speak of "the hermeneutical circle."

3. See Jack Miller's book, *God: A Biography*, a Pulitzer Prize winning book, that address the many ways that God is spoken about in the Bible, underlining how we tend to create God in our own image, our circumstances and our emotions. See as well the book by Kwok Pui-Lan, *Postcolonial Politics and Theology: Unraveling Empire for a Global Word*, a thoughtful articulation of the view that much of our theology was created in a context of colonialism and has assumptions from this era.

FAITH AS THE DEDICATED AND CONTINUING QUEST FOR TRUTH 45

A great many other questions arise as we seek truth in our religious beliefs and practices, but I want to move directly to the Christian faith and explore in what ways these forms of truth may be present in understanding the Christian Way. In a faith orientation, we often use the form of truth described as personal truth, one that serves as the foundation of a safe and loving relationship. It may be verbal, but it often has nonverbal dimensions as well. So, when we say that it is a true relationship, we imply that is full of honesty, trust, and deep love. We do speak often about being in relationship with God in this way, and that this relationship is profoundly true in the sense of an authentic personal connection.[4] Of course, we also care deeply about other forms of truth as well, such as describing accurate history, using clear and logical arguments in order to make sure our religious statements are wise and helpful to others, and that our spiritual experiences are healthy and nurturing.

We acknowledge that our belief in God is difficult to prove, although there are a number of so-called "proofs for the existence God" such as the need for a first cause in order to understand the "cause and effect" flow of creation. Or we ask why there is order and structure in the universe and attribute this condition to God's creation because we think that such a universe did require a creator and an all-knowing mind. These forms of "truth" may be helpful, but do not go beyond just suggesting that the existence of God is one possible explanation for these realities. These classic proofs, about five of them with some variations, have been more reassuring for believers rather than proving the existence of God; they may make sense, but lack absolute proof that the God we understand to exist was behind these realities. We may argue that God exists because there must be a first cause of the expanding universe, all the galaxies, and indeed for all that exists. Someone or something had to push over the first domino. This "first cause" argument has some appeal although it also has some limitations, such as not identifying who or what pushed over the first domino. Even if it were free of this or other limitations, it would not necessarily take us to the God of Abraham, Moses, Jesus, and Muhammad.

There is also the statement that what has been taught by a great religious leader such as Moses points us to a deep moral truth, one that

---

4. See Marcus Borg's book, *God We Never Knew*, in which he speaks about how his view of God changed from his childhood faith to his well-informed contemporary faith. He stresses the presence of the divine in our lives and the world around us rather than a God who is distant and only occasionally has been present in human life.

is universal in scope. We think that it is so profound and inclusive that it must have been given to the human family by God. For example, he prescribed the Ten Commandments, and we have understood them as universal in scope. We may argue that they are not limited by culture or history and, therefore, must have come from God. It is possible to make the case that what he taught is ethically the right thing to do (a truthful ethical norm), as well as pointing to what we should not do because it is harmful and wrong. Yet this observation may be more of an understanding of the greatness of Moses and his guidance of his followers than it is a proof for the existence and character of God. Buddha taught profound ethical guidance as well, but did not suggest it came from a personal God.

What we do affirm is that many religious "truths" do fall into the category of personal truth. And standing within faith, we affirm that these beliefs point to metaphysical truth. In essence, we trust that there is a God of love and light that stands behind it all. It may be a bit easier for us to say that our beliefs are "true" in that they lead to what is good for the human family and even the good of the earth. There is also the additional sense of truth as we line up these beliefs and state them in an orderly, logical, and consistent pattern.[5]

My way of speaking about my Christian faith fits more easily into the category of personal truth, although I care deeply about my faith being true in other categories of truth. The perfect example for this more personal understanding of truth is the statement of Jesus: "The truth will set you free." As we grasp the truth about our existence, understand healthy ways of living, and reject superstitious beliefs, we are enlightened and liberated from unhealthy practices, myths, projections, and biases that may be harmful rather than helpful. The truth has set us free, and made it possible to have an authentic relationship with God.

I am hopeful that my faith orientation does contain elements that point to a way of understanding all of reality in a truthful way, that is, that there is a gracious God who stands behind it all and engages with what S/He created and actually communicates with the human family. In particular, I hope and even trust that my understanding of Jesus is based on critical historical research that demonstrates that the actions of his life were described accurately and really happened, and also that his teaching is true for me, that is, it puts my life together in a mature and healthy way.

---

5. There are several excellent books that argue and attempt to demonstrate that that God exists. See Richard Swinburne, *Coherence of Theism* and David Bentley Hart, *Experience of God: Being, Consciousness, Bliss*.

I do try to have a thoughtful and credible faith, yet also one that I realize is the sort of faith that invites me to continue on the path of a dedicated quest for truth. Regarding a spiritual outlook and ethical way of life, my hope is to continue to cultivate what the apostle Paul affirms is our guiding center, the very mind of Christ (1 Cor 2:16).

FAITH AS THE THOUGHTFUL, CREDIBLE, DEDICATED, AND CONTINUING QUEST FOR TRUTH

Earlier, we stressed the need for a thoughtful faith, and noted Paul's admonition "to be adult" in matters of faith. Not all people of faith, nor even the majority of the people of faith, can do a systematic evaluation about the truthfulness of their beliefs and practices. With honest humility, we acknowledge that fully to understand the New Testament account about the life and teaching of Jesus will require a good measure of careful study of history, culture, and language. We are grateful that some of those who were his contemporaries and followed him did attempt to put his teaching in order and gave shape to the patterns of Christian belief in a way they hoped was a truthful account. There was a guiding belief that there were those who were "called" and indeed "inspired" who had a vocation and the gifts of putting the faith together in true and understandable ways and then teaching and proclaiming the life-giving message.

In time, the new church developed a kind of system that recognized those with such a vocation, those with special gifts to undertake different dimensions of articulating the message, others with gifts of organization, and still others with pastoral skills to help new disciples nurture their new faith. Initially, there was an oral tradition regarding these matters, in part because it was an oral culture and many new disciples lacked the ability to read. It took several decades for the story of Jesus to be written, drawing upon the testimony of those who were present, observed it, and were guided by it. The apostle Paul, a well-educated Jewish teacher, introduced the first writings about the Christian faith, and following his writing, the Gospel accounts emerged, with Mark the first Gospel. Matthew and Luke used Mark's account for their Gospels and information from oral traditions, and the Gospel of John appeared later and is quite different that the other Gospels. They all wrote prior to the rise of historical critical practices and from the perspective of their time and new beliefs.

Scholars across the centuries have studied this development of the New Testament, and over the last approximately two hundred and fifty years, there has been a great interest in finding the "real Jesus" buried to some extent in this literature. It is called the quest of the historical Jesus, a title translated from the German title of Albert Schweitzer's book, a classic in this endeavor. This effort has been incredibly thoughtful and dedicated, and it continues in the present. Several quite specific methods of study have developed, and an array of judgments in this "quest of the historical Jesus" have surfaced.

I have joined this quest with energy and gratification across the fifty years of my academic career, arriving at the following conclusions. The first one is that I believe that the church's desire to have an inspired and accurate version of the life and teachings of Jesus has been positive, although I know that what was written and later put in the form of the New Testament still needs critical historical study in order to be fully understood and credible. A simple faith statement that the Bible is the inspired Word of God, free from error, is not altogether convincing except for "true believers." The biblical records may be true in the sense of personal truth, yet still need technical study for us to be sure about many of the historical questions. I find the message true and life-giving; and I could stop there, but I can learn even more by using the methods of critical historical inquiry in the quest for the historical Jesus. We engage in this form of study thoughtfully and carefully because we want to understand the life and teaching of Jesus, and as we do, we are transformed by it.

Second, this form of historical inquiry provides us with valuable information and does lead us to a deeper understanding of the life and teachings of Jesus. What I learn enriches my life and gives it new dimensions. It is the case that some scholars and interpreters of the life of Jesus have moved away from the traditional understanding of Jesus. I have a few books that have been so eager to place Jesus in the context of their beliefs that they have almost ignored the historical study of Jesus. Some of the distortions are "amazing creations," although they are without historical support. Still others have suggested that we must be cautious and have humility about what we learn about Jesus in the Gospels because they were written many years after the death of Jesus and prior to the rise of critical historical study. New Testament scholars in the mid-twentieth century, such as Rudolf Bultmann, have said we can know very little from the biblical records, yet we can "know truly" by faith. These observations about the challenge of finding the historical Jesus have been somewhat persuasive in New Testament scholarship, yet over time this point of view has had some thoughtful challenges, and there was a new outlook in New Testament scholarship that suggests "we can know enough" for guiding the church in belief and practice. I join with those who are saying that careful study, with the above observations in mind, still gives us a good picture of the life and teachings of Jesus. Careful study will give us a relatively accurate portrayal of the Jesus of history, and we go the rest of the way, as believers, to the Christ of faith.

Third, I join with those who say we have what we need. It is possible for us to be deeply sympathetic with those who need another level of reassurance because we know how difficult the historical quest has been. But I do not say as easily as some that "the Bible is the inspired Word of God" and then ignore the realities of history. It may be a better direction to use critical historical study of the biblical accounts of the life and teaching of Jesus and affirm, because it is best record we have, that it contains the "Word of God," that is, it gives us sufficient information to make judgments of faith and belief. We work diligently so that the information we receive is *credible*, and we place our faith in Jesus, as we are invited to do in the accounts we have.

And fourth, I continue to be *dedicated* in the search for all aspects of the life and teachings of Jesus. We need to take advantage of works such as John P. Meier's lifelong study and four volume work, *A Marginal Jew: Rethinking the Historical Jesus* and many other dedicated and scholarly works (and there are many!), acknowledging that only few people in the community of faith have this calling and the required skills. We continue our study, as we are able, and ask those with the special gifts to help us. We take advantage of the many ways and means that the ecumenical church has to guide our continuing study.

A PERSONAL AFFIRMATION

Perhaps a personal note will be helpful, giving some of the reasons why I now find this biblical foundation for my faith both moderately accurate and also trustworthy. As I am mindful and thoughtful, I discover in the "Jesus-event" a way of understanding religious truth; it has guided and empowered me to move toward maturity, find meaning in life, and be guided by universal ethical norms. I can honor excellent scholarship, not see it as a threat or heresy, place my faith in God, and learn about following Jesus from the best scholarship possible using the records we have. I have found that Jesus was "full of grace and truth" and by God's power and presence, I too can move toward ultimate love and light.

I came to my faith orientation in my last year of high school; I was invited to make this leap of faith by gifted and kind people in the church that my high school girlfriend attended. And it was a leap of faith, uninformed as I was. I was encouraged in this step of faith by those who worked in a parachurch organization focusing on ministry to high school students. As my interest increased, I attended two different churches, one a moderate Presbyterian Church that was true to its heritage, and one that was an independent church with kind and good people, although deeply rooted in a conservative and dispensational perspective. In both of these church settings, I was treated with respect and was helped gradually to begin to understand the Christian faith. I knew very little about the differences between churches and the variety of traditions and ways of putting faith together at that time.

In my college years, I continued to attend the university ministry of a conservative church and participated in another parachurch ministry. I began to learn in these settings and also to be challenged by several university courses with a major in history and a minor in philosophy. I began to learn that it is not that simple and easy to say that Christian belief is based on true assumptions about reality and history, and that we have the authority of a divinely inspired Bible. Increasingly, I saw the need for a credible and thoughtful faith orientation. Even the admonition, have "simple faith," often used by well-meaning people as I asked questions, became useful as I turned it upside down. It took on new meaning for me as I began to understand "simple" as one, as a coordinated and integrated whole and that this is the nature of truth.[6] Simple faith was not naïve and uniformed, avoiding dedicated study and asking hard questions. For me, it was wanting to probe diligently for the ultimate truth about the cosmos.[7] I also had some discomfort with those who were in what appeared to me to be in "the cult of the absolute." I learned to be cautious around those people who had no doubts.

6. The story is told about the Dalai Lama, during his visit to New York, went out on the streets to a hot dog stand. When asked what he wanted, he replied: "One with everything."

7. I have been helped by the thought of the American philosopher, Ken Wilber, whose books nearly all point in the direction of order in creation, and the need to capture this "oneness" in religious thought. See Ken Wilber, *Religion of Tomorrow: A Vision for the Future of the Great Traditions.*

I did preserve and advance my relatively new faith as I attended a relatively conservative, yet scholarly seminary. It was a positive experience, although looking back, I now see that I was not fully exposed to the range of ideas and interpretations of the Christian faith. There was a slightly defensive edge to the culture of the seminary, yet I am grateful for the rigor they demanded in my studies. Following seminary, I continued my study of philosophy in a graduate program at Stanford. I was again nudged toward being more open to alternative ways of understanding the world around me and my faith. I began to question some of the assumptions of what appeared to be a quite conservative view of faith to which I was introduced. I left my graduate study at Stanford and took a position back in Eugene, Oregon in campus ministry. I was again situated in a conservative church, but assigned to a very scholarly and question-asking environment at the University of Oregon. I began making a transition from a faith orientation rooted in American culture and carefully protective of its evangelical faith to one that welcomed questions, learned from other faith orientations, and trusted careful scholarship. The faith orientation that claims to have the truth about belief and practice and asserts this faith over against other expressions of faith was not as attractive to me. I came from a family tradition that did not see questions as a threat, and, following my doctoral studies in theology and biblical studies at the University of Edinburgh, I felt free of a somewhat narrow tradition and open to the wonderful world of scholarship and a world culture filled with diversity of thought, customs, and religious life.

I valued the growth and understanding that I was gaining. In a gratifying way, I have continued what became a lifelong process of welcoming questions, deepening my faith understanding, and expanding my vision of a life of faith that is thoughtful, credible, and dedicated to continued growth and enrichment. I enjoyed and valued the deepening of my understanding. I was no longer afraid of knowledge and began to understand what Jesus meant when he said, "The truth will set you free," which was the welcoming sign on the University of Oregon library.

I have spent a career, both in the church and the academy, diligently trying to love all those who are on the pathway of faith, careful about judging those with whom I differ, and honoring the lane that has taken them to their current location. I loved teaching courses in world religions, an assignment in which I continued to learn. I have stayed active in the Presbyterian Church, true to my Scottish heritage, and have spent the majority of my life as a teacher and scholar. I continue to be profoundly "taken" by the Jesus of history and have written two books on that subject.[8] I also continue to ponder the possible differences between the Jesus of history and the Christ of faith and have sought to keep them together as I serve in the church. I try to emulate Jesus, full of grace and truth, and have found the life dedicated to truth and love, serving those in need and who want to learn a most fulfilling way of life. I genuinely enjoy engaging in the quest for the historical Jesus.[9]

An essential part of faith is the dedicated and continuing quest for truth. A life-giving faith is to put one's trust in that which is true. So, I am gradually learning to live with a wealth of wisdom, drawing upon all that we have learned in the several decades of our lives, knowing that wisdom gives us peace and guidance.

Terms, Resources, and Discussion Questions

Terms

1. Truth: the state of being the case; an accurate account of reality; a body of statements that describes what is.
2. Credible: an affirmation or statement about reality that is based on evidence and logical reasoning.
3. Historical Critical Study: a way of pursuing the accuracy of events and descriptions of occurrences based on careful historical study and evidence.
4. Faith: placing one's confidence and loyalty on that which is true and trustworthy.
5. The Quest for the Historical Jesus: The pursuit of understanding the life and teachings of Jesus that is based on sound historical practice rather than the assumptions of a particular Christian tradition.

Books to Read and Consult

1. Dale C. Allison, *Constructing Jesus: Memory, Imagination, and History*

---

8. They are titled *The Radical Teaching of Jesus* and *The Radical Invitation of Jesus*.
9. The title of Albert Schweitzer's classic work, translated into English and published near the beginning of the twentieth century.

2. Marcus J. Borg, *Jesus: Uncovering the Life, Teachings, and Relevance of a Religious Revolutionary;* and *The God We Never Knew: Beyond Dogmatic Religion to a More Authentic Contemporary Faith*
3. John Dominic Crossan, *Jesus: A Revolutionary Biography*
4. Ilia Delio, *The Unbearable Wholeness of Being: God, Evolution, and the Power of Love*
5. Duncan S. Ferguson, *The Radical Invitation of Jesus*
6. John P. Meier, *A Marginal Jew: Rethinking the Historical Jesus,* in four volumes
7. N. T. Wright, *The New Testament and the People of God, The Resurrection of the Son of God,* and *Jesus and the Victory of God*

Questions for Thought and Discussion

1. In what ways should we study the New Testament documents in order to understand the life and teachings of Jesus?
2. How do we read these documents in order to get the most accurate description of the life of Jesus?
3. How do you understand truth, and how can you be sure you are accessing, describing, and living the truth?
4. In what ways can we be reassured that our faith is based on that which is true and trustworthy?
5. In what ways do you think the Bible is the "word of God"?

CHAPTER FOUR

Faith as the Deep and Abiding Trust in Divine Wisdom

"Now when all of the people were baptized, and when Jesus also had been baptized and was praying, the heaven was opened, and the Holy Spirit descended upon him like a dove. And a voice came from heaven, 'You are my Son, the Beloved; with you I am well pleased.'"

(LUKE 3:21–22)

"In those days Jesus came from Nazareth of Galilee and was baptized by John in the Jordan. And just as he was coming up out of the water, he saw the heavens torn apart and the Spirit descending like a dove on him. And a voice came from heaven, "You are my Son, the Beloved, with you I am well pleased."

(MARK 1:9–11)

"Now after John was arrested, Jesus came to Galilee, proclaiming the good news of God and saying, 'The time is fulfilled, and the kingdom of God has come near;'repent and believe the good news.'"

(MARK 1:14–15)

"Six days later, Jesus took with him Peter and James and his brother John and led them up a high mountain, by themselves. And he was transfigured before them, and his face shone like the sun, and his clothes became dazzling white . . . . While he was still speaking, suddenly a bright cloud overshadowed them, and from cloud a voice said, 'This is my Son, the Beloved, with him I am well pleased; listen to him.'"

(MATTHEW 17:1–5)

"Then Jesus went with them to a place called Gethsemane, and he said to his disciples, 'Sit here while I go over there and pray.... Again, he went away for the second time and prayed. 'My Father, if this cannot pass unless I drink it, your will be done.'"

(MATTHEW 17:42)

"It was now about noon, and the darkness came over the whole land until three in the afternoon, while the sun's light failed; and the curtain of the temple was torn in two. Then Jesus crying in a loud voice, said 'Father into your hands, I commend my spirit.'"

(LUKE 23:44–45)

THE QUEST FOR DIVINE TRUTH

JESUS HAD A PROFOUND commitment to truth, truth as the accurate statement of what is and what has happened, truth when a statement or argument is logical, truth as a personal and transforming experience such as an encounter and connection with a dear friend, and ultimate Truth, a relationship of faith in, dedication to, and communication with the divine. During his public life, Jesus would often listen well and then, in response to an observed occurrence or a comment from another person, would gently expand the comments of others with a profound insight that would confirm the truth of what was said and done, often deepening the love and trust in the relationship. Matthew, early in his Gospel, records that Jesus "went throughout Galilee, teaching in their synagogues and proclaiming the good news of the kingdom and curing every disease and every sickness among the people" (Matt 4:23). His fame spread and people longed to hear Jesus speak life-saving truth and be healed from an illness. He lived a life teaching and healing, full of profound insight and liberating truth, deep love and empathy, and always with integrity and authenticity.

Following this introduction to the travels and teaching of Jesus in the Galilee, Matthew then begins his extraordinary account of the ministry and teaching of Jesus, placing his actions and speeches in the settings when and where they occurred, and then writing what he believed was a true account of what Jesus did and taught. The accuracy of his account is undergirded by other writings, such as the Gospel of Mark,[1] an oral tradition that preserved much of the teaching of Jesus, and Matthew's own personal experience as a disciple. Matthew's Gospel is remarkably well organized and invites listeners to hear the message of Jesus, accept its truth, and be converted to living a life of integrity and healing love. Matthew, who had the benefit of meeting Jesus and having first-hand knowledge of the message of Jesus, provides a marvelous account of the life and teaching of Jesus.[2]

In the historical time and setting of Jesus, there were other healers and magicians who also traveled, interacted with listeners, and spoke to crowds who longed for wisdom and care. Their actions and message had a portion of truth in them, yet, as far as we can tell, some of them were often less concerned about providing helpful information and life-giving insight and more concerned to persuade listeners to give money and allegiance.

Matthew, however, transformed by his encounter with Jesus, had a deep concern to understand Jesus correctly and communicate what Jesus did and taught accurately, although his account did not have the benefit of critical historical methods as we now understand them. He was deeply committed to providing a "good news" (gospel) account, sermonic at times with the motivation to help people and provide guidance to the young church. The truth about which Jesus spoke and Matthew records comes to us with clarity, wisdom, and as guidance for a life of faith. It is especially helpful to those of us in the evening of life.

As people across the years of history have listened and studied what Matthew wrote, they have been deeply moved and often healed by the account in Matthew concerning the wisdom and insight of Jesus. It is clear from the records we have that Jesus believed that what he was teaching was filled with divine wisdom about the meaning of life and the ethical norms of living in an authentic way in a complex setting. Matthew's account is a succinct summary of the foundational axiom of Jesus: "And the truth will set you free."

---

1. Matthew, clearly had the Gospel of Mark in his possession as he wrote.

2. Scholars, across the ages, have studied the Gospel of Matthew and attempted to measure its authenticity, acknowledging that it is an "extended sermon" more than a biography based on critical historical study, yet an authentic account having Matthew's personal observations and experience.

We are safe to say, following the accounts in Matthew and reading as well the accounts of Mark, Luke, and John, that people listened carefully, initially to Jesus, later to his disciples, and then as they were able, read the Gospel accounts in a way that gave them information, insight, and healed their souls. They learned that Jesus taught his followers the truth about life, offered ways of healing, ethical teaching and guidance, and a foundational direction in life. They also learned that Jesus truly believed that what he taught was divine wisdom, a message from God that would heal individuals, restore the community of faith, and inspire people to work for peace and justice.

What made Jesus nearly unique and fully trustworthy is that he spoke the truth in love and lived with such integrity that he had to be taken seriously; he was what he taught, a rare expression of the best of humankind. Those who longed for a good life sensed that he was one who brought divine wisdom to transform lives and create a just and peaceful social order. They saw him as opposed to those whose quests were for power and wealth rather than healing souls and caring for those who were hungry and sick. Jesus, in many of his speeches and actions, had the audacity to challenge the power structures, the religious leaders, and the religious establishment. He offered alternative ways of putting life together and creating a just social order in healthy and transforming ways.

THE UNDERSTANDING AND COMMITMENT OF JESUS

At his baptism by John, Jesus more fully understood and experienced the truth of his calling. He had a mystical experience; deep in his heart and mind, he heard the voice of God, "You are my Son, the Beloved; with you I am well pleased" (Mark 1:9–11).[3] Jesus, not unlike other revolutionary prophets, had a keen sense of being "called" by God to a spiritual vocation. He would have likely been in conversations with other Jewish teachers about their belief that there was one who is coming to restore Israel, and terms such as messiah ("Christ" in Greek) and Son of Man would have been used to point to the one who was to come in order to guide and lead in this restoration.[4] These titles and expectations may have

---

3. Some have wondered what the Scripture passages mean when they teach that "Jesus heard the voice of God." I am inclined to think that it was a metaphorical way to describe Jesus as having a deep insight that gave him direction.

4. There was a fervent hope by many of the Jewish people at the time of Jesus that God would intervene in their lives and deliver them from the oppression of foreign

prepared Jesus to understand his calling and to hear the guidance of God. He sensed the presence of God and that people were ready to receive the truth and live freely and faithfully. Jesus may have had a developing messianic identity.

Although our information is somewhat limited about the early adult life of Jesus, we know that as a young man he worked with his father, Joseph, as a carpenter, likely making and repairing boats for the fishing industry in the Lake of Galilee and perhaps assisting the Romans in the building of a new city in Galilee called Sepphoris, a mere three miles from Nazareth. At approximately the age of thirty, while living as a faithful Jew where he had grown up, he sensed the leading of God to change his vocation from a carpenter to a teacher and prophet in order to help nurture the religious life of the Jewish people. He did so initially in Galilee, then expanded his vision to revitalize the spiritual life of all of Israel with a focus on teaching and speaking truth to power in Jerusalem.

As he sensed and embraced this divine calling, he decided that he needed to learn more about this vocation, left the region of the Galilee, and traveled south into the region of Judea. It was there, a few miles outside of the center of Jewish life in Jerusalem, that he visited his cousin John. John was called the Baptist because of his mission as a prophet to revitalize the faith of the Jewish people by inviting them to be baptized, an act of cleansing and making a commitment to live as faithful follower of God.

Jesus was welcomed by John, and he identified with the community that had formed around John. A large number of people from Jerusalem and other locations had come to learn about John's ministry and message. Like the others, Jesus asked that John baptize him as his first step toward his new life as a rabbi (teacher of divine wisdom) and a prophet. John, somewhat reluctantly, consented, but underlined in his conversation with Jesus that it was he who needed the guidance of Jesus rather than the other way around. Jesus prevailed and was baptized by John. It was a deeply spiritual experience for Jesus and a powerful first step in his new vocation. The baptism had a profound impact on him, and he would have understood it as cleansing act that "washed away" all the previous reluctance and questions that Jesus may have had about his new life calling. It was also an act of dedication to God and a commitment to join with John in proclaiming the message of the coming reign of God. This act of

---

governments and a life of poverty. They hoped that a messiah would come, set them free, and restore a government that was just and bring peace.

baptism renewed his conviction that he was now called by God to a new vocation, the living and sharing of divine wisdom that would transform individuals and guide them in creating a more just and humane society.

The Christian community has understood Jesus across the centuries as sinless and totally faithful in his service to God. It has understood the baptism of Jesus as not so much an act of being washed clean of sin, but more of an act of identification with those who had come to John for renewal and a commitment to a mission in life. For Jesus, it was a major step in his dedication to his life of service.[5] While there is not a simple and clear account of all that he learned, a careful reading would suggest that there were at least three dimensions in this dramatic change in his life.

The first dimension would have been his deep desire to *understand and follow the guidance of God* in all aspects of his life. It was the confirmation that he was being called to a profound vocation, one that he understood as the proclamation and implementation of the reign of God (the kingdom of God). It was a moment when Jesus more fully understood his divine vocation, sensed a need for guidance, and especially sought divine wisdom that would enlighten and empower him to follow the will of God.

As one engaged in Christian mission across the adult years of my life, I have heard the stories of many people seeking to understand God's will for their lives. "How do I learn what is the will of God?" is a common question, one that seeks a more literal step by step process than the general goal of a life filled with love and compassion. These people have expressed in their question the need to know and follow the will of God for their lives, but were unsure of how to discern the will of God. They have also asked about how they might cultivate the inner strength to follow God's will and way once it is known. In these conversations, I have spoken with these seekers about learning from the example and teaching of Jesus as one who sought the will of God, grasped it, and followed divine wisdom. This account of the dedication of Jesus, fully expressed at his baptism, has been a special guide to them. Jesus heard the confirmation of God in his baptism and seemed to know where it would lead. As I have talked with these sincere people, I have sensed that they are inspired by the story of the baptism of Jesus, yet want to know as clearly as Jesus seemed to know where it would lead. They have sincerely wondered

---

5. The baptism of Jesus has not been seen by Christians as an act of cleansing from sin; rather it has been viewed as an act of commitment to identify with this new community and join with John in the proclamation of the reign (or kingdom) of God.

about next steps. They have asked how to hear the voice of God and grasp the guidance inherent in deep faith, and then learn and follow the will of God as Jesus must have done.

Initially, I have tended to suggest that the starting point for these people is to place their full faith in God, and in so doing, open one's heart and mind to the "voice" of God. It was the way of Jesus. I then turned in the conversation to the example of Jesus as the model of how to follow the will and way of God. As Jesus made life choices, he did so with deep faith in God and with a profound sense of divine guidance; he heard the voice of God and faithfully followed God's will as expressed in the Jewish Bible and the teaching in the community of faith. We, too, have the Bible to guide us and a community of faith to support us.

As one traces the next steps for Jesus, following his baptism, we note that he needed to prepare himself for his life calling. We read his story and learn that what he sensed to be God's will did not always lead him to a peaceful and joyful life.[6] He faced great difficulties, and the record of his life decisions to follow the will of God seldom led to his comfort and security. His first step was to go on a retreat in the wilderness, and there he fasted and sensed the presence of God as he prayed. It was not an easy time in the wilderness. For example, it was there that Jesus faced the great temptations that could lead him away from his calling. He faced them directly, and the indirect message to us is we may have temptations as well. In our act of dedication, we may face the temptation to respond to our bodily needs, the temptation to seek power, and the temptation to have wealth and possessions. We may hear the voice that these "possessions" are goals in life and are what make life enjoyable and manageable.

As he entered fully into his vocation, there were occasions in which the cost was so great that he did have to say and pray, "not my will, but yours be done." He is quoted in John's Gospel as saying: "I can do nothing on my own. As I hear, I judge; and my judgment is just, because I seek to do not my own will but the will of him who sent me" (John 5:30). Later, in Gethsemane, anticipating a possible arrest, his prayer was: "Father, if you are willing, remove this cup from me; yet not my will but yours be done" (Luke 22:42). What we learn from the life of Jesus is that we go in faith, trusting the wisdom of God, even if the way is difficult.

It is important to emphasize that Jesus was a great teacher and prophet, guiding us as we seek to know and follow the will of God. In

---

6. We too often expect that any "message" from God will be comforting and easy to follow.

many ways he was also a mystic, one who believed that he encountered God directly, and that knowing and doing the will of God came in a personal way, not one that urged us to follow a few simple steps. Neither was it formal learning, reading the history of the Jewish people and receiving the institutional guidance of a community. He did not disdain the process of learning from others; in fact, he endorsed a great deal of the traditional wisdom contained in Jewish Bible and the formal learning offered in the community of faith. Yet, he sensed an inner connection to and relationship with God, listened carefully to the divine voice, and felt the assurance that he had received divine guidance.[7] He sensed and received the wisdom of God in prayerful contemplation and deep faith.

I have been privileged to serve and teach students in university settings, and I found that one of the most common concerns of students who were exploring the life of faith was to understand how to prepare for their futures. I reassured them that guidance would come from both extraordinary wisdom from great scholars and teachers, and a more personal experience of sensing in their heart divine wisdom. I often heard the expected questions that would have started early in the developmental process of these young people: What should I study? Whom should I marry? Which of the many vocational choices should I make? It was not quite enough for many of these students merely to select a major in the area of their interest and talent or to follow the advice and traditions of their family. It was more complicated than simply discerning the next steps for getting through the challenges of today and tomorrow. To go into the family business was perhaps one dimension of the process; it wasn't enough. They wanted to sense at a very deep and authentic level how they might discern the will of God for their lives and what choices might lead to a life centered in the will and way of God. Neither was it enough to just be attracted to a possible life mate; this attraction may be an important first step, but they wanted to make sure that in the marriage relationship, there would be a unified calling to follow divine guidance.

7. Many followers of the divine way have sensed a direct connection with God, not one that was learned and cultivated by the intermediators of pastor and priest, with the worship practices of common prayer, music, and worship. There are classic works and contemporary expressions of this mystical way. See, for example, the classic work of Evelyn Underhill, *Mysticism: A Study in the Nature and Development of Man's Spiritual Consciousness* and a more recent study of mysticism by Denise Lardner Carmody and John Tully Carmody, *Mysticism: Holiness East and West*. There are also a number of biographies of mystics including people such as St. Francis and Julian of Norwich. The author, Adyashanti, underlines this mystical experience in *Resurrecting Jesus: Embodying the Spirit of a Revolutionary Mystic*.

Indeed, many students wanted a divine vocation and they longed for *hagia Sophia,* divine wisdom. They sought the guidance of the Spirit of God to transform them and prepare them for a life of service. In many ways, Jesus was their model.

A second part of their longing for guidance was *the assessment of their talents and gifts,* and their hope and belief that God would use these talents and gifts and lead and empower them to fulfill their calling. The discussion of talents and gifts often led to separating the two, hoping their talents would enable them to do the work of God in an excellent way and their gifts would empower them to do the work of God with the right spirit and a positive attitude. It was not always easy to separate talents and gifts, but the guidance of Scripture was often enlightening. For example, to have an agile mind and use it for a good academic experience (talents) would be joined with the gifts of the Spirit; love, joy, peace, patience, kindness, generosity, faithfulness, gentleness, and self-control (Gal 5:22–23). The students found this articulation of the differences between talents and gifts helpful. These conversations soon led to more specific guidance regarding their future in the service of God. Students were able to sense that they had God-given talents, and that the Spirit of God would empower them to join their talents with the gifts of the Spirit of God in the quest to understand and follow the will of God.

A closely related third dimension of their longing for guidance had to do with the *sense of empowerment by God.* For most students, it was enough to study hard and make wise life choices about the future. Those with a deep dedication to understanding and following the will of God found some comfort in just doing well in their daily lives, yet many others wanted more direct guidance and confirmation that they were on the right track. To do well with the right spirit was a wonderful pattern of life, but there was a longing by many of these students to want more direct guidance. Often, there was the question of whether knowing and doing God's will was just a matter of being disciplined, working hard, and using good sense. Some were content with this answer, yet many wanted a more tangible assurance that they were in the center of God's will. The wanted to hear "the voice of God" as Jesus did.

At times, I found it difficult to guide these students who were inclined to interpret every detail of life as having a message from God. I listened carefully, yet sensed that there was a risk of expecting and finding what they thought was God's will in every twist and turn of a given day; the message they heard may have been more about their needs to find a place in life or how to pass an exam than about a divine communication. Basically, a lost coat is a lost coat, not a clear message from God. It was not always easy to guide those students who spiritualized a common cold or a sprained ankle as such a message.

There were many times when a particular incident, conversation, or choice did have the additional component of the inner confirmation of the Spirit. I would rejoice when this occurred, but more often I would want them to use common sense and make judgments on the basis of what appeared to be the best way to move forward with their goals. This, too, may be understood as an expression of the will of God.

There is risk in an attempt to see every detail in one's life as divine signal. It is too easy to confuse a deep need or frustration as the "voice of God." Discernment is necessary in grasping the will of God. Some of the students with whom I worked longed for infusion of God's Spirit, a legitimate desire, but I also urged them to read the signals of having a clear sense of vocation, a realistic appraisal of their needs for education, and a sense of the discipline required to engage in a life of service. This realistic appraisal, coupled with a genuine spiritual turning-point, was a good place to start in finding one's way.

I urged these students to review with care the way that Jesus followed as he left his work as a carpenter, traveled to visit his cousin John, and then had a deep and life-changing mystical experience in which he sensed divine confirmation and the reception of divine wisdom. I wanted them to hear God's voice as Jesus did: "You are my beloved one, and with you I am well pleased." The students wanted to understand the implications of this affirmation of Jesus, and saw it as guidance in the understanding and experience of the way that Jesus understood his sense of being called by God.

THE PREPARATION OF JESUS

Jesus did leave his visit with cousin John with a deep inner confirmation that he was called to serve the will and way of God. The life-changing experience of his baptism gave him the assurance that he was being guided by divine wisdom. Wisely, he sensed that there was a need for more preparation in order to fulfill what he understood as his God-given mission. It was one appropriate step to gain clarity about his calling, but another step was to be prepared and ready to fulfill his calling. He needed the spiritual preparation in order to be faithful to his calling. With some sadness, I expect, he left the company of John the Baptist and traveled to a wilderness area, probably not a great distance from the Dead Sea, to make sure he was spiritual prepared to do the will of God. He knew there would be distractions and even temptations not to follow what he understood as the will of God.

Matthew describes this next step in the following way: "Then Jesus was led up by the Spirit into the wilderness to be tempted by the devil. He fasted forty days and forty nights, and afterwards he was famished" (Matt 4:1–2). Jesus removed himself from the rush and challenge of daily life, went to a wilderness area to be alone, and began to engage in fasting and meditation to prepare himself to be faithful to his life calling. He went to a spiritual seminary.

The wilderness area was not a region of forests, lakes, and rivers, but more likely a dry desert region with few natural resources. He was alone, he fasted, and he engaged in a profound spiritual retreat. His goal was to deepen his commitment to his calling and to engage in spiritual practices that called for extraordinary discipline that would prepare him for what was to come. This endeavor would cultivate the discipline and convictions he would need to sustain himself in the conflicts and distractions that might lead him astray and remove him from the challenges of the future.

We pick up the story from Matthew's Gospel. "The tempter came and said to him, 'If you are the Son of God, command these stones to become loaves of bread.'" It is a bit difficult to provide a clear description of what is meant by the title of tempter, but there is a sense in Matthew's account that there was the belief in a personal being, the tempter, who will try to lead Jesus astray.[8] The first temptation for Jesus was to turn away from his calling and listen to the voice of evil, or we might say, to turn away from his commitment and dedication to hear the divine calling and give up his disciplined fasting. "If you are the Son of God, command these stones to become loaves of bread. But he answered, 'It is written, "One does not live by bread alone, but by every word that comes from the mouth of God."'" The temptation of Jesus was twofold, to turn away from his pathway of discipline and accept bread to meet his physical needs, and even the more serious temptation, to listen to the voice of temptation rather than the voice of God and begin to give up his mission in life. I find

---

8. In the time of Jesus and Matthew's writing, there was a common belief that temptation and evil was often personified, a reference to the devil.

the insight of this story very powerful; it may be that one of our greatest temptations in life is to continue the normal flow of life, to eat some bread, and to meet your physical needs. We do get hungry. It doesn't initially sound like a decision to move away from the will of God; after all, you have been fasting and are hungry; why not ask God to change the stones to bread and eat. It may be that yielding to physical temptation is one of easiest of ways to move away from the will of God. It is so easy to rationalize and justify to ourselves that, "all I am doing is just being human and following the natural course of life." Jesus, deep in his spiritual consciousness, recognizes the temptation. He has been called by God to disciplined preparation for his life calling, a calling that will require difficult choices. Jesus, deep in his soul, hears another voice that says that you do not have to follow your disciplined practices in your retreat. "Give in to this other practical voice of meeting your physical needs. Go ahead and move away from God's will." Jesus, sensing the calling of God to prepare himself for his life calling, says: "One does not live by bread alone, but by every word that comes from the mouth of God" (Matt 4:4). Jesus stays faithful to the will of God, even though the temptation may seem somewhat innocent, merely meeting taking care of one's physical needs and desires. The divine voice and wisdom, on occasion, should prevail over the voice of basic needs. Yes, we do need to eat, sleep, stay healthy, and be close to and have affection for another person, but there are times when the greater good calls for some discipline and sacrifice. It is especially so in those situations when it is so easy to justify harmful behavior with the rationalization of "I was just meeting my needs," but by doing so, one fails to stay on the path of a disciplined retreat.

"Then the devil took him to the holy city and placed him on the pinnacle of the temple, saying to him, 'If you are the Son of God, throw yourself down, for it is written: 'He will command his angels concerning you,' and 'On their hands they will bear you up, so that you will not dash your foot against a stone.'"" Again, the tempter is persuasive: just think of all the power you would have! As you look across the landscape from the pinnacle and truly trust God, you know that God will take care of you. In fact, you would even have power over God. The divine One works for you, not you for the divine One. You will become close to God in power, and can even persuade God to do what you want God to do. Jesus replies: "Again it is written, 'Do not put the Lord your God to the test.'" In this temptation, Jesus is invited to believe that he has power over God, and that God will do what you ask God to do. Jesus is invited to test God rather than to trust and obey God. He continues to be faithful to his calling to do the will of God. The message for us is not to think we have the all the wisdom and power of God and that we tell God what to do; rather our calling is to sense the will of God, be filled with divine wisdom, and yield to the love and care of God.

Yet the evil one is not ready to give up: "Again, the devil took him to a very high mountain and showed him all the kingdoms of the world and their splendor; and he said to him, "All these I will give you, if you fall down and worship me." Jesus said to him, "Away with you, Satan, for it is written, 'Worship the Lord your God, and serve him only.' Then the devil left him, and suddenly angels came and waited on him." Jesus was not in a quest for power and control, nor driven by a desire to have wealth and possessions, but sought to be led by and to follow the loving presence and wise guidance of God.

It is clear that Jesus, while in the wilderness, is facing the greatest temptations in life and must be victorious over them in order to prepare himself for his life work, his true divine calling. In each of these temptations, he is invited to turn away from God's will and yield to some of the most dangerous temptations in life, although they come to us in innocent disguise.

The first is to yield to the temptation to give one's physical needs the highest priority, believing that then you will be satisfied. Most of us know better because we have tried it, and in most cases, deeply regretted it. From these failures, we have learned the deep and abiding truth that it is in doing God's will which brings us peace. We have learned how to place our needs in the proper category and give them the appropriate place in our lives, not a place that goes against the deepest values of our faith, our personal walk with God, and one filled with love and truth.

The second temptation that Jesus faced was to think that God does our bidding and follows our guidance, not that we serve God and follow divine guidance. It is to believe the great lie that we have all the wisdom and power. It may be that we think we can "use" God and the divine power to seek our own goals and desires or that we know better than God and that we should have the right to seek our own way. This pattern of life will lead to disaster; we see it daily; it is all around us. But deep in our hearts, we know that in trusting the will and way of God, we and others whom we love and serve find the way to fulfillment and contentment.

The temptation of Jesus was to yield to the belief that if you have all the most valuable possessions and rewarding experiences possible in life, you will find true happiness. Our culture in the United States epitomizes this attractive, yet false promise. If we substitute physical gratification and the accumulation of money and possessions as our goal in life, we will be forever in an endless and empty search for true contentment. Gradually, as one follows this tempting way, we discover that there is no end to our wants and desires. We learn from Jesus that it is God's loving presence and dedication to the divine will and way that bring us deep and abiding peace.

In the wilderness, Jesus faces in his imagination all of the ways that he might turn away from God's will and calling and place his desires and will above the will of God; he is tempted to substitute his own needs for possessions and power. He has faced the great temptations that would distract him and take him away from his calling. The time of discipline and reflection, of discipline and prayer, and of self-searching and to live with integrity, has prepared Jesus to undertake his life-calling.[9] He is our model as we prepare ourselves for our life calling. Empowered by God's Spirit, he moves into his ministry, trusting in divine wisdom.

THE FAITHFULNESS OF JESUS

Jesus has prepared himself for his life mission. He has sought the will of God and has a grasp of divine wisdom. He leaves the region of the Dead Sea east of Jerusalem, makes his way back to the Galilee, his native region, and begins his public ministry, trusting in divine wisdom (*hagia sophia*). *The primary way to recognize and receive divine wisdom is through faith.* Faith is to place our trust in a benevolent power greater than ourselves who understands all of creation and is managing the universe and our earthly world.

Jesus invites us to a life of faith and to trust in the Truth. He teaches by his life and words that faith in that which is untrue is dangerous. We do live in a time when there is much in the open market of religion that is dangerous and untrue. Faith can be understood as a way of knowing, that is, to discern and have the truth about life and to place our lives in the love and care of the Truth. The Greek word for faith, *pistis*, is a sure

---

9. These stories have the ring of truth. They do capture, as placed in the consciousness of Jesus, the great temptations of life. Jesus is clear in his response; it is God whom we honor and God's will that we do; to place one's own limited and distorted views about the nature of life as our goal and guide is a betrayal of God and disaster for finding fulfillment in life.

and certain understanding of the heart, a way of knowing that gives us confidence in our values and upon which we can set our course in life.[10] As one at home in the Christian faith, I believe the great first century rabbi, Jesus of Nazareth, as he struggles with the powerful and misleading promises in the story of his temptations, guides us wisely and well in the evening of life. He chose the wisdom of God rather than the alluring temptations of evil. As we struggle with the challenges of aging, we turn to Jesus for guidance:

1. We place our faith in God, personal Truth, and God becomes the foundation of our lives.
2. We are clear about what brings us guidance and peace, divine wisdom, not empty pleasure, the accumulation of possessions, and the quest for power.
3. We live for others, relating to them in love and care, and we serve in ways that encourage justice and peace.
4. We live authentically, have integrity, and our lives are filled with truth.

Terms, Resources, and Discussion Questions

Terms

1. Mysticism: the experience of union with the Holy or Divine; direct communion with ultimate reality. Also, it is the belief that direct knowledge of God, spiritual truth, or ultimate reality can be attained through subjective experience, such as reflection and prayer.
2. Meditation: a focusing of one's thoughts; a quiet reflection upon or pondering over what is important and true, and living in the present moment.
3. Contemplation: a form of emptying prayer in which a person seeks to pass beyond mental images and concepts to a direct experience

---

10. All too often, we consider the way of faith as turned against the way of knowledge and wisdom. It is better to understand the way of faith as our pathway to true knowledge and divine wisdom. The word, *pistis*, is the root of the English word epistemology, the study of how we learn and know.

of the divine; prayer which transcends the intellect, leading to resting in the presence of God.
4. *Hagia Sophia*: holy wisdom available to us by faith.
5. Faith: Confidence and trust in God or ultimate truth that leads to an authentic life of love and inner peace.

Resources: Books to Read and Consult

1. Brené Brown, *Daring Greatly: How the Courage to be Vulnerable Transforms the Way We Live, Love, Parent, and Lead*
2. Denise and John Carmody, *Mysticism: Holiness East and West*
3. Thomas Keating, *Open Mind, Open Heart*
4. Ronald Rolheiser, *The Holy Longing: The Search for a Christian Spirituality*
5. Evelyn Underhill, *Mysticism: A Study in the Nature and Development of [Human] Spiritual Consciousness.*
6. Youtube: The Method of Centering Prayer—Part 1, with Thomas Keating
7. Youtube: The Power of Vulnerability, TED Talk (2010) Brené Brown

Discussion Questions

1. As you reflect as one living in the evening phase of your life, what would you say are the three biggest challenges? What would those who know you best say are your strongest assets for dealing with these? Were these assets inherited from your parents or developed by you, especially as you have chosen a spiritual pathway?
2. After leaving his birth family, Jesus created a "family" of those open to and committed to his vision of love and service. Whom do you claim as your primary family at this phase of your life? What are some ways you can cultivate new relationships with people of all ages who care about the same things you are committed to?
3. Reflect on the ways Jesus recognized God's Spirit in his life, and the times he relied on his relationship with this Spirit of divine wisdom. Looking back, what were some times in your life when the Spirit

was especially present with and for you? What wisdom did you receive? Are you open to a deeper connection with the Spirit during this evening of your life?

4. Recall some regrets or lost opportunities in your life, and rethink them now in light of the Spirit's blessings and challenges that Jesus faced. How might you identify the ways God is working in your life and what God's Spirit is creating for you out of these losses?

5. There are suggestions offered in this chapter about how to understand and follow the ways that Jesus encountered and sensed the presence of the Holy Spirit and received divine wisdom. Which of them strike you as helpful and in what ways? Can you imagine engaging in a retreat, or journaling, or prayerful introspection as a way of opening yourself to the Spirit's Holy Wisdom?

CHAPTER FIVE

Faith as the On-Going Commitment to the Divine Mission

> "And as he sat at dinner in the house, many tax collectors and sinners came and were sitting with him and his disciples. When the Pharisees saw this, they said to his disciples, 'Why does your teacher eat with tax collectors and sinners?' But when he heard this, he said, 'Those who are well have no need of a physician, but those who are sick. Go and learn what this means, "I desire mercy not sacrifice." For I have come to call not the righteous but sinners.'"
>
> (MATTHEW 9:10–13)

FAITH AS ACTION: THE PROPHET

WE HAVE SPOKEN ABOUT the need to cultivate a faith orientation that is deeply rooted in the truth, a way of understanding what truly is and a way to see what has actually happened. To live wisely and well is to live in a truthful way, based on a truthful foundation. We also explored another meaning of truth, that is, a *true* relationship with others and God, an authentic experience that forms a true connection and relationship; it is the cultivation of a deep and life-changing, even mystical experience, one that advances our understanding, heals and reconciles, and then improves our mental health. To live wisely and well is to be truthful in our relationships and to encounter others and God authentically. As we do, we are set free from that which enslaves us, as Jesus teaches: "So if the Son makes you free, you will be free indeed" (John 8:36). We in the evening of life need and long for this kind of connection and freedom.

We turn now, drawing upon our understanding of truth and our spiritual experience of being transformed by a genuine experience of the divine, to explore how these understandings of truth play out in our daily lives. We place our faith in what we understand as the very essence and foundation of truth, God, and then seek a deep and true experience of God's presence in our lives. In this divine encounter, we gradually begin to experience grace and truth in our day-to-day lives. We have been informed, reformed, and transformed by truth and love. As this occurs, we are then asked to engage in a mission of sharing this truth and love with others. We do that in a truthful and loving way as we make our commitment to the divine mission in the world.

The mission is centered on those with a deep need for healing, consolation, and restoration; it is a divine calling to show mercy and compassion that includes, as Jesus did, living in solidarity with the poor and prophetically challenging unjust social structures and conditions that keep people in poverty, marginalized, and disenfranchised.

The ways of expressing and sharing the divine love and truth may vary as we search for a way to express love in tangible ways. We need to find sensitive and caring ways to express love, not by interfering and intruding, but with understanding and empathy. As we find our way of sharing divine love and truth, we seek the empowerment of God, embracing and receiving the presence of God's Spirit in order to fulfill our commitment to the divine mission. Again, we turn to the example of Jesus, one full of grace and truth, as a model for taking on this responsibility.

As we read about his way of fulfilling our calling, we see the several qualities in Jesus, and we pray they might be present in and for us. We will focus on our understanding of the mission of Jesus as prophet, as a healer, and as a teacher (rabbi), and we note that all three of these dimensions of his mission were often present simultaneously in his encounters with people and his actions.[1]

The first and most obvious quality of Jesus in all three of these dimensions of the identity and mission of Jesus was his gracious unconditional love for all who came into his circle, even those who were critical of his mission. He especially focused his loving ways on those in deep need,

---

1. Other categories and titles for Jesus are available to us as well, and each one provides a slightly different perspective on the identity and mission of Jesus.

those who suffered, and those who had to navigate through social systems that were unjust. He also cared deeply for those in the evening of life.

We read about his way of loving as he met the woman who was accused by the elders of adultery.[2] As she came to him in tears, he received her warmly and empathically, honored her as a person created in the image of God, and then provided her with attentive care and guidance. Others, as was the custom and in the legal system, sought to condemn her and kill her by throwing stones at her. We know all too well how many different kinds of "stones" there are, and unfortunately, on occasion, we select and use our stones as we harshly judge others. Jesus said to those who had condemned her: "Let anyone among you who is without sin be the first to throw a stone at her. And once again he bent down and wrote on the ground, calming the situation and relaxing the woman. When those who condemned the woman heard the words of Jesus, they went away, one by one beginning with the elders, and Jesus was left alone with the woman standing before him. Jesus straightened up and said to her, 'Woman, where are they? Has no one condemned you?' She said, 'No one, sir.' And Jesus said 'neither do I condemn you. Go your way, and from now on do not sin again.'"

He loved this woman with compassion; she was one who had been used and abused, and he did so in spite of the opposition from local leaders. He challenged the interpretation of the Law by the elders, which they claimed gave them the authority to stone her to death. For Jesus, it was a courageous act of love, giving the highest priority to the healing of one who needed acceptance, understanding, and healing. Jesus was willing to take the risk to stand over against the unfair power structures of his time. There are times, often and especially in the evening of life with years of experience behind us, that we should follow his example. We are now responsible adults with the capacity to challenge harmful behavior and to live with some resistance and criticism as we embrace these values. We are sufficiently mature and secure, knowing there may be some resistance, yet we are reassured that we are taking the right action.

Jesus, also, in helping those in need and deep suffering, took appropriate action to take care of those with deep fear and the feeling of being lost and alone. In Mark 1:40–45, we read:

---

2. John 8:2–11. Note, I am aware that this passage may have been a later addition to the text.

> A leper came to him begging him, and kneeling he said to him, "If you choose, you can make me clean." Moved with pity, Jesus stretched out his hand and touched him, and said to him: "I do choose. Be made clean!" Immediately the leprosy left him, and he was made clean. After sternly warning him, he sent him away at once, saying to him, "See that you say nothing to anyone; but go, show yourself to the priest, and offer for cleansing what Moses commanded, as testimony to them." But he went out and began to proclaim it freely and spread the word so that Jesus could no longer go into this town openly, but stayed out in the country; and people came to him from every quarter.

Jesus not only healed the leper,[3] but made sure that the healing was recorded by the authorities. He attempted to stay within the social norms that were present and asked the ill person to report his healing so he would be allowed to go into public places. Jesus healed in love and made sure that all the details were recorded; it was a very responsible action of love, not just a vague feeling or a passing concern. When we love, we often take on responsibility and are invited to make sure that the one whom we help is able to re-enter society and have a normal life. We sometimes forget this last act for full healing. Those who are ill do not always and easily enter back into normal life. In addition, Jesus also wanted to have some relief from the crowds as a result of the healing, but the healed person told everyone about it, and the crowds sought to be in the presence of Jesus. When we love, we may experience resistance and harsh judgment as we help those who are part of a social system controlled by those in power. To help wisely and well, we factor in a number of social concerns that are part of the healing process. We exercise wisdom.

There are many other records that describe Jesus giving special attention to individuals who were suffering and in need of healing and loving guidance. In story after story, we read that he demonstrated that he cared deeply, not only about their immediate needs, but also about the social structures that kept people in situations that were unjust and harmful to them.

Jesus was also an extraordinary prophet.[4] For example, Matthew records the account of Jesus healing the man with a withered hand (Matt 12:9–14):

---

3. Leprosy was a common word used for more than just what we now know as leprosy. People with this disease were required to live in an isolated region so as not to spread the disease.

4. See noted New Testament scholar, Richard Horsely's book, *Prophet Jesus and the*

> He left that place and entered into their synagogue; a man was there with a withered hand, and they asked him, "Is it lawful to cure on the Sabbath?" so that they might accuse him. He said to them, "Suppose one of you has only one sheep and it falls into a pit on the Sabbath; will you not lay hold of it and lift it out? How much more valuable is a human being than a sheep! So, it is lawful to do good on the Sabbath." The he said to the man, "Stretch out your hand." He stretched it out, and it was restored, as sound as the other. But the Pharisees went out and conspired against him, how to destroy him.

In spite of the risks of getting resistance to relieving suffering in this setting, he healed the man, even knowing that there would be strong opposition as he challenged an unjust law. There are times when we must have the courage to follow the pathway of Mohandas Gandhi or Martin Luther King, Jr. or Mother Teresa, models of those living wisely and well as they acted courageously in reference to the suffering of others caused by injustice. The prophet takes great risks.

Likely toward the end of his public ministry, Jesus went to the temple, a setting that was in some ways a center of human activity. It was not just a religious building where people went once a week to worship. It was where one took care of many needs such as shopping for meals, finding clothing, or meeting friends. But primarily it was where one addressed needs of a religious nature. The people believed that it was a setting where God was present, although open access to this center where God was thought to be fully present was restricted. It was in the temple, of course, where people went to express their deepest religious feelings and to receive forgiveness and guidance. Jesus was concerned about abuses in the temple, and there is one well-known story of Jesus showing compassion for those who lived in poverty and who were abused by the practices of those at the temple and who were part of the social and religious systems.[5] Jesus comes to the temple and discovers that the poor, who have come to the temple to express their deep religious feelings, are asked to give alms in support of others in need and to support the activities of the temple. Because there were different kinds of money in circulation, as for example Roman and Jewish, people often had to exchange their money

---

Renewal of Israel.

5. See Matt 21:12–22. There is a question about whether this particular story occurred early in the ministry of Jesus or towards the end. Matthew places it toward the end, while John places it much earlier as Jesus begins his public ministry (John 2:13–22). Although unlikely, some scholars have suggested that it occurred twice.

in order to give alms in the acceptable kind of coinage. Jesus notices that the "blind and the lame" were not given the accepted and fair exchange rate, receiving less than the worth of their money. He takes bold and courageous prophetic action against this practice, expressing deep concern that unfair practices could exist in the temple of all places! He turns over the tables of the money changers and declares so that all can hear: "It is written, 'My house shall be called a house of prayer; but you are making a den of robbers.'" The crowds noticed this action as did the authorities who saw it as a disruption, a continuing practice of a trouble-making prophet. There may be times in the evening of our lives when we must, given our wisdom and place in the social context, express strong resistance to practices that discriminate against those with few resources and little power. Prophetic action may be and should be on our agenda in the evening of life. With experience and less to lose, we may see more clearly and have the courage to act on behalf of those who suffer from injustice.

I tend to be more of a peace keeper than a prophetic action taker, although over the years I have learned a great deal about social injustice and the need to challenge it. Early in my career in the late 1960s, I served the church in a setting that was conservative in both theological and political outlooks. The people in the congregation were kind, well-meaning, and very supportive of my work, yet I did feel the need to be aware of those who might criticize my work with university students. The church and the academy were two different places, and I had to learn how to navigate the two different cultures. The University of Oregon was a large multicultural university with a diverse student population and a setting that was very accepting of different points of view and styles of life. It was also the 1960s, a time full of social change and new ideas.

On one occasion, I was asked by a young woman, a university student who had been raised in the church I served, if I would perform her wedding. She had met an international student from Africa, fallen in love, and wanted to get married in the church, her spiritual home. She did acknowledge some fear of opposition to her marriage and mentioned that she had already felt some resistance because her fiancé had the dark skin of those with African descent. I, of course, said "yes, I will perform the marriage ceremony." I knew that this was a quite mature young couple, well-educated, sophisticated, and accepting of all people. I did hear from several people in the congregation that it was a bit risky for me to go forward with the marriage ceremony. One woman, well-liked and well-educated, although raised in the South, was a church leader and came to me with her concern. She said to me very directly, "I, of course, accept all people, but there are differences, and we should acknowledge this reality. There are different races, and even though we accept other races, they should be kept separate. They can live in their part of the city, and we can live in our part. I don't think you should perform this ceremony in our church." As a young person of the 1960s, I thought her comments were out of touch, not only with the dramatic social changes of the time, but with the Christian value of respect and love for all people. While I thought it and didn't say it, I knew that Jesus may have had the darker skin of the people of the Galilee in the first century. I was also persuaded that all people are created in the image of God, and while there are different cultural norms, we should honor and accept all people with unconditional love.

I trusted the maturity of this couple and went ahead with the wedding. I did receive some affirmation, but also sensed that there were those in the congregation that were not quite consistent in applying their Christian values nor in touch with their feelings about what they called "mixed marriages." The statement by the woman in the church reflected the attitude of many in the congregation: "I, of course, accept all people, but they should stay and live within their settings, heritage, and culture." It was more prejudicial than she realized. I did sense a deep need to be supportive of the young couple. The marriage went forward, and the couple has had a wonderful life, living both in the United States and Africa, yet they did have to manage the quiet questioning by some whom they encountered, as I did in my service to the church. Looking back, I would change nothing with the possible exception of being more open and making an attempt to facilitate the church's mission to challenge racism in all of its many forms.

FAITH AS ACTION: THE HEALER

Jesus took bold action as a prophet. He also demonstrated deep love for those who were poor, had limited resources, and who were ill or had disabilities. In fact, the common people may have come to Jesus as much or more in order to be healed than to hear a great teacher whose insights gave them a new lease on life and promised social change in those areas in society where there was discrimination against those who were different. We have already spoken about the leper who asked Jesus to heal him and how Jesus responded to this request. We return to this theme of healing. A great deal has been written about the capacity of Jesus to heal, and often there is the question of how he did it, living prior to the rise of scientific medical care and the advanced development of medicines, technology, and surgery.[6] Some have suggested he really did have the capacity to perform miracles in his healing ministry. This thesis is accepted by many, yet there are others who find that the category of "miracles" problematic, and one that is not all that easy to accept on this side of the rise of science. They have sought other ways of explaining his healing ministry.

One commonly held view is that Jesus, given his charismatic presence and loving behavior, healed those with illnesses that had a social and psychological cause; and these diseases were healed because of the "emotional intelligence" of Jesus.[7] His great insight and deep love were healing. Others have suggested that some of names used in the New Testament to describe different forms of illness have been difficult to translate and describe in contemporary language. We may not know for sure what the disease may have been. Some may have been illnesses that are now understood as a severe disease. The symptoms may have suggested the disease, but again, the descriptions may not provide enough information for us to identify the disease with the title we would now use in modern medicine. Some of these diseases may have had a psychological cause that could be treated by understanding, love, and insight. Yet these explanations simply do not cover the range of his healings. One then has to acknowledge that in many cases, he did have miraculous healing power to heal or the stories were told from the perspective of the first century understanding of disease. As the stories were retold, they took on the character of a miraculous healing. I do not have a final answer about whether "miracles" are possible, but I do sense that Jesus had a remarkable ability to heal, and an integral part of the healing was because he gave unconditional acceptance and empathic understanding to those who were ill; he acknowledged and honored them, and took time to be with them. There are contemporary reports of this

---

6. See, for example, the description of the healing of Jesus in Crossan, John Dominic, *Jesus: A Revolutionary Biography*, 76–84.

7. See the book by Roy M. Oswald and Arland Jacobson, *Emotional Intelligence of Jesus: Relational Smarts for Religious Leaders*. They provide several examples of the emotional intelligence of Jesus such as the feeding of the five thousand, and walking on water when fishing with his disciples.

kind of "miraculous" healing, and the reports are often described with a reference to a healing miracle.

It is this aspect of the capacity of Jesus to heal with deep love and empathy that we must emulate. We, too, can take time to be present, offer genuine concern, demonstrate love by offering to help with details that the ill person can't tend to, and to meet the ill person with respect and genuine care about their suffering. In a review of the several stories of the healing by Jesus, there is the dimension of careful listening, avoidance of self-referencing, and empathic identification with the suffering of the ill person. Those who were ill, lonely, and discouraged found renewed life and even a measure of healing as Jesus intelligently and lovingly listened, took them seriously, honored them, and cared for them by his presence. It is a ministry that we can undertake in the evening of our lives. We have empathy and experience and may need to cultivate better listening skills!

FAITH AS ACTION: THE TEACHER

There are many examples in the Gospels of the social justice and healing ministries of Jesus that have an authentic ring about them, ones that are models for us. In addition to these ministries of social justice and healing, Jesus is also and perhaps best known as an extraordinary teacher. He was called a rabbi, meaning a teacher of wisdom, one who gave guidance to those seeking to live in a joyful, peaceful, and loving way. As he met people, he shared his extraordinary insights and wisdom, empowering those who heard him to take bold steps toward maturity and service.[8] One might say that his teaching has had as much influence on shaping human behavior as anyone who has ever lived, sharing this remarkable way of guiding and enriching human behavior with just a few others such as Moses, the Buddha, Muhammad, the Dalai Lama, Ilia Delio,[9] and thousands of other women whose names are just below our awareness.

The four Gospels, for which we are grateful, record much of the teaching of Jesus. The pattern of recording what he taught was a bit complex, unlike ways we would use in our time. In that it was largely a non-literate society, people who had listened carefully to his teaching would

---

8. See Cynthia Bourgeault's book, *Wisdom Jesus: Transforming Heart and Mind—A New Perspective on Christ and His Message*.

9. See Dr. Delio's book, *Unbearable Wholeness of Being: God, Evolution, and the Power of Love*. She is an exceptional scholar and one who wisely guides us in understanding the Christian faith.

share it others, often in small groups. In a way, it was their method of remembering what was important; they had no "Jerusalem Times" or the national news every evening, or phones or laptops to use. These accounts, shared in small groups, would then be passed on to others, and in time, there was a fairly substantial oral tradition circulated among the new churches. By the middle of the sixties of the common era, this oral tradition began to be put into writing, and the author of the Gospel of Mark (likely written by Mark, the disciple and companion of both Paul and Peter) used this oral tradition, some of the available writing, and wrote his Gospel. Later, both Matthew and Luke, using Mark's Gospel and other oral reports and manuscripts, wrote their Gospels. The Gospel of John, written later, had additional sources, both oral and written. John's Gospel has a different approach, and he may have used some different resources that were available. Careful study of these documents and many others have been used over the centuries to capture the contours of the life and teachings of Jesus. There is a mountain of information, a mountain that I have attempted to climb during the last sixty years.

As we attempt to discern and summarize the teaching of Jesus, we will refer to all four Gospels, yet tend to draw heavily from Matthew because of his systematic organization of the teaching of Jesus. Matthew begins by describing the family tree of Jesus, his birth, his calling, his formation of a team of disciples, and the beginning of his ministry in the Galilee. Matthew then presents us with a remarkable summary of the teaching of Jesus, an essential part of which is called the Sermon on the Mount.[10] It begins with Beatitudes and it then moves on to a great deal more of the teaching of Jesus on several topics (Matt 5:1–7:29).

The Beatitudes, perhaps as well-known as any part of Jesus' teaching,[11] begin with the primary foundation of the teaching of Jesus, the kingdom (or reign) of God. Jesus often references this theme in order to ground his teachings. He speaks to his listeners and tells them that the power and presence of God are available now; he then invites them to open their hearts and minds to the reign of God (Matt 5:1–12), and to pray, "Your kingdom come, your will be done, on earth as it is in heaven" (Matt 6:10). The apostle John writes that God sent his Word (*logos*) to the human family in Jesus, as one filled with grace and truth, the essence of

---

10. It is unlikely that Jesus preached this vast array of material in one setting. There is a location on a hill above the lake in Galilee that has been identified as a place where he may have taught, one from which he may have spoken on many occasions.

11. It includes the Lord's Prayer and the Golden Rule.

FAITH AS THE ON-GOING COMMITMENT TO THE DIVINE MISSION   81

God's identity. (John 1:14). Therefore, as we open our hearts and minds to God's reign, we will then begin to have these God-given qualities; we will gradually be those filled with grace and truth. John adds, in the amplification of this notion, that God's presence may be understood as God's Spirit, the very presence and power of God, who will fill our lives (John 4:24). John understands God in a quite personal way, as being a loving Presence and Guide, empowering and sustaining us.[12]

We read that Jesus says that the reign of God is available to all, and to open one's heart to God is transforming and redeeming. "Blessed are the poor in spirit, for theirs is the kingdom of heaven," that is, all those who suffer and worry about the demands of life that seem overwhelming may receive the power and presence of God that will "bless" them, that is, make their lives better, full of peace and joy. It is a remarkably simple message, that acknowledging the presence of God and receiving God into one's heart and mind will give deep peace and meaning to life. Those who mourn will be comforted, those who long to be righteous will be empowered, those who suffer will receive mercy, and those who are pure in heart will see, understand, and be filled with the presence of God. Those of us in the twilight of life will flourish, even with the challenges of aging, as we embrace and receive the reign of God.

This wonderful truth becomes the foundation of much of the teaching of Jesus and, of course, he then models in his behavior what he teaches as he speaks. He goes on to say that those who have embraced God will be the salt that seasons all of human life with goodness. Those filled with the presence of God will be the light that guides all who seek direction (Matt 5:13–16). He teaches that the Hebrew Bible has provided ethical guidance with the Law and the guidance of the prophets, and this guidance should be followed. He then goes on to add the life-changing message of God's gracious presence in our lives. As we open our heart to God, we will be those who do not let anger take over; we will be truthful in our relationships and faithful in marriage, careful about oaths that cannot be kept, remain true to our promises, and we do not retaliate and get even. Rather, we should even love our enemies and forgive them. All of this is possible by living a truly spiritual life, one filled with the very presence of God which we sustain with commitment and prayer and through our prayerful communication and on-going relationship with God.

12. It is important to note that the word in Greek for Spirit is also the word for wind or gentle breeze. God's Spirit is like the gentle breeze on a warm summer day that refreshes us.

Matthew, in his summary of the teaching of Jesus, pauses as he references prayer and provides guidance with a model for prayer, often called the Lord's Prayer (Matt 6:9–13). The Christian church has used this model of prayer over the centuries. Matthew then continues with his summary of the teaching of Jesus. He references the risk of being hypocritical regarding religious commitments and practices and asserts that we must be *those who have integrity and who live in harmony with our deepest values.* We need to be sincere in our dedication to God and live in a way of life that is authentic as we engage in spiritual practices such as fasting. He urges his followers to be clear about values and priorities in the use of money. He underlines that one cannot not have two masters, that it is not really possible to love both God and possessions and money. These loyalties will conflict. God alone deserves our love and loyalty, and money and possessions can be used in daily life and to help others.

He then stresses that worry should not take over one's life, and it is likely that those with whom he spoke were filled with worry, were insecure, and had fears just about survival, given their poverty. Jesus says (and shows!) that God will provide ways of coping with our problems as we seek first the kingdom of God and live righteously. He strongly urges his followers not to judge others, but seek God with a gentle knock on the door and God will be present. In short, he underlines what is called the Golden Rule: "In everything do to others as you would have them do to you; for this is the Law and prophets" (Matt 7:12). He then adds that we should not deceive ourselves; it is so easy not to face what is truly inside of us. We need the empowerment of God for self-reflection and growth toward integrity and love. Enter the narrow gate of God's presence and be true to your faith. In short, be doers, not just hearers of the truth.

What is truly remarkable is that Jesus lived his message with remarkable faithfulness, taught with great clarity and insight, and loved all who came his way with wisdom and active compassion. It would be hard to find a trace of inconsistency in the life of Jesus. Although because he was so direct, occasionally challenging the religious establishment, there was some resistance to his teaching and presence. Toward the end of his public ministry, which had been primarily in the Galilee, he opted to take his ministry of teaching and healing to Jerusalem, the center of the Jewish faith. It was there where the regional Jewish government, the Sanhedrin, was present and a setting where there was a strong Roman presence as well. He saw this region as a setting in which he must proclaim his message of the reign of God. He felt he must go to the center of Jewish life to complete his vocation and calling, the seat of power for the religious establishment and the different levels of government. He was warned about the risks, yet felt that his mission would not be fulfilled if he were not to go to Jerusalem.

THE FINAL WEEK

Joined with and largely supported by his band of apostles and disciples, Jesus makes his way to Jerusalem. There were stops along the way, conversations with those close to him, a moving mystical experience called the Transfiguration, and an interesting encounter in Jericho with a Jewish tax collector. Jesus completes his trek to Jerusalem, staying with friends who were just outside the city in a village called Bethany. Books have been written about his time and experiences in and around Jerusalem during this final week, and it is beyond our scope to address all aspects of his final days. We have chosen to focus on the faith and courage that Jesus demonstrates in completing his commitment to what he understood to be a divine mission.[13] For us, it is another picture of what it means to live wisely and well in the evening of life.

Jerusalem, at the time of the arrival of Jesus, is a troubled and busy city. It is a holiday period, and the population of the city has expanded dramatically. Faithful Jewish people had come for the feast of Passover, the remembrance of the way that the Jewish people were protected (passed over), a time of deliverance of the Jewish people from the plague that swept through Egypt. The plague, part of the Exodus experience, did not affect the Jewish refugees who sought delivery from slavery and a return to their homeland. It was a time of celebration of this great occasion in the life of the Jewish people.

Yet the celebration, a grand holiday, did not remove the problems that existed for the Jewish people as Jesus entered the city. The problems centered in two primary arenas of power and authority, governmental and religious. The government was a complex mixture, confused by the existence of different levels of responsibility and power. There was the Jewish level, centered right in the city, called the Sanhedrin, which functioned in many ways like the high court for Jewish cases in which people had broken the law. It was made up of both aristocrats and religious

---

13. I will draw upon the account by Marcus Borg, and John Dominic Crossan, *Last Week: A Day-by-Day Account of Jesus's Final Week in Jerusalem*.

leaders, and they were concerned about the presence of Jesus with whom they had disagreement and were prepared to adjudicate his case. For the most part, they saw him as a trouble-maker, although he had the respect of a few of these Jewish leaders.

A second level of government was centered in the family of Herod, an Idumean group in the south of Israel, which had been appointed by the Romans to keep order. By the time of Jesus, the original Herod, called Herod the Great, had passed away, and the Romans appointed his sons to rule in different regions of Israel, with Herod Antipas having authority in the region in the north called Galilee where Jesus lived and centered his early ministry. There was also the presence of the Romans, led by Pontius Pilate, who served as the governor of the region of Judea in which the events of the last days of the life of Jesus took place. As it turned out, Jesus would face all three of these governments in his trial, with the ultimate sentence of crucifixion coming from the Romans.

In general, it would be fair to say that this governmental system had difficulty managing the region of Judea, and especially Jerusalem in a time of a holiday where there was an infusion of visitors. Jesus faced a confusing system in his trial, one having less focus on justice and more on managing the chaos of the holiday season with a dramatically expanded population. Secret meetings were held at odd hours, and Jesus was questioned in these settings.

It was a chaotic time in Jerusalem, and in the background was the reality that many of the people in the region already faced various forms of political oppression. New Testament scholar Marcus Borg described the oppression in three categories of domination.[14] There was the economic oppression, with those in positions of power using taxation and control over the economy to ensure that the Romans and their appointed leaders kept more than their share of the funds available. There was political oppression, with minority groups not being allowed to have power in the government or even much control in their isolated settings. And there was a form of religious oppression, in that it was the religious leadership that gave sanction to the inefficient, unjust, and confused legal system. Jesus had to face the harsh irony that it was hard to argue with "god" if the governmental and religious establishments were sanctioned "by God" in the Sanhedrin.

---

14. Borg, *Jesus*, 225–60.

FAITH AS THE ON-GOING COMMITMENT TO THE DIVINE MISSION

It was these conditions that caused poverty and hardship, political unrest, and religious confusion that in many ways set the agenda for Jesus in the last week of his life. It was on Sunday that he entered Jerusalem, and it would be the following Sunday that the Easter story became the heartbeat of the new Christian movement. Jesus understood that it was his calling to proclaim his message of truth, love, and justice during his visit. He did it in several ways that reflect how he lived wisely and well in the evening of his life, in spite of the reality that he should not be arrested and could not get a fair trial as he got arrested.

Jesus had arranged to stay with friends just outside of the city (Bethany), and the disciples had arranged a place for meetings and meals during the week. It was on Sunday, the first day of the Holy Week, that he chose to enter the city on a colt with his followers using Palm branches to clear the way, a humble entrance that was in contrast to the power of Rome with their soldiers riding in an imperial procession suggesting power and control (Mark 11:1–11). He was greeted with joy by many people who either knew him or had heard about him, and there was the chorus of those who said, "Blessed is the one who comes in the name of the Lord." It was a bold statement, challenging the authority of Roman power. Perhaps a new King David had arrived, and the foreign government could be over throne. It was a statement about political oppression and the need for the people of Israel to have their own government. Ordinary people heard him, recovering their sense of identity and desire for justice and freedom. Jerusalem, on this special day, was the right place for confrontation with the Jewish and Roman authorities. At the end of the day, he returned to Bethany.

On Monday, the challenge and proclamation continued (Mark 11:12–19). On his way into the city, he engaged in a symbolic act as he approached a fig tree, thought to be a symbol of Israel and its government. He found no fruit on the tree, cursed it, and it died, and the disciples saw this act and heard him say, "May no one ever eat fruit from you again." He came into Jerusalem and went to the temple, the symbol of the religious life of the people. He observed what was going on in the temple, saw the table of the money-changers who were prepared to provide the right coinage for alms and perhaps other purchases, and then noted that poor, even the lame, were not getting a fair exchange for money. He overthrew the tables of the money changers and said so all could hear: "My house shall be called a house of prayer for all the nations. But you have made it a den of robbers." It was another dramatic statement, and the people flocked to hear him speak and were "spellbound by his teaching." It was a long and dramatic day, and "Jesus and his disciples went out of the city."

Tuesday was a day of his continued teaching, proclaiming the need to open one's heart to the reign of God. His message of love, truth, and justice was unsettling for the religious establishment. His authority to teach was challenged, and Jesus responds in wisdom by asking by what authority did John the Baptist preach. The authorities, aware that John was well respected, did not answer, and Jesus knew that if they acknowledged the truth of John's message, they would have to acknowledge the truth of his message. He quieted them. The issue of Roman authority also came up and again he silenced them with a coin, showing the head of the emperor, and saying, "Give to the emperor the things that are the emperor's and to God the things that are God's" (Mark 12:13–17). Again, he silenced his detractors. On Wednesday, he continued to teach and his detractors sought for a way to arrest him. On Thursday, Jesus met with the disciples for a Passover meal, and one of his own followers, Judas Iscariot, left early to betray Jesus, and then told the soldiers where he could be found away from the crowds. It was that evening that Jesus and his disciples went to the Garden of Gethsemane. Jesus knows that the end is near, and he invites his closest friends to pray with him. It is in the middle of the night and with many of them asleep, Jesus prays for deliverance: "Abba, Father, for you all things are possible; remove this cup from me; yet not what I want, but what you want" (Mark 14:33–36).

Jesus is arrested and taken early to the temple authorities and speaks with the leaders in the Sanhedrin, answering their questions. With confusion over which government has the authority to deal with Jesus, he is taken to the Romans who have the power of capital punishment. He is presented to Pilate for the final phase of the trial. Somewhat ironically, Pilate makes an effort on behalf of Jesus as he offers the crowd to free one of three prisoners. The crowd does not support Jesus, and then he is then crucified.

All through the week, Jesus remains firm, deeply committed to his mission, and speaks the truth boldly. Even in the last hours of his life, he cares for others and remains faithful to God. It is hard to say that he was ever truly found to be guilty of a crime, although he is finally arrested by Rome and on the vague charge of sedition and revolt.

His last words on the cross are very revealing of the identity and character of Jesus. The first word reflects his deep empathy for those who have been forced to carry out the horrendous death of crucifixion.

Instead of shouting in anger toward the soldiers, he says, "Father, forgive them; for they know not what they do" (Luke 23:34). He prays that God will forgive them, as he has done. The second word, coming in conversation with a prisoner who is deeply afraid and waiting to being crucified next to him: "Truly, I say to you, today you shall be with me in Paradise" (Luke 23:43). Even at the end, he cares for the prisoner next to him and gives him reassurance of God's eternal love.

The third word is about his mother and dear friend John. "Meanwhile, standing near the cross of Jesus were his mother . . . . Jesus saw his mother and the disciple whom he loved standing beside her; he said to his mother 'Woman, here is your son.' Then he said to the disciple, 'Here is your mother.' And from that hour the disciple took her into his own home" (John 19:25–27). In the end, Jesus cares for his mother.

The fourth comment from the cross, as Jesus is close to death, is the prayer, "My God my God, why have you forsaken me?" (Matt 27:46). Quoting from Psalm 22, he reveals his sense of loss. The very human Jesus suffered profoundly.

The fifth word from the cross comes after Jesus fully understands that his life is over; he says: "I am thirsty" (John 12:28). He remains human, yet direct and mature. The sixth word is, "It is finished" (John 19:30). Jesus knows that the end is near. And, finally, the seventh word is: "Father, into your hands I commend my spirit" (Luke 23:46). In the end, we see a Jesus as one who will never betray his commitment to love and truth, the heart of living wisely and well, even in the most severe circumstances imaginable.

So, live with careful courage, unafraid of death and taking delight in what we are still able to experience and contribute.

Terms, Resources, and Discussion Questions

Terms

1. Prophet: One who speaks truth to power, often challenging a person or governmental polices that are unjust.
2. Justice: Ensuring that all people will be treated fairly and that social structures protect the common good.
3. Compassion: A sympathetic consciousness that discerns the distress and suffering of another person and seeks to alleviate it.

4. Emotional Intelligence: The capacity to be empathic with those who struggle in life and a way of communicating to them a deep concern for their well-being.
5. Sanhedrin: A council of Jewish religious leaders in the time of Jesus given the capacity to act as judges regarding the Jewish law, interpreting it and making judicial decisions.

Books to Read and Consult

1. Kenneth E. Bailey, *Jesus Through Middle Eastern Eyes: Cultural Studies in the Gospels*
2. Marcus Borg, *Jesus: Uncovering the Life, Teachings, and Relevance of a Religious Revolutionary*
3. Günther Bornkamm, *Jesus of Nazareth*
4. John Dominic Crossan, *Jesus: A Revolutionary Biography*
5. Bart D. Ehrman, *Jesus: Apocalyptic Prophet of the New Millennium*
6. Paula Fredrikson, *Jesus of Nazareth: King of the Jews*
7. Frederick J. Murphy, *The Religious World of Jesus*
8. Michael J. Sanders, *Justice: What's The Right Thing to Do?*
9. E. P. Sanders, *Jesus and Judaism*

Discussion Questions

1. Do you see yourself participating in the divine mission in the world and if so, what might your role be?
2. Would you have joined with Jesus or at least supported Jesus in the overthrow of the tables of the money-changers?
3. What were the primary qualities of Jesus in the last week of his life?
4. How would you interpret the healings of Jesus described in the New Testament?
5. How would you describe the "emotional intelligence" of Jesus?

SECTION TWO

Sustaining Hope across the Years

> "Here is my servant, whom I have chosen, my beloved with whom my soul is well pleased. I will put my Spirit upon him, and he will proclaim justice to the Gentiles. He will not wrangle or cry aloud, nor will anyone hear his voice in the streets. He will not break a bruised reed or quench a smoldering wick until he brings justice to victory. And in his name the Gentiles will hope."
>
> (Matthew 12:21)

THE GREAT PROPHETS OF the Hebrew Bible, speaking to a people in continual transition and filled with anxiety, urged these Jewish people to have hope, even with the challenges of internal unrest and external threat. The prophet Isaiah speaks about one whom God has chosen who will not only guide and lead the Jewish people, but also one who will "proclaim justice to the Gentiles." These great prophetic voices spoke again and again about the need to remain hopeful as they faced one crisis after another. There is a compassionate and wise one who is coming who will not "break a bruised reed or quench a smoldering wick" and who will "bring justice to victory."

We turn now in this new section to the second part of the "still more excellent way," one which has three undergirding and foundational values. "And now faith, hope, and love abide, these three, and the greatest of these is love" (1 Cor 12:31, 13:13). For us to live wisely and well in the evening of life, we must embrace, cultivate, and apply the great virtues of faith, hope, and love. We have spoken of the ways that faith undergirds and guides our lives. We want now to explore how hope will sustain and empower us as we seek to live wisely and well, knowing that the world is in crisis and that night comes soon as we live in the evening of life.

CHAPTER SIX

Hope as the Attitude and Spirit of Gratitude

> "As God's chosen ones, holy and beloved, clothe yourselves with compassion, kindness, humility, meekness, and patience. Bear with one another and, if anyone has a complaint against one another, forgive each other; just as the Lord has forgiven you, so clothe yourselves with love, which binds everything together in perfect harmony. And let the peace of Christ rule in your hearts, to which indeed you were called in the one body. And be thankful. Let the word of Christ dwell in you richly; teach and admonish one another in all wisdom; and with gratitude in your hearts sing psalms, hymns, and spiritual songs to God. And whatever your do, in word or deed, do everything in the name of the Lord Jesus, giving thanks to God the Father through him."
>
> (COLOSSIANS 3:12–17)

THE ESSENCE OF HOPE

As I speak with people in a given day, even in casual conversations, I find that they often reveal whether they are those with hope, giving them a very positive outlook on life, or those without hope, those feeling a bit overwhelmed by personal, family, local, regional, national, or global concerns. Often their hope or lack of it are related to personal concerns. Of course, there are many categories that describe this range of people

I meet. I suspect that there might be dozens of other categories that accurately point to or at least hint at their demeanor and identity, giving hints that reveal the kind of person they are. Yet not all of these first impressions point back to what is foundational in the person's life. Only a few words, such as mature, faithful, loving, positive, happy, sad, angry, contented, honest, authentic, fulfilled, and wise, suggest that which is the true character of the person's inner life rather than just a passing observation of a mood or the reflection of a momentary thought or feeling.

On occasion, I am asked by a friend to tell them what I think about another person, usually because this person has come into their life in one way or another. From time to time, there is the request: "Tell me about this person; my daughter may be going to marry him" or "I will be in a working relationship with her and I want to know how to make it a productive partnership." One often struggles with just the right word or sets of words and sentences that do justice to the question or request. One wants to be both accurate and fair.

One common category is the contrast of being either "positive and hopeful" or "a bit negative and overly critical, perhaps a bit cynical." In the evening of life, I hope that my friends, if asked about me by another, will be able to say, "hopeful and full of gratitude." I've had a recent experience that has taught me more about this spectrum of hopefulness-hopelessness. The church I am attending is planning a new initiative in adult education. I raised my hand at the wrong time and am now helping to guide the initiative. As we think about committee appointments, we are seeking to find a group of people with good experience and a positive outlook on the success of the new program. I want the ones with hope, not the ones who can just identify all the reasons why it will be hard and perhaps even impossible to have success in the endeavor, not that we shouldn't be aware of potential problems.

It is in the evening of life that the profound value of hope is vitally important. As one ages, there is the gradual decline of one's physical strength and skills, a shift in relationships as children mature and leave home or there is a divorce, an unexpected illness finds its way into our lives, and one's life work and vocation shift to a retirement mode. I have often asked myself how it is then possible in the evening of life, given these changes, to remain hopeful and full of a positive spirit about the prospects of each day. These changes take their toll. I am persuaded, after a few years of pondering this challenge, that one basic component of hopefulness and a positive outlook on life is gratitude. It keeps me going forward in a project and guides me in the ways I manage life. I look back with deep gratitude and forward with comforting hope. I have loved and been loved, have a wonderful family and many friends, have been fulfilled in my life work, and now have ways of living that are in some ways the result of being so blessed across the years, although not without a range of challenges. I am grateful and hopeful. My feelings and thought process might be identified in the following way: *My hope is based on the sense of being in relationship with God, grounded in the life and values of Jesus, and the integration of my faith and values with all the advances in the humanities, technological developments, social theory, and natural sciences.* For this foundation, I am profoundly grateful, not that I have fully accomplished the goal of being fully informed and totally hopeful; it is a process. I assume it as I face each day feeling hopeful and have deep gratitude for what I have been given.

The writing of the Colossians letter, attributed to the apostle Paul and from which the opening quotation is found, finishes two segments of the quote with: "and be thankful" and "giving thanks to God." Gratitude flows from our trust in God and the good work being done in the world. The author summarizes the heartbeat and deepest values of the Christian life, underlining at the end of each component and experience of the Christian way, the reminder of the deep need for gratitude. I am learning this practice and saying thank you for all the goodness that has filled my life.

Hope and gratitude flow together in a remarkable way. Hope may be understood as the attitude and spirit of one who anticipates that more goodness is yet to come. It is our horizon of understanding; it is the expectation and anticipation that the future will bring that which we need and cherish. I have my deep faith, the primary foundation of hope, and I believe that careful study of the human condition, the exploration of the natural sciences, the rigorous development of the social, technical, and natural sciences, and the appreciation of the arts, can take us into a safe, wonder-full, and hopeful world. As we are blessed by our faith, informed by our knowledge, and enriched by the arts, we sense that we are on the right track. As we stay on this track, we expect with confidence and hope that many of our goals will be realized. From this realization, we have a deep inner peace. We have been accepted and led by God, our lives have been filled with compassion and kindness, we have learned how to be patient and forgiving, and we now have the love that binds us together in perfect harmony. The peace of Christ has and will continue to be present in our hearts. Our faith gives us the profound assurance of God's love, and we are then hopeful and grateful.

With this foundation, we then turn to our knowledge about the world, how it works, and this union of faith and knowledge points the way forward. We are assured that we are on the right path. As we let the word of Christ dwell in us, we will have the wisdom to be lovingly related to one another. We will engage in working for a more just and humane world, believing that there is a way to bring a profound peace and contentment to one another. In spite of all the advances of harm and hurt in the world and all the challenges we face such as climate change, I still believe that we can help to create a better world. So, we are hopeful and with grateful hearts we give thanks to God.

We especially give thanks to God because of our knowledge about life, the world, and the cosmos. To fully grasp the content of our hope and gratitude and make it less of a platitude, we need *to continue to advance our knowledge of the ways that religious faith and scientific understanding find common ground*. Much has been done in that domain, yet we still have "miles to go before we sleep." There continues to be a gap between two worldviews. Our present task, as it is been for earlier generations, is carefully to integrate our faith with the scientific understanding of the world. With at least partial integration as a foundation, we are able to move forward with a hopeful outlook. We can and must work together to create a world of enlightened knowledge, compassion, justice, and peace. As we make progress with this integration, we become people of gratitude and a hopeful spirit. Better informed, we are able to do the complex and challenging work of love, emulating the first century teacher and prophet from Nazareth. We join the thousands of others who have sensed the same calling and gone before us.

We can do this work in small ways all around the globe. One of my assignments as I was working at the Presbyterian Center in the role of co-ordinating the support for mission in higher education. I traveled internationally, visiting institutions of higher education that had been founded by the Presbyterian Church in the United States. There were challenges in this assignment, juggling different visions of the mission of high education rooted in different time and place, and limited by a very modest budget. But what was quite clear from start was the need to find ways to have a strategy that integrated the values of justice and compassion with the advances of science. Many of the institutions that I visited were in a position to make a significant contribution to improving the lives of certain target populations in their region. They often lacked the financial resources to realize their dream of creating advances in programs that had the potential to improve the lives of the people whom they served. What they did fully agree on was the importance of creating programs with a scientific base that would advance the goal of preparing students from poverty-stricken backgrounds to return to their communities with the knowledge to improve the lives of those of those from their home regions. They sensed that it was necessary to have a mature understanding of care and compassion that could be linked to scientific expertise in order to create a more just and equitable social order. It was clear to the leadership of these universities that they had the responsibility to offer through education a deeper and more extensive understanding of values that could be integrated with science-based programs. This values-faith orientation, integrated with a contemporary understanding of the world, would indeed give those whom they served hope and a sense of vocation that had the goal of addressing the needs of a world in crisis. The issue for them and for us as well was how to educate students which helps them to live in a way that heals and transforms a threatened world.

THE REASONS FOR HOPE

At the heart of being hopeful is the grateful acceptance of the belief that God is what the biblical record affirms. There are only a few "God is . . ." statements in the Bible with most of the biblical authors likely assuming that when the word God was used, the readers would understand its primary meaning, although the nuanced meaning was varied and diverse at that time given the several cultures and countries present in the region. In addition, there is a cautious, reluctant, and wise reserve on the part of the biblical authors about trying to define and describe God, intuitively grasping that God is beyond our limited and partial definitions. Our words cannot contain God. Most of the time, our described God is way too small. Because of this risk and the limits of language, there is a tendency on the part of the biblical authors and leaders to use metaphors, analogies, and comparisons when speaking about God. For example, there is the common expression that God is like a loving parent who cares for the children of the world, with all humans being dear and needing love. Or God is like a shepherd who cares for sheep, ensuring that they are fed and do not get lost. There are these three "God is" statements as we turn to the Bible for guidance, and there are a few others that border on this way of describing God. I want to look carefully at the three statements.

1. That God is light: the Word of God came to us in Jesus whose life "was the light of all people. The light shines in darkness, and the darkness did not overcome it" (John 1:4–5). We have the guidance of the "light of the world" (John 8:12), and with this accurate and truthful guidance, we can see and at least partially understand God and begin to find our way. God is light, a metaphor for truth, and this light came to the human family in Jesus and shines in our hearts and guides us in our daily circumstances. In faith, we encounter and link with ultimate Truth, the ground of being. As we connect with God, the Center of it all, we "see" our true direction and find our way on the difficult trail of life, overgrown with thorny bushes and full of danger. There are snakes on the path. Yet we know that we will find our way on this path with the values of our faith, knowledge of how the world works, and the guidance of scientific inquiry. We need lots of light.

2. That God is love: "God is love, and those who abide in love abide in God" (1 John 4:16). This statement is not just a description of God's attributes, but also an ontological grasp and description of the identity of God. As we connect with God, we encounter Love (as well as Truth), are truly loved, and learn how we might be those who have and give love. We give love in the best possible way when we are in relationship with God, when we are informed about God's way in the world, and when we are rooted in understanding of how the world works.

3. That God is Spirit: "God is spirit, and those who worship him must worship in spirit and in truth" (John 4:24). Spirit, in this passage in John's Gospel, is an interesting metaphor, one that implies that God is personal and omnipresent, always with us, and then transforms us as we receive and embrace God's presence. We sense and then learn that the "Hound of Heaven" will always pursue us when we don't place our faith and trust in God. As I mentioned, the word for spirit in Greek is the same as the word for wind or breeze, and to say that God is spirit is a way of saying that God is everywhere like the wind, and when we step outside on a warm day, we feel a gentle breeze and feel refreshed. We are in the presence of God whether we acknowledge it or not, and we can be guided and empowered by God.

These definitions/descriptions of God give us hope in times of great challenge, serious danger living in a world in crisis, and the common feelings of being impotent, lost, and alone. We begin to find our way through the maze of contemporary life as the Light shines in our lives; we then become better able to see and understand the world and the challenges we face. We discover the truth of our condition and how to cope. For example, as the human family struggles with the reality of climate change and the deterioration of the environment in which we live, we turn to God and seek knowledge to find our way. We know that our only way through and past this enormous threat is to understand it in all of its complexity and to invite our finest universities and scientists to guide us through this jungle. We must understand the harsh realities of what we face and find sufficient light to grasp and create answers for overcoming severe climate change.

One is reminded, as we face this challenge, of the passage in Genesis that suggests that humankind is responsible to be the good stewards of the creation. "Then God said, 'Let us make mortals in our image, according to our likeness, and let them have dominion over the fish of the sea, over the birds of the air, and over the cattle, and over all the wild animals of the earth, and over every creeping thing that creeps upon the earth. So, God created humankind in the divine image" (Gen 1:24–27). We must let this ancient account, indeed this ancient parable, teach us about our responsibilities for the created world. God is light and love, and God will guide us with light and love. We can dare to be hopeful. Or to say it in a more scientific way, we are the result of 4.5 billion years of evolution, and we should understand how we got here, why we are here, and act in reference to this foundation of light and love. We are to be good stewards of the earth.

We have sound reasons, then, to hope and be grateful; God is a present reality in our cosmos and in our lives. God is light and shows us the way, God is love, guiding and empowering us as we seek to be good stewards of the earth, and God is with us as we go into the future seeking a healthy and just context for our small little planet, earth. We are grateful that God is ever present in guiding and empowering us in our responsibility to be good stewards of the earth, that is, to care about its general health, and to show compassion and to seek justice for all of God's creatures. We are to care for all of life, and especially for humankind, that species which often makes mistakes, but has the capacity and responsibility to create a good and sustaining earth for all of its creatures.

ON SUSTAINING HOPE FOR THE GOOD EARTH

The faith communities of the world have a special responsibility for the welfare of the earth, viewing it as a divine gift and one for which they have some responsibility. Most of these faith families across the centuries have sought ways to fulfill this responsibility, especially at this time as the earth is in peril. All three of the Abrahamic monotheistic religions, Jewish, Christian, and Muslim, joining with the many other families of faith have agreed, at least in principle if not always in action, that the human family must fulfill their responsibility in caring for the earth, its living creatures, and its many components and dimensions.

While not always faithful in this endeavor, the best of these families of faith have engaged in the task of being good stewards of our home. Yet, as we have observed in our checkered history, these related families have not always agreed on how to undertake the care of the earth, but have now acknowledged that they must join together to face the harsh realities that threaten the earth. Nearly all of the great leaders of these families of faith have agreed as well on the need for the spirit of gratitude, grateful that there is life in its many forms and a special kind of life for humankind. Many of the leaders of these religious families have spoken with gratitude and hope. It is a common refrain that we are truly blessed and that life can be and generally is good. Almost with one voice, there is the chant of gratitude in prayers and liturgies, although with somewhat different beliefs and perspectives. There is the multi-voice refrain of gratitude to God and a deep thankfulness that is the foundation of hope. God or Presence or Transcendence, understood in a variety of ways, has blessed us, and because of this great blessing, we have both responsibility and hope for the future.

All three of the Abrahamic monotheistic traditions, a family which I know best, agree that in this time of crisis and threat, humans have a special responsibility, one that involves intelligent caring and making wise decisions about the way we care for mother earth. We are grateful that most of the religious families of humankind are in agreement about the kind of care and the general direction of the kind of care which the earth needs and deserves. They agree that there is the need to seek to know and be faithful to the best ways of improving the condition of our planet.[1] For

---

1. See the wonderful account of "mother earth" in Thomas Berry's book, *Dream of the Earth.* See as well the book by Matthew Fox, *One River, Many Wells: Wisdom Springing from Global Faiths,* and the book by David Christopher, *Holy Universe: A New Story*

most of these faith families, the starting point for them is that we go in faith and that the God of love and light is present with us. There is the common affirmation that God is the creator of all there is and the One who created our earth and the life and character of the earth. Admittedly, there are many different descriptions about this common affirmation, some related to history and culture, some related to advanced or limited educational exposure, and some even clouded by needs of power and control. But at the root of most cultures and their religious expressions, there is a sense that God has created our life on this small planet, that we should be profoundly grateful for it, and that we have the responsibility to be good stewards of it. It is faith in the God of creation and the God of compassion that binds us together, gives us hope for the future, and guides us to the best ways to be good stewards of the earth.

We are now faced with a gigantic threat to our home, and we must now find a way to cooperate and collaborate. We need to emphasize the common bonds we have and not fight over the insignificant details of caring for the earth and some differences of belief that might suggest different directions for care. *We need unite in a faith that is rooted in the continuing quest for truth, faith as the deep and abiding trust in divine wisdom, and faith as the on-going commitment to the divine mission of love and justice as we attempt to fulfill our responsibilities of being good stewards of the earth.* It is faith as the continuing quest for the truth that is especially urgent at this point on earth and in human history. Our common faith must be guided by the sciences, not the voices with naïve and superstitious belief that they can predict the end of time with obscure references to isolated passages in ancient literature or obscure events in history as revelatory about the future. Our best direction is to integrate the sciences with our profound belief in a personal God of compassion and ultimate truth. Our faith communities, linked to the best science, have the responsibility to guide their constituents in the truth of what we must do to care for our earth home and all who live in it.

This last emphasis, understanding faith as the continuing quest for the truth and finding good solutions to pronounced problems, has its foundation in a deep and abiding trust in divine wisdom and the continuing quest to learn. This sentence is much easier to write that it is to apply on the global level. In fact, many would say that it is not true that God is present in our struggle, and that those who believe it are misguided,

---

of Creation for the Heart, Soul, and Spirit.

even superstitious. They underline the classic issue: If God is good and all powerful, why would God allow all of this evil, danger, and harm to happen? On occasion, I am tempted to accept that I am misguided about my faith in God's goodness and care as the problems continue and get more complex and severe.[2] I live with some doubt. When doubt is present, I turn in two directions, one is to accept the reality of my good fortune to have been exposed to excellent science and the other is to understand in a general way the variety of belief systems of the human family. The range of these religious belief systems is vast, and not all of the beliefs and practices of the religious traditions can be synchronized and integrated with scientific understanding. Yes, there are religious beliefs that are harmful and even some religious practices that are destructive. Yet my hope is that we will be able to do this most important work of integration and achieve a profound understanding between the values of religious faith and the truths of the humanities and the social, technical, and natural sciences. As we do, we can draw upon the values of the great religions, use the wisdom of the study of the human family, and apply the great discoveries and applications of science to save our earth home. It is this vision, filled with knowledge, wisdom, and motivation that has the capacity to lead us into the future. With gratitude, we have hope that in their own language and way, many of the wise leaders of the world religions, the finest scholars of the humanities, and the great scientists of our world will find a way to be in accord about caring for the earth. I have hope that this will happen; I am grateful and encouraged by the limited way that scientists and religious leaders and scholars are beginning to talk.

ONE WAY FORWARD

As I have participated in a few discussions and read accounts of other conversations on these critical issues of earth care, I have found that *listening and educating* are a better strategy than arguing about different religious views and profit margins of the companies who misuse our natural resources. It may not be possible to reach an agreement on all of the details of advancing the petroleum industry and caring in a spiritual way for the earth, although leaders in both domains need to talk together. There is much at stake.

I have also found that statements that imply "you are wrong and I am right," often present between scientists and theologians, lead to

---

2. The tragedy in Gaza has just occurred.

frustration and separation. It is better to say, "please explain a bit more so that I will understand." When this happens, on occasion, there are then more collaborative discussions that have the potential to lead to a more refined statement of the problems and the solutions. Conversations about the stewardship of the earth often do get derailed by closed systems of thought, a preoccupation with an irrelevant issue, a personal bias, or a hidden prejudice. These conversations are often filled with objections rather than, "I am still learning; tell me more."

Over time, I have begun to find a few ways of conversing about beliefs and assumptions that do not drive those conversing apart. Rule number one *is to honor those who are engaged in these conversations, and especially those who have different views.* We need to listen well and then to read widely and carefully in order to be as informed as possible. As I learn and listen, I have often discovered that a legitimate point of view is often covered up by one's idiosyncratic ways of describing it. It may be rooted in the assumptions of a historical timeframe, specific cultural norms, and a specific language that one does not often use. Then, of course, there are the personal preferences, experiences, and even prejudices on the part of the listener. As I listen, I try to hear the deeper truth that stands behind the array of distinctives of the religious tradition and their expression in a particular time, language, and culture. As I listen well, and then carefully restate the disguised truth, I may find an openness and find common ground. Not infrequently, there is the acknowledgement that many of our religious traditions may be chasing after the same deep insight, belief, and course of action, ones which are integral to the task of integrating scientific understanding with the best values and beliefs of the religious communities of the world. There is room for us all in the dance of survival.

Rule number two, of course, is to *find that elusive common ground,* that is, some agreement about the challenges to the whole human family and the many ways that religious insights and values have the capacity to bring helpful and guiding insight to the solutions that are being offered by the scientific community. I often reflect on the native traditions of human family in particular. Inherent in them, one often sees a common religious understanding of their place on mother earth and a semi-scientific agreement about how to listen and respond to her. Taking a lesson from those who have lived close to nature may inspire us. Then we need to say, "yes, that is one way of looking at it and we must consider it as we do the work of science." We might even save the coasts of Alaska or reverse the rising waters on the coast of Bangladesh and other threatened areas with faith in the goodness of nature and its integration with science. We must work hard to find common ground as one affirms that mother earth has smiled on us and told us to tend the garden in thoughtful scientific ways. The voices may be referencing the same Being and Presence with different names. Yes, there are those who live in the realm of "the cult of absolute truth" and cannot open their hearts to those with a different tradition and another perspective. The religious voice may shout at the scientific voice, and often the shouts are returned. But by showing respect, building trust, and listening carefully, we may be able to reduce tension between those with different views and open doors to understanding, find common causes and possible solutions, and take unified action.

It is also essential that we get others to accept the reality that human belief systems are rooted in our language, history, and culture, and may be limited by them. With some humility about our views, we are more apt to find ways to join hands in the care of the earth, show compassion for all those who suffer, and then address the need to challenge practices that harm the environment and create social injustice in its many forms. We are then able to offer good solutions that are the product of good science and apply it with the compassion that is integral to the world of religious faith.

There are many who do agree that the heart of thoughtful and informed faith is a deep and abiding trust in divine wisdom, although they may find it harder to say what that divine wisdom may be. It may have a different definition among the many religions and be absent in secular science.[3] I continue to believe and then share with others that "God" speaks many languages. I know that all of the languages of humankind that describe ultimate reality, whether they are religious or scientific, are partial. They are often complex and contained in within a particular language and culture. So, in some cases, we may have to reach across and enter into a different understanding with empathy. We need to find a way to hear and grasp the point of view of others. God is present with us all, and we are his children learning how to listen and how to describe, hear, and understand by faith, reason, and scientific exploration.

It is generally easier to bring people together by talking about the great need to address the range of human problems we all face than it is to get them to agree on the specific beliefs and ways of how to do it.

---

3. See the book edited by Joseph Runzo and Nancy M. Martin, *Ethics in the World Religions,* for detailed illustrations from the world religions about justice and peace.

Agreement on the nature of the problem, especially one that open to a range of possible solutions, is needed and very possible. Yet it is often made more difficult to get diverse groups to agree when there is the use of religious language from different cultures and scientific language in the same conversation. It may be hard for some people to say that we are called to the on-going commitment to the divine mission and then join with scientists who find the word divine to be problematic. But there may be a common commitment if we use the language of reducing suffering, the technical knowledge of the sciences, and the goal of seeking justice and peace. At times, in these conversations, I have dropped the word "divine." Yet I have occasion spoken about this dimension of divine care about human suffering in India to Hindus, in Japan to Buddhists, in Pakistan to Muslims, in China to those following Confucius, in Ireland to Protestants and Catholics, in Alaska to Native Americans, and in Moscow to atheists with a sensitive conscience. I have often been heard. I have learned, in some cases the hard way, and in other cases a more gentle and universal way, that there is element of compassion and gratitude in nearly all human hearts. As humans understand the depth of human suffering, the range of domination systems, and the larger threat to life on earth, they tend to soften, often setting aside for a few moments their own hard and fast beliefs and narrow perspectives.[4] Frequently they show understanding and compassion. As they do, they edge toward trust in the continuing presence of good science, an appreciation of human wisdom, and move partially toward sensing that there may be a divine mission in the world.

THE EMERGENCE OF HOPE: ON LEARNING HOW TO CARE FOR AND LISTEN TO OTHERS

Often what happens, when we truly care and listen, is that we begin to feel deep joy in being alive. Our hearts and minds, in harmony, begin to celebrate life, and then we sense a deep gratitude for all that we have been given, the hope it brings, and our desire to make life better for those who suffer. This thankful insight often expands to caring more deeply about others form different cultures and religious traditions and who have little in their experience that gives them hope. It is an essential part of our responsibility to find ways of bringing hope to those whose lives have been

---

4. I confess that I almost lose hope as I see the suffering in Gaza.

stunted and shattered by hunger, illness, lack of opportunity, injustice, violence, being ignored or set aside, and not having opportunities to improve one's life. Unfortunately, there is a large portion of human beings, and indeed of all sentient beings, that dwell in the land of hopelessness. This reality requires that we who have must assume some responsibility for those who are among the "have nots," and to do so without an old-fashioned and outdated condensation or cultural bias. It is often people in the evening of life, who have acquired deep empathy because of their vast experience, who sense this responsibility to address human suffering in all of its diverse forms. It is a way for us with years of experience to live wisely and well, using our vast experience, accumulated knowledge, and unique gifts in a constructive way. The deep values of love and compassion join with the humanities, the sciences (technical, natural, and social), to find ways to care for those who suffer and to hear those who desire to heal a broken world.

There are some clear lessons to learn as we read this ancient letter to the Colossians. In fact, we do need to study the past in order to move wisely and well into the future, especially in the direction and spirit of love and collaboration. This new church, one that was founded by a close companion of the apostle Paul, had, as any new church might have, some growing pains. Paul and his companions in ministry saw that aiding these new congregations was a central component of their ministry. The challenges faced by these new congregations involved both learning about the content and newness of their belief and the behavior expected by those with their new found faith in Christ.

Colossae was good-sized and substantial city in Asia Minor, east of Ephesus. It was important to the region as a city with industry, and the citizens of the city may have been in the process of some rebuilding because of a damaging earthquake. It was a busy city, full of energy and vision. It was also a city full of ideas from the ancient world, ones that had to be adjusted and reinterpreted in some different ways as the new church sought to find its way in a new and changing world. The author of the letter, with care and remarkable insight, is seeking to assist these new Christians to understand their faith in light of their circumstances and the prevailing worldview.

One example that Paul and his companion writing the letter take into account is that the region and city had the heritage of some Jewish ideas as well as the ancient practices and beliefs of astrology. They were asking questions about the observance of festivals that were attempts to live in harmony with the new moon and the movement of stars. Present was the discussion between what was thought to be science and how it was related to religion. They had been taught to follow a range of Sabbath observances and dietary restrictions as well as how to worship angels. The crossover to simple faith in Jesus Christ and his way took some adjustment, just as it does for us as we shape the contours of our faith in reference to dramatic changes and severe problems. In fact, their challenge was not totally unlike the ones that we face on a regular basis as we seek to live wisely and well in the evening of life.

Let me attempt to summarize the intent of the letter, one that we quoted from above. The first challenge was to rearrange their belief system and to accept a simple faith in Christ, "for in him all things in heaven and on earth were created, things visible and invisible, whether thrones or dominions or rulers or power—all things have been created through him for him" (Col 1:15–16). The whole earth is the subject, religious and scientific. The author, likely Paul or one of his followers, introduces this foundational statement for these new Christians.[5] He adds, "As you therefore have received Christ Jesus the Lord, continue your lives in him, rooted and built up in him and established in the faith just as you were taught, abounding in thanksgiving" (Col 2:6–7). The summary in chapter two of the letter stresses five modes of living in a Christian way, ways that may guide us as we seek to live wisely and well in the evening of life in the midst of a troubled world.

1. Remember that you have been chosen by God and are now holy (set apart for deep peace and loving action) and beloved.
2. So, act accordingly: "clothe yourselves with compassion, kindness, humility, meekness, and patience."
3. Bear with (be patient with) one another and forgive each other, just as you have been forgiven.
4. Above all, be loving; it will bring you together in harmony.
5. And then you will have inner peace and become thankful for this profound blessing.
6. Help each other by sharing wisdom, and then celebrate with song.

---

5. In fact, the early church used this passage and others in Gospel of John to speak about the cosmic Christ, the very *logos* or meaning of all of reality. See the description of this thought in Jaroslav Pelikan's book, *Jesus Through the Centuries*, 57–70.

7. "And whatever you do, in word or deed, do everything in the name of the Lord Jesus, giving thanks to God the Father through him."

I am reminded and inspired by this simple message about how to live wisely and well, any time, in the past or present. I know there is the use of a new Christian language that may be strange to many, but it is a message that points to peace, love, and justice. It gives me hope, as I approach the end of life. With this hopeful spirit, I try to do the work of integration of faith and science in reference to our global crisis. As I do, I give thanks to God.

We live with honest hope, humility, and loving behavior, facing the complexity of life, knowing that we have limited knowledge, yet have a range of experience that can be used for the good of the earth.

Terms, Resources, and Discussion Questions

Terms

1. Hope: to cherish and anticipate a positive experience and change, to desire with a positive expectation.
2. Gratitude: the state of being thankful.
3. Truth: the state of being the case, what is said and what has happened; sincerity in action and speech.
4. Love: affection for another, acceptance of another, and care for another.
5. Spirit: an animating or vital principle; in Christian thought, the power and presence of the divine—the Holy Spirit.

Books to Consult and Read

1. Ewert Cousins, ed, *Hope and the Future of Man*
2. The Dalai Lama, *Toward a True Kinship of Faiths: How the World's Religions Can Come Together*
3. Kate Davies, *Intrinsic Hope: Living Courageously in Troubled Times.*
4. John Macquarrie, *Christian Hope.*
5. Joanna Macy and Chris Johnstone, *Active Hope: How to Face the Mess We're in with Unexpected Resilience & Creative Power*

6. Jürgen Moltmann, *Theology of Hope*

Discussion Questions

1. Are you a hopeful person or do you tend to be a bit skeptical about your future, the future of your country, and the future of the world?
2. What is it that threatens your hope, and then what gives you encouragement to be hopeful?
3. Do you generally understand your hopefulness as the internal message of your feelings (intuition, etc.) or do you base it on the circumstances around you? Or both?
4. Are we living in a time in which it is justified to be hopeful or in times that we should genuinely worry about our future?
5. How did Jesus sustain his hope, and did it continue in the last week of his life?

CHAPTER SEVEN

Hope as the Quest for Justice and Peace

"By the tender mercy of our God, the dawn from on high will break upon us, to give light to those who sit in darkness and in the shadow of death, to guide our feet into the way of peace."

(Luke 1:78–79)

"Woe to you, scribes and Pharisees, hypocrites! For you tithe mint, dill, and cumin, and have neglected the weightier matters of the law; justice and mercy and faith. It is these you ought to have practiced without neglecting the others."

(Matthew 23:23)

SUSTAINING HOPE ACROSS THE YEARS

WE HAVE MAINTAINED THAT an essential component of hope is the attitude and spirit of gratitude. Because we have been blessed in the past, we anticipate being blessed in the future, and for this hope and the anticipated blessings, we feel profoundly grateful. These anticipated blessings as they arrive bring us a deep and abiding peace. As we continue in this spirit of hopeful gratitude and the resulting peace and contentment, we trust in God's will and way for our lives. Knowing that God is Truth and Love, our deep faith in God's blessing in our lives is secure. We rest in

God, and in this lifelong mode of being, we are filled with life-giving hope, even in the challenging times. Hope sustains us as the threats to our well-being are internal (I am not sure I can cope, given what I feel) or external (the challenges in my setting are overwhelming).

There are, of course, many blessings that come our way even when we are not preoccupied with either internal unrest or external threat; there are wonderful moments when we are free from fear and discouragement. For example, we can often have an authentic and simple hope when we are with our families, have our picnics, and plan for our summer vacations. As a boy, I loved those times; they were filled with joy and anticipation. My brother and I would go to our room and talk about the big lake where we could swim and the diverse and beautiful landscape in which we could hike. We would then marvel at the snowcapped mountains that would surround us. We loved to hike and explore, and we would often see some of the great animals of the Northwest, the deer of course, but also the occasional eagle, moose, fox, beaver, otter, and certainly traces of bears and cougars. We did see the bears at Yellowstone National Park and were warned about getting too close to them.

These rich and joyful memories have stayed with me for decades, but so has the reality of fear and insecurity. There were times of being anxious, especially when my father joined the military service in the early 1940s. We were at war, and the young men of our country were called into the service. Summer vacations, if and when they occurred, took a different turn, as my mother visited her military husband in Texas and later in Florida. We were left with our grandparents who were very kind. Yet, with the start of World War II, our hopes for family vacations we once had were diminished as dramatic injustice and violent warfare took over the world. These conditions severely limited the times and circumstances that allowed for family vacations in the mountains, streams, and lakes of the Northwest.

Luke, as he writes his Gospel, quoted the writing of that ancient source of Zechariah, a small prophetic book in the Jewish Bible (Luke 1:17–18). He wrote to people who were threatened by injustice and war, as we were, and promised that God would send one "to guide our feet into the way of justice." Jesus, the Prince of Peace, said to his followers as he faced injustice: "Peace I leave with you; my peace I give unto you; I do not give to you as the world gives. Do not let your hearts be troubled, and do not let them be afraid" (John 14:27). The disciples of Jesus were worried as he told them that he might have to leave them; and as was his way, he still gave them hope: "Peace I leave with you" was his closing comment.

Peace is intimately interwoven with love and justice, and it clashes with its opposites, discrimination, violence, and war. These opposites bring unrest and worry, and both internal and external peace become rare commodities. In times of crisis, our hope for the good life is diminished. As Jesus said: peace is given, "not as the world gives," to suggest that deep and true peace does not often come from external circumstances, although there may be moments of joy that come from our surroundings. Lasting peace comes with the guiding and comforting presence of God.

My brother and I began to learn this lesson as we missed our vacations in the wonderful wilderness of the Northwest. We hoped that our father would return home safely, and that the family vacations might reoccur. He did return to the family setting in 1945, and we all climbed into the car and drove to our new home, one we hoped would be a paradise, and Menlo Park, California at that time was close to that description in last half of the 1940s and well into the 1950s. I can't remember the precise feeling we had as we moved, but I do remember that we hoped for a life of peace and joy across the years of our lives. My parents, having experienced worry, fear, and the disruption of our family life in the war years, were especially hopeful for a new way.

We thought the move to California was a step in the right direction. While this hope came and went with the details of family life, the message of those years remains with me, that my life, based on hope that brings great peace and joy, is only partially linked to external circumstances. The rolling hills out behind Stanford University were wonderful places to explore and hike. Yet, as I got a bit older, I learned that deep peace is rooted within, although I learned as well that it may be sustained in the settings where we live and where justice and peace prevail.

The circumstances of those years of growing up taught me a great deal about the connection of hope and its linkage not only with my day-to-day activities, but also with justice and peace in my nation. As a young person, I really did have hope, related in large measure to my personal circumstances in California and in part to national and international politics. I soon learned, sometimes the hard way, that doing well in school was also connected to my hopeful vision of what I might do in life and how I could and would spend my adult years with a good measure of happiness. I did reasonably well in school, even with a few too many moves and an array of schools; I learned despite the challenge of adjusting to several different elementary schools. Fortunately, given the national unrest and international conflict, I was just a bit too young to be drafted for service in the Korean war and bit too old with some education-related protection for service in the war in Vietnam. I slipped past these two conflicts and learned that my hopes for a professional life in ministry and higher education could have easily been derailed by these conflicts. Had I been drafted, it would have had a profound impact on my personal life, as those were the years of preparing for a career and of finding a life mate, a partner in life who could contribute to my sense of peace as I sought to go forward in life.

These personal hopes and dreams during these years were at least partially dwarfed by the larger reality, the racial injustice in our country and the violent warfare in Korea, Vietnam, and later in the middle east and the war in Iraq. The violence, destruction, and the enormous injuries and loss of life spoke eloquently to me about the connections between injustice and peace. When one added the ever-present fear of nuclear war, it became quite hard for so many to have hope, both the hope that comes from one's own life and circumstances, but also hope that comes when our country and our world are at peace. I wonder, looking back with more understanding and with the deep commitment to the value of peace, if major parts of these conflicts could have been avoided. I often fantasized about writing a book entitled: *The Stupidity of it All: There is an Alternative Way* as I thought about the conflicts in Vietnam and Iraq.

PEACE AND HOPE: PERSONAL AND CORPORATE

I was not prepared and sufficiently informed to write such a book, although my feelings about these conflicts were quite intense. I did, from time to time, participate in peaceful protests. I also found that I was inclined to illustrate presentations to students with stories in which the themes of justice and peace and the risks and tragedy of war were central. These themes were on my mind.

It was during these years of moving fully into my career in the 1970s that I began to piece together the many parts of my thinking and deep feelings about human suffering and the loss of personal peace. I had received a position in a church-related college, now a university, as both chaplain and assistant professor in religious studies. This combination, although it certainly made for long days, was ideal, enabling me to care for the growth and development of students and to introduce the causes and issues of our troubled world in an academic way. One particular student, with whom I was in a counseling relationship, epitomized this mixture of a deep need to find relief from his suffering that occurred in his service in the war in Vietnam. He did want to hold on to his childhood faith in a loving God, yet he could not bring these different dimensions of his inner life together. He asked with some intensity: "Why does God allow war and deep human suffering? My suffering!" He sought personal peace through pastoral care and also sought answers about why there is so much suffering. He hoped that his study of religion with an emphasis on the God of love and justice would provide as least some perspective.

He was a returning student, a bit older and had been wounded in the Vietnam war. He desperately wanted to find some personal peace and some answers. He did understand the ways that warfare caused deep suffering, and he wondered why a God of love did not intervene. He couldn't find that connection and asked me to help him integrate these two opposed realities, the love of God and suffering caused by war. He felt that his personal well-being and his faith were at stake. Although I tried, I don't think I was able to help him fully to integrate the promise of God's love for the human family and the terrible suffering that occurred in Vietnam. I listened well and became his "go-to" friend, but personal peace was absent for him; he remained deeply troubled.

One result of this counseling relationship, rooted in the suffering of one who participated in warfare and was suffering from it, was that I learned that personal peace does not always follow when warring countries achieve a measure of peace. The damage of war remains. Post-traumatic stress syndrome is real, past suffering does not leave us, and national and personal peace are not always integrated and often remain two separate domains. The larger lesson of these realities for me was to commit my life to help those who suffer from engagement in the violence of war to find a measure of hope. Was it possible to recover from the damage of violence and regain the presence of personal peace?

I did care about the suffering veterans and tried to help them. But I also wanted to be diligent about helping to reduce the conflicts between different peoples and nations; it is hard to estimate and describe the level of suffering that violent warfare causes. Thich Nhat Hanh, the recently deceased Buddhist monk, faced this range of questions about peace directly in his book, *Creating True Peace: Ending Violence in Yourself, Your Family, Your Community, and the World.* He writes:

> True peace is always possible. Yet it requires strength and practice, particularly in times of great difficulty. To some, peace and nonviolence are synonymous with passivity and weakness. In truth, practicing peace and nonviolence is far from passive. To practice peace, to make peace alive in us, is to actively cultivate understanding, love, and compassion, even in the face of misperception and conflict. Practicing peace, especially in times of war, requires courage.[1]

He develops this theme with several insights and suggestions including his counsel that peace really does begin with us as we have the right understanding, are truly present in our interaction with others, face directly and in depth the causes of conflict, and seek reconciliation. It was the pathway he followed in reference to the war in his homeland, Vietnam. He was profoundly aware of the ways that military conflict created deep personal trauma for many of his country's citizens. In a remarkable way, he connects personal peace to the best ways to seek peace between conflicted regions and nations.

There is comparable wisdom in the Bible, and it often revolves around the several nuances of the Hebrew word *shalom*.[2] Its root meaning is wholeness and well-being, and it is used in reference to finding peace in both personal and corporate situations as well as religious and secular settings. The word also carries the meaning that peace comes by engaging the two-pronged strategy of avoiding the causes of suffering *and* finding ways to cultivate peace.

At another level, I have found it interesting that *shalom* is used as a greeting as one meets a friend and says *shalom* or closes a letter or says good-bye with *shalom*, often followed by a signature indicating good wishes. It is an expression of hope that those who are addressed will have peace and security, and in some cases, even prosperity.

The word is often used as well as an expression of hope for peace when difficult conflicts occur between regions and nations. The way to resolve the conflicts is not war, but *shalom*, the hope that the nations will find ways to overcome their differences and not have to resort to violent war. Just below the surface of these clear and direct expressions of hope is also the implication that nations will need to face the truth of their

---

1. Nhat Hanh, *Creating True Peace*, 1.

2. I have been helped in my understanding *of shalom* by *Harper's Dictionary of the Bible*, s.v. "Peace," 766–67. Its meaning became more deeply ingrained in me as I wrote an article on *shalom* for a publication of the Presbyterian Church U.S.A.

troubled condition directly and live faithfully and righteously in order to achieve peace. The practice of shalom is to reject ignorant and false claims that are used to justify the resort to warfare and to find a different reading of events by opposing the justification for war by both sides of those in conflict.

In the Hebrew Bible, the word is used as an expression of a gift from God, and there is the underlying assumption that God wants peace between individual people and especially between tribes and nations. The great prophet Isaiah laments warfare and understands that God wants peace. "O Lord, your hand is lifted up, but they do not see it. Let them see your zeal for your people, and be ashamed. Let the fire of your adversaries consume them. O Lord, you will ordain peace for us, for indeed, all that we have done, you have done for us" (Isa 26:11-12). Peace is a gift from God.

The same teaching and underlying assumptions are present in the New Testament as well. Again and again, we read that *shalom* is the goal, and every effort should be made to eliminate conflict and war. Paul frequently exhorts Christians to be at peace with one another. "Owe no one anything except to love one another; for the one who loves another has fulfilled the law.... Let us then pursue what makes for peace and for mutual understanding" (Rom 13:8, 14:19). Jesus teaches a complementary goal and even goes so far as to say we should love our enemies: "You have heard that it was said, 'An eye for an eye and a tooth for a tooth.' But I say unto you, do not resist an evildoer. But if anyone strikes you on the right cheek, turn the other also; and if anyone wants to sue you and take your coat, give your cloak as well; and if anyone forces you to go one mile, go also the second mile ... But I say to you, 'Love your enemies and pray for those who persecute you'" (Matt 5:38-42).

It is when conflict and retaliation are put aside that we find political peace, and it is when we resolve internal and personal conflicts that we experience personal peace. As we overcome conflicts at all levels, we recover our hope for a life of peace, purpose, and joy. The biblical witness not only addresses the pathway to personal peace through a deep faith in God, but encourages peace with others by being generous and loving toward them. The Bible also addresses the issue of living in peace in a setting where justice prevails and conflicts between groups are reduced. Hope is dependent upon these several levels of peace. Our hope becomes a reality with the realization of the reduction of personal conflict, when there is a just social order, and the conflicts between tribes and nations are resolved. The prophet Micah captured it so well: "He has told you, O mortal, what is good; and what does the Lord require of you but to do justice, and to love kindness, and to walk humbly with you God" (Mic 6:8). And again, to quote Jesus who speaks as a prophet to power: "Woe to you . . . for you have neglected the weightier matters of the law: justice, mercy, and faith. It is these you ought to have practiced without neglecting the others" (Matt 23:23).

Our history teaches us the same lessons, and it has been so hard for us to hear the desperate need for and practice of the quest for justice in order to restore hope to those who are on the outside looking in. Day by day, our newspapers and news broadcasters tell us about the condition of those on our southern border who have fled from the injustice of their governments in central America and sought justice and restored hope in the United States. For a variety of reasons, it appears that we have been unable to receive many of them and welcome them into what we hope would be their relocation in settings where there is justice and equal opportunity. American history, while its documents and laws are designed to preserve equality and justice, also demonstrates that we as a nation have not always been able to live up to our lofty goals. Minority persons and those with racial and ethnic differences have frequently been the victims of discrimination. It has not been exclusively those with African descent, but also Latino, Asian, and Jewish people continue to feel the harsh edge of discrimination. The same is true for the LGBTQ+ community. Yes, progress has been made, yet more recently we hear stories about the resurgence of discrimination, unequal treatment, and even violent abuse.

Those of us in the evening of life long to be treated with fairness and compassion as we cope with the changes in our lives. Retirement is not always easy; not only health concerns can rob us of our ability to live wisely and well, but social injustice can push us to the edge and make it nearly impossible to live a life full of contentment in an unjust society. We want peace at all levels.

PRACTICES THAT RESTORE HOPE: SELF-UNDERSTANDING AND LIFE-GIVING RELATIONSHIPS

There are ways of making some progress toward personal peace and peace between those with conflicts, ways that give hope to those in the evening of life. Some of these ways have to do, of course, with our nation's policies and region's practices, and those in the evening of life often lack the access to the power structures in order to make changes at these levels. There may be limited access to the decision makers in order to ensure there is justice in the settings in which we live. And, unfortunately, nearly all settings have sharp and discriminatory edges. Yet there are some ways to help and do our part in our mature years by committing ourselves to create and engage in practices that include "the other" and lead to justice.

As I reflect on these conditions, I begin by being grateful for fairness and justice in many of the settings in which I have lived. In this reflection and deep in my heart I find myself thinking about personal relationships, their challenges, and the deep peace and joy that they bring. I find that honest and loving relationships bring me a sense of inner peace and gratitude; my life has been good and full of joy because of them. I do value just and peaceful conditions globally, nationally, and regionally, and locally, and as I can help to increase justice, I do it with as much wisdom and commitment as I can. I get involved as some level in which I have competence and motivation. I can lend a hand by using skills and wisdom that I have cultivated over the years.

Further, I sense that my deepest happiness is linked to my ability to develop profound and lasting relationships with others. In the evening of life, my peace of mind has a great deal to do with building and sustaining honest and loving relationships. I am taught by my faith about the many dimensions of love and continue to learn how to love unconditionally, deeply, intelligently, and compassionately.

Most of these kinds of love relationships will be established and sustained in the community in which we live, although there are many life-giving relationships with those from whom we are separated. For example, my wife and I find our relationship with our son and his family one of the most important relationships we have in life, yet we are separated by nearly two thousand miles. We have learned, even in separation, that there are ways to improve the relationships that bring us deep joy.

I have been helped in sustaining these life-giving relationships by increasing my self-understanding and improving my skills of listening and communicating. First a word about self-understanding. Across years in my several roles, I have been invited to learn more about myself in order to fulfill my responsibilities and also to experience satisfaction and sense of accomplishment in the work that I do. There were the courses in counseling, years of experiencing ways to heal others, and then ways of understanding the depth of my own being. I am so grateful for the exposure to the great minds who have provided tremendous insight, increasing our self-understanding and the ways to live a fulfilling and productive life. I have also been grateful for those who have taken these great insights and found ways to make them practical in terms of self-understanding and ways of assisting others in their growth toward maturity. I want briefly to mention a few instruments and ways that may assist us in self-understanding, ones that have been helpful to me. The first is the Myers-Briggs Inventory with its categories and its four sets of personality types. After some testing and reflection, I began to discover how I process information, how I use my energy, what are my personal priorities, and what I value. I was careful in the process of learning, especially being conscious of over-simplification, yet was grateful for increased self-understanding. I also exposed myself to the ways of achieving self-understanding and a deeper spirituality using the Enneagram, and exploring styles of processing information with the categories of thinker, one who intuits, a feeler, and a sensor. These exposures increased self-understanding and were especially helpful as I served as a chaplain, as a faculty member, and as a senior academic officer. I had some idea of my style and my strengths and limitations; it was important learning and increased my sense of how to lead, make changes, and ways to manage life in better ways.

Drawing on some from these exposures and learning, I want to look at the ways we may be able to build relationships in a better way. I will speak personally, but want draw upon a study that has been done at the University of Kansas that has a range of practical suggestions about creating life-giving relationships.

The study suggests the nature of building and sustaining relationships in the community in which I live.[3] The suggestions on the lists tend to be quite practical. The title is: "How Do You Build Relationships? An 11-Step Program."

1. Build relationships one at a time. . . . there are no shortcuts.
2. Be friendly and make a connection.
3. Ask people questions.
4. Tell people about yourself.

---

3. I borrow here from a publication of the University of Kansas called "The Community Tool Box." It was prepared and used by the Work Group for Community Health and Development. No date is given, although it comes from a larger publication entitled "Core Functions of Leadership, Section 7i, Building and Sustaining Relationships."

5. Go places and do things with others.
6. Accept people the way that they are.
7. Assume other people want to form relationships.
8. Overcome your fear of rejection.
9. Be persistent.
10. Invite people to get involved.
11. Enjoy people.

Each of these suggestions is expanded in the document that I consulted. There are additional suggestions for building relationships with people with different cultural backgrounds, not uncommon in our time, and some of the suggestions may apply even among people with the same cultural heritage.

1. Learn about the person's culture.
2. Put yourself at the center of another person's culture.
3. Take a stand against the person's oppression.
4. It's okay to make mistakes. Smile and apologize.
5. Don't be intimidated by those who hold positions of authority and power. Be yourself!
6. Listen and withhold judgment.

How then do you sustain relationships?

1. Pay attention to people.
2. Communicate openly.
3. Appreciate each other.
4. Extend yourself.
5. Volunteer to do some work in a common cause.
6. Challenge each other to do better.
7. Back each other when things get tough.

What do you do when relationships get messy?

1. Take time to listen to one another.
2. Put yourself in the other person's shoes.

3. Look at what is true about what the other person is saying.
4. Separate emotions from reality.
5. Continue to appreciate and respect each other.
6. Speak from your heart.
7. Don't give up on your principles.
8. Hang in there when things get tough.
9. You can act independently to improve any relationship.

I now want to make some suggestions about dealing with the occasional necessity to confront another person.

1. Confront by attempting to understand the other person, and why their behavior disturbs you. To start, ask a polite question, such as how should the schools help transgender children or should they?
2. In general, do not confront harshly if you want to continue the relationship.
3. Be aware of why you feel the need to confront and be careful about making an unfair judgment; if you do, it will just provoke defensiveness and in some cases, anger.
4. Keep an eye on the goal of confrontation as a means to achieve a greater good, not just to release your negative feelings.
5. Be sure to note in the exchange that you want to improve a situation and deepen a relationship.
6. As far as possible, understand that there are different forms of confrontation: informational, interpretive, sense of being threatened, and a desire to improve or deepen a relationship.
7. Keep in the mind the following factors that will improve the exchange: empathy, timing, the nature of the relationship, being concise and authentic.
8. Remain open to the possibility of misunderstanding; keep it tentative.

Better ways of achieving communication that improve a relationship:

1. Listen carefully to avoid misunderstanding: ask yourself what you heard and whether your interpretation of what has been said are

accurate. If needed, ask for confirmation of your understanding of the exchange.

2. Establish rapport by being sensitive to the other person's feelings, see if your sensitivity is accurate, and then offer alternative ways of looking at the exchange.

3. Listen carefully to identify the problems in the exchange. Did you really find out what the other person wants and whether there may be other alternatives and solutions?

4. Stick with the issue and don't insert a list of your past experiences. Avoid the very real temptation to shift the conversation with continual self-referencing.

5. Maintain a calm level of emotion and maintain perspective. Avoid the tendency to use a series of "I-statements," shifting the conversation to you and taking attention away from the person with whom you are speaking. Stay with the original intention of the one with whom you are speaking.

6. As far as possible, end the conversation on a positive note, leaving room for further conversations. Ask if there are other feelings and thought that need to be expressed, possibly with a reference to ending the conversation if that is your goal.

Note the following: You are not listening to me when:

- You do not really care about me.
- You give me an answer to my problem before I have finished describing it.
- You cut me off before I am finished speaking.
- You find me boring and you are only pretend to be listening.
- You feel critical of my feelings, although I cannot fully control my feelings.
- You tell me about your experiences and seem to find mine unimportant.
- You are communicating with someone else while I am talking.

You are listening to me when:

- You come quietly into my world and let me be me.
- You really try to understand me.

- You grasp and accept my point of view even if it doesn't agree with yours.
- You don't give advice about how to solve my problems but allow me to grapple with them.
- You accept my gift of gratitude by telling me how good it is to be understood.

I have collected these lists over years of experience, several workshops, and a variety of meetings, but did not tag them with a title and date. I apologize in not giving full credit, yet I am grateful for the ways these suggestions have guided me. I use them because they make some of the more general statements and lessons about the love both taught and shown by Jesus, recorded in the New Testament, very practical. I can apply them daily. In fact, as I ponder potential avenues of reconciliation between Israel and the Palestinians, I find it possible to be guided by some of these principles in the endeavor to seek peace in Gaza. The Gospel of Matthew summarizes them so well in the Golden Rule: "In everything do to others as you would have them do to you; for this is the law and the prophets" (Matt 7:12). This saying, with comparable ones in other religious traditions, gives me hope and represents my quest for creating a community where there is a full measure of peace and justice.

We make our contribution to encouraging hope when we live with caring compassion for all who come our way, receiving them with joy and affirmation, and identifying with their pain and struggle.

Terms, Resources, and Discussion Questions

Terms

1. *Shalom*: Hebrew word meaning peace, both personal peace and peace among groups and nations.
2. Crisis: a turning point for better or for worse, although always a challenge to find ways to cope.
3. Post-Traumatic Stress Syndrome: Excessive lingering stress and anxiety as the result of being present in a violent conflict such as war.

4. Non-violence: A strategy for making social change to rectify injustice without resorting to use of weapons.
5. Contentment: the quality or state of personal internal peace.

Books to Read and Consult

1. Thich Nhat Hahn, *Creating True Peace: Ending Violence in Yourself, Your Family, Your Community, and the World*
2. Colin Grant, *Altruism and Christian Ethics*
3. David P. Gushee and Glen H. Stassen, *Kingdom Ethics: Following Jesus in Contemporary Context*
4. Daniel C. Maguire, *Ethics: A Complete Method for Moral Choice*
5. William C. Spohn, *Go and Do Likewise: Jesus and Ethics*

Discussion Questions

1. How does one assess whether resorting to violent war is justified? Are there any good reasons?
2. What are the primary steps that one should take in order to reduce conflict with another person? Between groups and nations?
3. What are the primary causes of conflict?
4. How would you define social injustice?
5. What are the best ways to correct social injustice?

CHAPTER EIGHT

Hope as Living a Joyful Life in God's Presence

"When they saw that the star had stopped, they were overwhelmed with joy. On entering the house, they saw the child with Mary his mother; and they knelt down and paid him homage. Then, opening their treasure chests, they offered him gifts of gold, frankincense, and myrrh."

(MATTHEW 2:10–12)

THE CONTOURS OF HOPE

WE HAVE BEEN EXPLORING the ways that we are able to live with life-giving hope, and we noted that the deep feeling of being joyful is related to hope; it is what we feel about the goodness that has come into our lives and what we anticipate will be the continuation of being blessed by a good life. Hope makes us joyful! We underlined that hope is the anticipation that we will continue to be fully present in the beauty and complexity of the world around us, deeply appreciative of the circumstances of our lives, and continue to find gratification in having a life filled with loving relationships and life-giving responsibilities. Joy comes to us if we have these circumstances and the spirit of gratitude about our lives; hopeful joy is sustained by continuing to have a positive outlook on life. We sing with Louis Armstrong, "I think to myself, what a wonderful world!" In a spiritual context, we express gratitude to God for the positive experiences of life, and we are then filled with the hope that we will continue to have those experiences which are fulfilling. They bring us joy, and we anticipate a good life ahead of us, the heartbeat of hope.

In addition, we may even have a measure of joy as we have been able to manage those experiences and conditions that were painful and challenging. We learn from them how to cope and manage life wisely and well, an experience that is a special gift to those of us in the evening of life. We have been surrounded by positive relationships, meaningful work, and an environment in which we have found our way, even with its challenges. In fact, in the evening of life, filled with a hopeful spirit and a broad range of experiences, we may be able to assist in the formation of a more just and humane social order that makes life better for others, one that gives them joyful hope. We stressed that hope is the motivating energy that guides and empowers us to continue the quest for justice, peace, and care for the earth. Reflecting on these life circumstances, difficult as they might have been, we remain committed to helping create hopeful joy for others. Being grateful and joyful about the circumstances of our lives, we discover that we have been and continue to be motivated to share our joyful spirit with others. We sense that we are able to contribute in creating an environment of hope for others, fully understanding that hope emerges from our positive surroundings (under control), our internal frame of mind (life will continue to be good) and our emotional state (I feel joyful about life). It is in the evening of life when we seriously ponder these questions about joy and hope, often grateful that they have been present in our lives, yet also reflecting on their absence in some periods of our lives and may be especially absent as we age.

As one deeply rooted in the spiritual traditions of the Christian faith and aware of the spiritual practices of many of the other religious traditions of the human family, I have discovered that the spiritual connection with the divine is a source of great hope and joy, much needed because we cannot always depend on having positive life circumstances and enriching and loving relationships. A deep and profound connection with God sustains us and brings us joy, even in the midst of difficulties and challenges. Hope is rooted in the healing and empowering presence of God, giving us deep joy and peace.

From time to time, I look back to the moments in which I was most hopeful and filled with gratitude and joy. There have been many of these times, and occasionally their opposite, feeling discouraged, almost overwhelmed by life's demands and filled with anxiety and borderline depression. As a young university student, I had moments of feeling overwhelmed by the demands of disciplined study and the need to get excellent grades while still facing the challenge of learning how to study and cultivating the discipline to be consistent and complete the assignments day after day. I am so grateful that, somehow, I was able to study with diligence and do reasonably well with my course of study. I look back to those years as well with gratitude for good friendships and the occasional relationship that I thought might lead to marriage, a concern for most people at that age. I truly wanted a good life partnership. It was one of my deep hopes as I reflected on the somewhat troubled relationship of my parents.

In my college years, I had begun to be more realistic and accepting of the fact that my parents had their own problems and could no longer be my emotional base of support, not that it was fully there earlier in my life. I also sensed that my financial support was somewhat limited, as my parents struggled some with their finances. I did make some decisions that helped with this realistic appraisal. For example, in part because of continuing injuries, I told the football coach, based on the doctor's assessment, that I could no longer be on the team and wondered how my financial aid might be impacted. The coach was understanding, and he was able to help shift my athletic scholarship to an academic scholarship. I began to study with more focus and diligence and my grades improved. I became involved in student government and found it more fulfilling than the three hours a day on a wet practice field, although I still loved Saturday afternoons. I turned inward and felt affirmed by what I understood to be the guidance and presence of the Spirit of God. I also had good and supportive friends, and my life turned from a measure of worry and discouragement to one with more hope and joy, not that all of my life's circumstances suddenly became easy to manage. But I had an attitude shift in reference to them, and I began to feel more confident as the grades improved. I found myself more in that wonderful world of gratitude and hope, although I still had to work hard and make good decisions! The lessons of those years were an exceptional gift, and they pointed me to a more disciplined and spiritual life.[1]

---

1. It was admittedly a somewhat naïve orientation, yet in time it progressed to a much deeper understanding of a sustaining spiritual orientation.

SECTION TWO

WALKING WITH GOD

One of the frequently used metaphors for living a spiritual life is directional movement, that we go forward in a spiritual way by walking with God. The Gospel of John describes Jesus as often using the metaphor of walking as he guides his followers:

> Again Jesus spoke to them saying, "I am the light of the world. Whoever follows me will never walk in darkness but will have the light of life." Then the Pharisees said to him, "You are testifying on your own behalf; your testimony is not valid." Jesus answered, "Even if I testify on my own behalf, my testimony is valid because I know where I have come from and where I am going, but you do not know where I have come from or where I am going" (John 8:12–15).

In this account, as Jesus speaks to the Pharisees, he says to them that his life has a direction, although they (the Pharisees) may have been unsure of the undergirding divine origin and meaning of the life of Jesus.

In this frame of reference, Jesus teaches his disciples that life is like a long walk, and it is easy as we come to corners and hills to make a mistake and feel exhausted in the direction we are going. He taught them about *wrong turns*. I expect that most of us have suffered from them, and it is not uncommon to have a few "if onlys" as we reflect on our past. We know that we need guidance in finding the right direction in life, not only in the early years as we set our course, but also in the evening years as we finish the walk and have less energy, deep needs, and troubling questions as darkness comes.

The Pharisees question whether Jesus has the wisdom and knowledge to suggest the right direction in life for his listeners and followers. They ask: "Has he been adequately trained and formally sanctioned to teach and suggest the right direction for faithful Jews?" Jesus replies that he has been sanctioned by God and that his teaching gives guidance and light so that his listeners will see clearly and be guided in the right direction to walk toward a good, healthy, and fulfilling destination. He underlines that he has been sent by God to give light to those who struggle to find their way in life; "I am the light of the world." Having this light as a guide enables us to be joyfully hopeful as we walk. As we set out on our hike through life, we want to be sure that we don't take a wrong turn and step in a ditch or get on a path shared with a rattlesnake. We want our life to be filled with joy as we walk; we want it to be filled with hope that we will have a joyful life and, in the evening of life, to anticipate finding rest in the loving arms of God.

As we walk, in order for us to remain hopeful, especially as we age, we must have the right motivation and right orientation to sustain us, and it may be difficult to have these dimensions in life as we age. Jesus often speaks to these concerns as does the apostle Paul. In what is called his second letter to the young Christians in Corinth, Paul says that we can be confident that we are going in the right direction, not because of our own sight and calculations, but because we are guided by God. "So, we are always confident; . . . for we walk by faith, not by sight" (2 Cor 5:7) We do use our mind and senses as we set out on our walk, but deep down, our joyful journey is one of faith in God, sensing that the presence of the Holy Spirit will lead us safely to our destination. If we turn away from God and seek our own destination, based perhaps on fear or ego gratification, we may truly lose our way. Jesus is quoted as saying that those who seek their own way may discover that: "Those who find their life (seek their own way) will lose it, and those who lose their life for my sake will find it" (Matt 10: 39). Luke words this counsel from Jesus in just a slightly different way as he writes: "Those who try to make their life secure will lose it, but those who lose their life will keep it" (Luke 17:33). We walk by faith, filled with God's light and love.

THE STEPS THAT LEAD TO A JOYFUL LIFE IN GOD'S PRESENCE

As we explore the several ways of walking through life with hopeful joy, I want to acknowledge that our environments are filled with many paths and trails to follow. Some lead us to health, happiness, and purpose; others may lead to disappointment and the sense of being lost. I know this reality exists for people in the United States and I am sure that it is true for people also in other parts of the world. As I have traveled in other parts the world, I have been with joyful people who have found their way within the history, culture, circumstances, and faith traditions of their life setting. Often, I would realize that their way was not mine, but I discovered that these people were profoundly contented as they walked the pathways of their setting. I gradually learned from them about the wisdom of their way rather than judging them for not going my way. It is not uncommon for those of us in the Christian context, and even because we live in in the United States, to say that our way is really the only way. Yet the cultural norms and wisdom traditions in other countries do provide guidance and comfort to their people. I also found that their wisdom traditions often complemented the wisdom inherent in my way.

I have found my way in my setting in the United States with its many pathways, some which are healthy and attractive and some that are not always helpful and, in some cases, could be quite harmful. Yet it has been the context in which I have sought and found my lane. I have found guidance from my Christian faith, spacious and open in character, to guide me with hope and often fill me with joy. Now in my eighties, looking back across the years, I sense that I have found a good pathway. To a large extent, I have found ways to live wisely and well, and now, in the evening of life, I have a good measure of joy and peace with only a few regrets.

It is bit a difficult to fully explain why this is the case; there are so many factors and circumstances. But I want to try because I think it is important for me in order better to understand how I have come to my current orientation; and I suspect that there may be some crossover to others. In fact, I am persuaded that this kind of understanding about which we are speaking will be helpful for others as well who seek guidance and understanding. There is some common wisdom that is more universal in character and may be helpful to nearly all people who are seeking to find a good direction in life. As people discover this common wisdom, they begin to realize that the evening of life for them will be a time for profound gratification and deep contentment. So, at the risk of some presumption, I invite you, the reader, to follow as I attempt in a general way to explain how my life has unfolded. It is my hope that my pathway will have traces of common wisdom that point to a flourishing life, one filled with love.

I want to focus on five major influences, that is, five different sets of circumstances, experiences, patterns, and habits that have made the difference in enabling me to move toward living wisely and well, not that I have consistently done so. I now have a measure of joyful hope because of these influences, and I want to share their character, hoping that others may see how their shaping influences may have the capacity to guide them to a modestly peaceful life. As I ponder these experiences, they give me hope for those near and dear as well as those I will never meet, sensing they may be able to find a good life with comparable influences. What

I do know with confidence is that they will need to walk through life with *wisdom*.[2] The threats and challenges to the good life are real!

The first condition and influence that has empowered me to live with hope and joy is that I have followed with only a few missteps a very *good direction*, given my background and pattern of life. For me, the direction was to move toward becoming a well-prepared teacher and scholar who might help others who were seeking to become healthy and whole persons, make good choices, be fully informed, and following a life-giving way. My direction was and is to care for the souls of those who have been and are in my circle of nearness. In doing so, my soul or the central core of my life has healed and become more mature. I soon discovered along the way that my soul needed to be grounded in truth and love; I needed this center for me to be able to invite others into a life filled with truth and love. Jesus, full of grace (unconditional love) and truth, was and is my model.[3]

My early location and circumstances did not guarantee that this direction would be the one I followed. My family life was not always positive and nurturing, although even the more negative challenges along with the opportunities contributed to my development. I learned what was not so healthy and life-giving with an alcoholic parent. It taught me about the pathways that could lead me in the wrong direction. Yet there were positive dimensions in my family life as well, and for those, I am grateful. Not the least of these was the value of education.

I was surrounded by good teachers, youth workers, and caring friends who helped me gradually to understand and stay on this course through the years of education. This period was at times difficult early on because I attended many elementary schools as my father often changed jobs. I generally felt a little bit behind the rest of the class and did not always feel secure. I was continually the new kid on the block. The high school years were more stable and positive. In these years, I did have good friends, fine teachers who taught with great skill, many adults who were mentors, and wide range of travel and study opportunities. I began to find my way and began more consistently to walk in the right direction.

---

2. Wisdom in seen as a great quality and fundamental value in both the New Testament and the Hebrew Bible. Solomon, the king of Israel, was viewed as having great wisdom, and Luke notes that Jesus even had greater wisdom than Solomon (Luke 11:31).

3. It is easy to project qualities on to Jesus that may not have been integral to his life; there is risk for us to create a Jesus that satisfies us and meets our need. I have tried to be sensitive to this temptation, careful with our limited history about his daily life.

The university years were comparable and mostly positive with good friends and challenging courses with a major in history and a minor in philosophy. I had a range of quite healthy opportunities to learn about the life of faith and how to navigate many of the contemporary challenges to living in a healthy way. Immediately following the undergraduate years, there were the years of seminary and then an initial appointment in youth and campus ministry, my first full time professional appointment. I felt secure with my education and comfortable in this appointment; I sensed I was going in the right direction. It lasted just nearly five years, a time of learning new skills and a time of investing my heart and soul in the lives of the youth of the church and the students at the University of Oregon. Although serving in church context, one in which I valued although it was not in a denomination that was part of my earlier life, I did discover in my campus ministry responsibilities that I really wanted to be a part of the university, not just a visitor. In fact, my grandfather, Henry Davidson Sheldon, began teaching at the University of Oregon in 1900, and my parents were students at the University in the nineteen-thirties. My brother and I were both graduates. I felt at home, although I knew there was still a long way to go to find my way and be secure in the course of my life.

With a Scottish heritage and wanting to learn about my roots, I applied for a post-graduate degree at the University of Edinburgh and was delighted to be accepted and receive some financial assistance. The years in Scotland were enjoyable and demanding, and they gave me a more mature outlook. I was freed to some extent from an exclusively American cultural frame of reference, a fairly narrow Christian outlook that needed more depth and breadth, and I was invited to embrace a more global outlook. I loved the hikes in the Scottish Highlands and the sandy shores of the bonnie, bonnie banks of Loch Lomond. And Edinburgh was and is a marvelous and beautiful city.

This graduate education, followed by some excellent appointments as faculty member, chaplain, and administrator, confirmed that I had made the right decisions and had found my direction in life. Perhaps I could teach reasonably well and wisely care for the souls of those I was called to serve. These experiences were very positive; I felt adequately prepared and confident in them. As I moved forward in my career in church-related higher education, there were the additional opportunities for research and writing. I was fortunate to be granted three sabbaticals at centers for research and writing, and, in addition, an appointment for the intensive study of management in higher education at Harvard

University. In short, I had an unusual array of good educational and writing opportunities.[4]

The work and service appointments were equally positive, serving as a chaplain in a university setting, a faculty member in three institutions of higher education, and as a senior level university administrator both in universities and the national offices of a mainline denomination. This last appointment with the denomination was the most challenging appointment in that I found that I was slightly more comfortable in the academy than in the institutional church. It was easier for me to engage in the search and discovery of truth rather than assuming I had an essential part of the truth and was called to spread it. All of these opportunities, mostly positive, were exactly on target to keep me headed in the right direction. I look back and rejoice, mostly because of the positive experiences, and even experiences that were more challenging that gave me the opportunity to learn and manage a range of difficult circumstances.

The second set of conditions and influences, in addition to walking in the right direction, were the *relationships* that I had across years of my career. As far back as the last year of high school, I was supported and nurtured by those with vast experience and deep empathy. There were many people from the church and parachurch communities in which I participated who kindly and patiently guided me. One part of my learning in these years was their example; I could not fail to aspire to be like these bright, able, thoughtful, articulate, and caring people. I was profoundly grateful for the attention and guidance that I received. I learned a great deal about how to care for others just by observing how they taught and counseled me and led the groups in which I found affirmation and acceptance; these were settings that nurtured positive growth and learning.

Many of these leaders were very able teachers, and their teaching in the areas of the history of human thought, contemporary theology, biblical literature, and the resurgence of spirituality gave me a firm foundation. I was especially drawn to those leaders and teachers who invited me to probe the mysteries of religious knowledge, not just accept what was the current religious outlook or one that connected me with a narrow and exclusive tradition. Some of the groups in which I participated did have what one might call an evangelical point of view. It was often filled with joy and love, but occasionally what was taught was viewed as the exclusive truth, the only way to understand the Christian faith and to give

---

4. I was able to spend two sabbaticals in Princeton Theological Seminary, one at the Institute for the Advancement of the Humanities at the University of Edinburgh.

one acceptance by God. I trusted these wonderful people, was nurtured in the groups which they led, but quietly I asked a number of questions. It wasn't long before I learned what to say and how to say it in order not to offend. But I knew that there were many traditions of faith and practice within the larger Christian church, and that there were millions of others who sought a spiritual way within the framework of their culture and history. I learned from Karl Barth and the Dalai Lama, Dietrich Bonhoeffer and Thich Nhat Hanh, Martin Luther King, Jr. and Mohandas Gandhi, Mother Teresa and Pema Chödrön, and the New Testament and Rumi.

I have also learned a great deal from a very special friend, Jamal Rahman, who is an Imam of an interfaith congregation in Seattle, and one of the well-known "three amigos" (a Jewish rabbi, a Protestant pastor, and Muslim Imam) who have traveled widely to encourage and cultivate interfaith understanding. Jamal has been faithful to the foundational teaching of Islam which I admire, and what has been most admirable is the way that Islam honors the great prophets of the ages, not just from the Islamic tradition, but also from the great prophets of Judaism and Christianity. Abraham, Moses, Jesus, and Mary are among those honored alongside of Muhammad.

The mention of some of the authors from *different countries and religious traditions* who were influential in my growth suggests a third major influence in my growth and development. I moved toward becoming a more mature and responsible person because of my experience in different parts of the world. I was most fortunate in my work across the years to have responsibilities that took me to several countries. In my work for the Presbyterian Church (U.S.A.), I had some assignments that were designed to continue to cultivate the relationship between the Presbyterian Church and the educational institutions which the church had founded in many parts of the world. The goal, of course, was to indigenize these institutions and grant them full ownership and responsibility. In that process, one major principle was to sustain what the church called a covenant partnership, one in which there would be an exchange of ideas and the sharing of resources in order to strengthen the partnership and encourage learning about the global character of the church, and indeed, the global character of the new world in which we live.

The third major influence in shaping my life and career has been the opportunity both to travel to over seventy countries in the world and to have the privilege of living in a few of these countries, learning about their history and culture, and how to work in a cooperative and collaborative way with their religious leaders and spiritual communities.[5] I have learned that God is honored in the beliefs and worship of the religious families of humankind. It has not removed me from my Christian orientation and, in many ways, it has enhanced it. I often reflect on the reality that Jesus was not Christian but a Jew and Muhammad was not a Muslim although Islam formed around his life and teaching. Yet their influence created two of the world's most populous religions, ones rooted in guiding their followers to a life of love and dedicated to serve the profound needs of humankind. I have learned that there are many ways, even with our differences, to join with others in the task of creating a more just and peaceful world.

These linkages with leaders and teachers of the world's great religious traditions have had a very positive influence on my life. I have been enriched by their wisdom, guided by their moral teaching, and emancipated from a narrow and exclusive view of the Christian faith. It has made me a better person and deepened my spiritual journey. I find great comfort in affirming a spacious Christian faith, one that is open to new ways of understanding and accepting of those with a different faith tradition. It has increased my capacity to live by the two most foundational dimensions of what we mean when we speak of God; that God is Love and that God is Truth. The Christian Scriptures are clear that God is love and light (John 8:12, 1 John 4: 12), and that Jesus was filled with "grace and truth" (John 1:17). These same values are foundational for many of the religions of the human family.

I want to mention two other opportunities regarding experiences and responsibilities in foreign travel that contributed to my understanding of other cultures and increased my awareness that we now live in a global context. One of the universities, founded by Presbyterian mission workers, was Forman Christian College, in Lahore, Pakistan, a city of over ten million people. This institution was founded in the mid-eighteen hundreds, and over many decades has been an influential private high school and university in Pakistan and the larger region of the subcontinent of India. Prior to the founding of Pakistan, Forman Christian College as it was called, educated many of South Asia's leaders. The institution found itself in a difficult financial situation in the last two decades

---

5. Time and space do not allow a full development of the place of interfaith understanding and cooperation, although I have found ways of linking with adherents of several religious tradition, found common ground in the areas of social service, spirituality, and care for the integrity of creation, and have been enriched by these relationships.

of the twentieth century, caused in part by a failure to find experienced and visionary leadership. It was also one of those situations in which the Presbyterian Church (U.S.A.) still technically owned this extraordinary school/university. It was situated on nearly one hundred acres in the middle of a vast metropolis. I was invited, along with several other leaders of the church, to assist in revitalizing the institution. It is perhaps unnecessary to say that this was a most challenging assignment, crossing cultures, the use of different languages, the presence of two major religions, and its location in a huge metropolis in a Pakistani metropolis; a complex and invaluable setting. We never did quite learn the value of the one hundred acres with excellent facilities in middle of a huge metropolis.

Our team's responsibility was to organize, inform, and guide this invaluable institution toward renewal. We had to adjust to the reality that we were in a Muslim country, partially wary of American influence and cautious about the Christian influence. Books could be written on this endeavor, but suffice to say that we managed to accomplish our goal. Our team met with a team of Forman's faculty and Pakistani leaders, knowing that the Prime Minister of Pakistan as well as many other government leaders including members of the supreme court, were graduates. For at least a century and a half, this institution was viewed as one of the best small universities in a vast region of the world. With good translators and a positive outlook, we managed to build trust and made progress. The lawyers and bankers dealt with property and finances, wisely informed alumni and leaders addressed the context and the place of Forman in the city and county, and still others with whom I worked dealt with restating the education goals and reorienting the curriculum of the institution. A few major decisions were made including the creation of a new infrastructure and educational mission. I'll just underline three of the specific and positive changes:

1. The first was to turn over the ownership of the institution to Pakistan and appoint a new board of trustees, made up of Pakistani citizens and alumni, to guide the future of Forman College. It was an extraordinary gift of the Presbyterian Church (U.S.A.). What was vitally important was that this action was in keeping with the church's mission principles. The church honored the Muslim context and worked in collaborative way with Muslim leadership, leadership which honored the Christian heritage of this extraordinary

institution. Muslim and Christian faculty and students worked in a collaborative and cooperative way.

2. There was the appointment of a new president, an American educational leader, recently retired from a college presidency in the United States and sensitive to the values and ways of other cultures. He brought years of experience, profound wisdom about crossing cultures, and a new educational philosophy based more on an American model than on the British model that was influential across the region in nineteenth and early twentieth century. It had a deep commitment to liberal arts learning as well as the focus of a major, pointing toward a career.

3. The American church made a modest commitment to continue the funding of the institution, although it put in place a way for the government and business leaders of Pakistan and Lahore to plan to take full financial responsibility. Within just a few years, the funds were raised, the campus was renovated, and the budget was balanced.

In this endeavor, I learned a great deal about other cultures, Muslim foundations, careful and strategic planning, a good process for making foundational decisions, and how to raise sufficient money to renew the life of the institution. Dr. Peter Armacost, the first of the appointed presidents in this new era, did a remarkable job; he was a person of vision, wisdom, and great strength. I was privileged to have a small part in this endeavor.

I was also influenced by one other initiative that taught me about crossing cultures and enhancing the lives of people in other countries facing severe challenges. As part of my work, I did travel on occasion to the British Isles, and on one of these trips, I was able to speak with a government leader in the British province of Northern Ireland. His responsibilities were vast, although one focus of his work was to improve the economy of Northern Ireland and thereby to assist in improving the economy of the Republic of Ireland. Both settings were suffering from an economic downturn and limited financial resources. As we talked, we explored the possibility of having students from Northern Ireland and, as possible, some from the Republic to come to the United States and study business practices that might help improve the economy of Northern Ireland and lend a hand in creating better understanding among Protestants and Catholics, at that time still in the era called "The Troubles." I suggested that some of the Presbyterian-related colleges and universities might be willing to assist, opening up perhaps two places for Irish students and offering free tuition and room and board expenses. My colleague thought the British government might pay travel costs and a provide a modest stipend for daily expenses. We were told by several people, both in the United States and in Ireland, and in the church and the government, that it would never work! Catholic and Protestant leaders would not even talk to each other; they were too busy condemning each other from their pulpits. There was a deep division. A collaborative program such as this did not "have a prayer." Even the American presidents of the church-related colleges and universities said that it would be hard to justify the free tuition and room and board costs when there were so many American students needing these few places in their institutions. But we got it started, with about twenty Irish students attending for either one semester or a full academic year in seven Presbyterian related colleges and universities. The Catholic priests and the Presbyterian ministers in Belfast spoke to each other for the first time in years; and then prayed together with tears flowing. In the second year, the American Methodist and Catholic related colleges and universities joined in the program, and the Lutherans were not far behind. In the third year there were over a hundred Irish students studying entrepreneurship in American colleges and universities. The program continues. Protestant and Catholic Irish students became dear friends, the economy of Northern Ireland improved for many reasons, one which was new and visionary leadership from the program. Letters of congratulation and support were sent to our office from the leaders of both nations. I learned that change is possible as people come together with open hearts and minds and a dedication to improving social structures with honest conversation, clear goals for creating more opportunities, and a commitment to just and humane practices. I will never forget those years, and Belfast, almost as much as Edinburgh, became a second home.

I do want to mention just two additional influences that have shaped my life, ones that have given it more depth and a deeper understanding and commitment to use what few gifts I have in lending a hand in creating a more just and humane social order. While in Louisville at the Presbyterian Center, I was asked to participate in trips in which service was provided to educational institutions in many parts of the world, not just in Europe, but also across Asia in Korea, Japan, and especially in India. There were also trips to universities in Africa and Latin America. What stands out for me, as I have had these few privileges and challenges, is that I have found *deep meaning and fulfillment in leading a life of service to others,* even when it was very difficult. I do know all too well that my abilities and experience were not exceptional and that mistakes were made, but my heart was filled with gratitude and a sense of profound privilege by having crossed so many geographical lines and had a small part in helping others. I learned again and again that education is the key component to improving our world. These experiences have had a profound influence on my life and were even gifts to members of my family as they on occasion were able to join me in many parts of the world. I want to summarize in a very brief way how these opportunities of service have contributed to my life and perhaps helped those whom we served.

1. The first way, of course, is that they were very *educational in nature*. I learned so much from serving the needs of others in many parts of the world. I learned about world hunger, global infrastructure, other cultures, the ways and beliefs of religions of the human family, and the place of education in the development and leadership of countries. My views were expanded and deepened by the wisdom of human family.

2. I did become a *better person* because of these years of service, not exclusively because of the international travel, but also in the day-to-day service of counseling, preparing, and implementing programs, teaching about values and alternative ways of living, and of course learning about my own limitations because of my own culture, family experience, and way of life.

3. I have also had the great privilege of *feeling profoundly fulfilled* and having meaning and purpose in life. When I began to think about how to use my life, and then began to understand it as having the responsibility of helping others, caring for the health of their hearts and mind, and making sure they have a good measure of joy and peace, I wondered how it all might turn out. Toward the end, would I have a sense of accomplishment, having used my limited skills and gifts in a constructive way, and been reasonably happy and content in the flow of my life? The answer is always a bit mixed as one is truly self-aware and honest, but for me, I would say that life has been good. My dear wife, our son and his family, and many friends have made it so. I would not change very much, only the few times when I have made mistakes of judgment. Yet these mistakes, with thanks to God, have taught me and did not stop the pattern of service.

I want to mention one other aspect of my life, a fifth one, that was another major influencing factor in shaping the pattern of my life, and that is my *commitment to a life of discipline and study*. No, I have not been a Buddhist monk living in poverty, nor a doctor serving the sick in a needy country, nor even one who has consistently fasted and taken personal retreats on a regular basis. Rather, I would say that my patterns of discipline have been relatively consistent in the flow of a normal life across many years. I look back and see the many failures, some caused by ignorance, many by a lack of good judgment, and some by having deep needs, with some hidden and therefore inaccessible and without sufficient insight to make necessary changes. But they have not stopped the bigger picture of growth, which has encouraged me to be as consistent and regular as possible in refining my skills, improving my health, and deepening my understanding of life.

This pattern of discipline is most obvious in its external form as a commitment to staying healthy and engaging in an active program to learn more about my immediate concerns and about the world in which I live and seek to find ways to serve. My way of staying healthy is to get regular exercise and to try to have a regular pattern of sleep and rest. Staying physically fit has not been all that difficult, although I am not always as careful as I should be with my diet. In part because of being involved in several sports in my younger years, I have managed to continue to stay physically fit with walking and engaging in various forms of exercise in local health facilities. I feel quite grateful for few illnesses and being relatively active in my mid-eighties, but do not take this healthy condition for granted. I exercise at the gym regular basis if we are not traveling, and when we do travel, there is still the opportunity to walk in the settings we are visiting.

A bit more to the point about discipline is that I read on a regular basis and engage in some writing. I also work at the preparation level as I have opportunities to teach and speak. Again, I have managed a consistent pattern of staying in touch with national and world affairs. I do feel informed.

One particular area in which I want to be informed, and which is part of my active teaching, is to be sufficiently aware of what is going on in the world that is constantly in change and deeply troubled. I have been especially conscious of the place of religion in our society and other parts of the world, hoping that it has had a positive influence. I have been very concerned about the place of religion in our culture, aware that certain types of religious faith are not adequately based on a solid foundation nor undergirded by good scholarship and healthy spiritual practices. There appears to be a large number of exclusive, tribal, and cultic groups. I do understand that most religious movements ask for a full commitment, and at times, this request may have a positive outcome. Yet all too often religion is used as an instrument of control and often invites a harsh judgment of other people with a different religious heritage and outlook. When a religion becomes judgmental, cultic, superstitious, exclusive, and absolute in its system of belief, it may become harmful. I sense some risk in the ways that conservative Christian groups too easily identify with a particular political outlook. I feel discomfort if the name of Jesus is used in support of a narrow, exclusive, and judgmental religious beliefs and practices. How I wish these groups, if and when they use the name and model of Jesus, would welcome everyone and understand the deepest religious truth of all, that God loves the whole human family.

I do not want to ever practice my faith in way that has these negative dimensions; I want it to be inclusive, open, spacious, informed, and deeply committed to love and truth that leads to justice, peace, and the care of creation. A good part of my religious service is to invite people to have an informed and growing faith, one that empowers them to help those in need, and even at times to resist those forms of religion that are narrow and uninformed. I do gain wisdom from the life and teaching of the Jewish teacher and prophet named Jesus who cared for all people with unconditional love, resisted unjust governmental systems, and gave his life for those in need. I find in his life and teachings my model of how to live, and I remain open to spiritual and religious practice wherever truth, justice, care for the environment, and love are present.

In short, I have been influenced by having a clear direction for my life and being supported by good friends and wise teachers. I have expanded my understanding of life by living in and learning from other countries. I have matured and become more appreciative of other cultures, so needed, in a deeply divided world. I have been enriched by engaging in a life of service and helping to those in need. I only wish I could do better.

I often remind myself to live with winsome wit, seeing the humor in life, and being able to relax and not take myself too seriously. I try to not be offended when I am joyfully teased, very needed whenever I am about to fail the test of humility.

SECTION TWO

Terms, Resources, and Discussion Questions

Terms

1. Joy: The deep feeling about the goodness of life and the anticipation that we will continue to be blessed by positive relationships and circumstances.

2. Hope: The profound sense that we will continue to have love, truth, and justice in our lives, and that these conditions will exist for others.

3. Life lane: A pathway or direction in life that is the expression of our history, culture, and life circumstances.

4. Mature outlook: A frame of mind that honors the truth and which empowers us to manage life wisely and well.

5. Imam: A person in the Muslim tradition that is a teacher and pastor who provides guidance and support in a congregation.

Resources: Books to Read and Consult

1. Jack Kornfield, *The Wise Heart: A Guide to the Universal Teachings of Buddhist Psychology*

2. Matthew Fox, *One River, Many Wells: Wisdom Springing from Many Faiths*

3. Hans Küng, *On Being a Christian*

4. Maryam Mafi, *Rumi Day by Day*

5. Thomas Moore, *The Soul's Religion: Cultivating a Profoundly Spiritual Way of Life*

6. Paul Tillich, *The Courage to Be*

Discussion Questions

1. What empowers us to have a good measure of hope and joy?

2. What conditions must exist for us to be truly happy, filled with contentment?

3. In what ways does a deep spiritual life increase our hope and joy?

4. What are the conditions in your life that contributed to a sense of hopefulness, or have contributed to a sense of distress and discouragement?

5. In what ways did Jesus manage life in order to sustain his sense of calling and his faithfulness to his beliefs and values?

SECTION THREE

Practicing Love in the Evening of Life

"Little children, I am with you only a little longer. You will look for me; and as I said to the Jews so now I say to you; 'where I am going, you cannot come. I give you a new commandment, that you love one another. Just as I have loved you, you also should love one another. By this everyone will know that you are my disciples, if you have love for one another.'"

(JOHN 13:33–35)

THE NEED FOR LOVE IN OUR CONTEMPORARY CONTEXT

WE ARE EXPLORING TOGETHER the foundations for flourishing in the evening of life, and we continue that quest with the focus on love and its importance for us as we seek to live wisely and well as we age. Drawing upon the apostle Paul's letter to the new Corinthian church, we are seeking to follow what he calls "a still more excellent way." He summarizes this more excellent way: "And now faith, hope, and love abide, these three, and the greatest of these is love."[1] Having addressed the way of life rooted in faith and hope, we now turn to the virtue of love, the capstone of a flourishing life.

1. 1 Cor 13:13.

SECTION THREE

The author of the Gospel of John has placed a number of the teachings of Jesus in a section that captures his final guiding and comforting words to his disciples, knowing he will soon be threatened and will likely not "go quietly into the night," but into the night he is going. Chapter 13 of John's Gospel begins: "Now before the festival of Passover, Jesus knew that his hour had come to depart from this world and go to the Father. Having loved his own who were in the world, he loved them to the end" (John 13:1). The stage is set, and out of his deep love for his disciples, he once again assures them of this love and gives them the message that they, too, must continue to be loving in all aspects of their lives as he leaves them.

CHAPTER NINE

The Love that Cares and Is Compassionate

"One of the scribes came near and heard them disputing with one another, and seeing that he answered them well, he asked him, 'Which commandment is the first of all?' Jesus answered, 'The first is, 'Hear, O Israel: The Lord our God, the Lord is one; you shall love the Lord your God with all your heart, and with all your soul, and with all your mind, and with all your strength.' The second is this, 'You shall love your neighbor as yourself.' There is no commandment greater than these.'"

(MARK 12: 28–31)

WHICH COMMANDMENT IS THE FIRST OF ALL?

JESUS LIKELY SPOKE TO his disciples in Aramaic, with possibly some Hebrew mixed in, but his words are remembered and recorded in *koine* Greek. The word chosen for love in the noun form is *agape*, which means unlimited and authentic love. It has been defined and nuanced carefully over the centuries because it is viewed as the central core of the ethical teaching of Jesus. Because of its centrality in his teaching, the word has crossed over into many of the languages spoken by Christians around the world. It is often placed alongside two other Greek words for love, *eros*, from which we get the word erotic, and its basic meaning is that the object of love is so attractive that it evokes the deep feeling of attraction in return. Another common usage of the English word love is to describe the close relationship of friends. In the Greek it is *philia*, and it was used by Aristotle in his teaching on ethics in which he speaks about true friends who are loyal and others who just pretend to be friends and often exploit the relationship. The founders of the city of Philadelphia claimed the word and named their city as "the city of friends."

English speaking people have used the general term, love, as a translation of these terms in Greek; and, indeed, related words for love from other languages as well. The result is that the word love in English has many meanings, well beyond the three terms in Greek. As we read about love in the Scriptures, and particularly in the New Testament, we are generally speaking about agape love. We are careful to define it as unconditional love, love that is present in the form of caring and compassion, even if the one who is being loved is not always "lovely" and, in many cases, quite difficult to love because of selfish and harmful behavior and a disruptive and hurtful spirit or attitude. In the evening of life, we want these several forms of love to be present for us, attraction to beauty in its many forms, friendships that are authentic and trustworthy, and of course love that is present for us regardless of our attractiveness and when we need it the most. God's love is always present, and we need it especially when we are not attractive, when we are ill, feel deeply wounded, and when we are not at our best self in a variety of settings, including our decline as we age. We are grateful for this love in the evening of life.

THE NEED FOR UNCONDITIONAL LOVE

The need for agape love is present in nearly all humans; in fact, our need for it seems to be built into the human condition. We need immediate loving attention and full acceptance when we are born, and the period of infancy is quite long in comparison with other creatures in the animal world. We arrive with only the potential of development and complete self-care. In nearly all cultures, the child, in order to be healthy and thrive, needs several years of adult care, with most children needing and often receiving good parenting well into the teen years. The care, of course, at least initially, is the kind of care that is consistently compassionate, providing security, a healthy diet, the teaching of a range of skills, and emotional reassurance that one is always cared for and of great value. Over a period of at least fifteen years, the child in the family needs parental care, filled with unselfish and self-giving love. It is also true that we need this kind of love in the evening of life as we decline.

Nearly all children have a dimension in their personality that occasionally goes against the grain, even in a healthy and loving family. It is a natural expression of the person who is moving in the direction of becoming independent. Parents create rules and structures that are designed to assist the child to become responsible and point them toward an ethical, responsible, and fulfilling life. On occasion, the child, often in the teen years, resists these rules and structures. Emotional and moral development, not unlike intellectual development, take years of careful guidance as the child "bobs and weaves" through childhood. Life has a range of written and unwritten expectations, and not all children are in touch with or want to act in accordance with these norms, especially when they are not clearly spelled out. A measure of clear expectations should be given to the child, including the "why" of a particular guideline and discipline if these expectations are not met. The good parent should nearly always have a good reason for the guidelines and should not just impose a bias or make a demand that only meets the idiosyncratic need of the parent.

In the Christian context, no less a person than St. Augustine maintained that we are actually born with the tendency to break the rules and eat the forbidden fruit (original sin). I lean toward a more developmental model and less toward a sort of life sentence i.e., I am born sinful. I understand the growth and development of the child in terms of movement toward maturity and ethical responsibility, a complex challenge across the early years and into adolescence. I am inclined to agree with my great teacher, Jesus, to understand God as a truly loving Parent rather than an angry judge who had to send his Son to die for my sins. He died to show us the need for love, how to love, and empower us to love, not to appease the anger of an uptight divinity.

All of this is to say that unconditional love, coupled with consistent and careful guidance and clear expectations, are needed in our years of growth and development. It is also true that the conditions in many of our families, our immediate context, our schools, and the society in which we live and have our being, offer us a precarious platform from which to move toward healthy growth and to have the capacity to express mature love. There may be some healthy and positive conditions on this platform, but many challenging and dangerous components as well. Perhaps some form of this lack of a healthy foundation for life has always been true, yet it does seem that the current conditions in which we grow up and build a life are especially challenging, even harmful.

It is also the case for those of us in the evening of life that our few remaining years will have abundant challenges. I am grateful for all of the good that has filled my life, a loving spouse, a responsible son with a wonderful family, and a career that has been filled with exciting challenges and gratifying experiences. I come to the evening of life filled with gratitude and with the continuing opportunity to flourish and live wisely and well. Yet as I read the accounts of those in my age range, and especially those who have limited income and live in dangerous settings, I realize I may be part of a truly blessed minority. This truth awakens me, helps me to see and appreciate all that I have, and makes me deeply grateful and, I hope, compassionate as well. It also underlines that there are many minorities that do not have what I have. For them, safe and comfortable housing may not be within reach, food is costly, and receiving experienced and competent care for children is rare and a profound challenge for many parents. Even medical and dental care are expensive and not easily accessed, and those living on the edge need to plan carefully as they navigate the guidelines of Medicare or dental care. The same conditions may exist with Social Security, and there is the threat that the program will be reduced. There may be some government assistance and limited retirement income, but these resources may become increasingly minimal.

In addition, there are several negative and threatening conditions that are dramatically present in our common life. For example, there is the threat of gun violence, often in our schools, the recent climate change with storms, hurricanes, and tornadoes, and our county's political conflict and unrest. These and many other conditions have exacerbated the dangers in the settings in which we live.

I have been especially sensitive to those who live with deep fear about how to manage life and who feel lonely and afraid. On occasion, in that I continue to be somewhat active in teaching and do some informal counseling, I am discovering that there is subliminal fear, almost existential in character, in many of the people whom I encounter. They desperately need empathic understanding, compassion, and assistance in managing life. An essential ingredient, and perhaps the foundation of these gifts of care, is unconditional love, the reassurance that these people have value and that life has the potential to be good. They want desperately to live wisely and well.[1]

THE WORLD IS THE THEATRE OF LOVE[2]

It is the desperate and needy people from whom we learn about the impact of the absence of love and care. In particular, I have learned from those in poverty what it is like to live without the basic resources for life. With some reflection on these conditions, we hear the divine voice that says that love is desperately needed and that addressing poverty needs to become part of the central core of our ethical life. As we move beyond our immediate settings and gaze at the wider world, we are reminded that there is an abundance of problems; it is not an exaggeration to say that our world is truly in crisis. Fortunately, we have many experienced leaders and gifted authors who have studied, listed, and described in detail the conditions that create this crisis. It is beyond our scope to describe fully these global problems, but perhaps a simple summary list, although not comprehensive, may remind us of some of the challenges with which we are dealing:[3]

1. The issues dealing with ecology.
2. The issues dealing with dramatic increases in the population.
3. The issues dealing with poverty, hunger, and disease.
4. The issues dealing with the global economy.
5. The issues dealing with violence, war, and conflict.
6. The issues and conflicts dealing with opposing religious beliefs and practices.

This range of challenges in our global and corporate structures have a hurtful and negative impact on individual lives. Again, I want to add a

---

1. See the section in my book, *Lovescapes: Mapping he Geography of Love*, entitled "The Need for Love in Contemporary Life: Love in an Age of Crisis," 1-27.
2. Irish proverb.
3. *Lovescapes*, 6. I have added an additional one, the issues dealing with religious beliefs and practices, in part because of what we see, for example, in the negative influence of religion in Afghanistan, and indeed in the United States.

summary and a suggestive list of how these conditions and subsequent challenges impact individuals.[4]

1. There is the challenge of receiving adequate health care, a situation that is especially urgent for those living in poverty in the evening of life.
2. There is the challenge of gaining access to high quality education, with some regions of the world having only limited and inadequate education even for children.
3. There is the challenge of having an adequate income; poverty is on all of our continents and with it is the lack of access to a nourishing diet.
4. There is the challenge of responding to rapid change in nearly all aspects of life, and, in particular, how to manage information technology and artificial intelligence.
5. There is the challenge of maintaining good health, physical, mental, psychological, and I would add spiritual, including the quest for meaning and purpose in life.

These challenges are very real. It is encouraging, as I travel and read, to learn that some of these problems are being dealt with in a responsible way in many nations of the world. Yet deep emotional pain, often impacting physical health, is rampant. Several descriptive words of these conditions come to mind, and I admit that they are in some measure quite personal. I once invited a class of reasonably healthy people to describe some of what they were feeling. The following words surfaced, often with intensity:[5]

1. Stress, unable to relax because of the demands of work, family, and social engagement.
2. Anxiety, not just worry about what comes next and how to do it, but a deep fear about how to cope with the overwhelming demands of contemporary life.
3. Depression: often the stress and anxiety lead to depression, a condition that makes it quite difficult to enjoy nearly any aspect of contemporary life and take care of basic responsibilities in life.

---

4. Ferguson, *Lovescapes*, 11.
5. Ferguson, *Lovescapes*, 20–2.

4. Loneliness, sensing that it was and is inappropriate to "complain" and talk about my problems and the inability to identify with and listen to the problems of others; I feel alone with mine.

At least a dozen other words surfaced, revealing how worried people are at this moment in history.[6]

This same group of people voiced the concern that these feelings created several warning signs about their wellbeing and symptoms bordering on ill health.

- Cognitive symptoms: memory problems, inability to concentrate, poor judgment, seeing only the negative, anxious or racing thoughts, and constant worrying.
- Physical symptoms: aches and pains, digestive problems, eating more or less than what is healthy, sleeping more or less than is healthy.
- Emotional symptoms: moodiness, irritability, agitation, feeling overwhelmed, sense of loneliness and isolation, depression or general unhappiness.

THE RELATIONSHIP OF LOVE AND HUMAN NEED

It is in the evening of life that these challenges can come very close to overwhelming us, and not infrequently, we withdraw into isolation and do not seek the help we need. If we are going to thrive, even flourish, we need to arrange our "world" in such a way that active love is present, present for us to give and present for us to receive. As we ponder this linkage between love and human need, it is essential that we have a clear idea of what love is, how it can restore us to a good measure of health, and empower us to live wisely and well.

I have affirmed and shared my belief that the ultimate source of love is God, and as we are filled with the divine presence (Love), we become those who know, deep in our being, that we are loved and empowered to love. Others rely on being centered and having foundational values that ground them in a life-giving way, and I affirm these directions as well. Yet the risk for all of us is that it may be a bit too easy to think that because we have spoken about love that we can easily just begin doing it. One way

---

6. Words such as insecure, confused, angry, afraid, guilt, irritated, and many others surfaced in these conversations.

to understand more fully how to receive love and to love is to return to the question of what we truly mean when we speak about love; to better understand its several meanings is one way that will help us become those who love.

We mentioned briefly the three Greek words that point to the different kinds of love, love as attraction, love as deep friendship, and love as receiving and accepting others just as they are as they come to us. These three dimensions of love are very helpful and suggest a simple and direct way to understand how we might both give and receive love. They suggest a place for us to start. Yet there are several other subtle dimensions of love that we need to understand, ones that deepen and go in different directions than the foundational three-pronged formula of *eros*, *philia*, and *agape*.

In fact, love is a very complex energy and feeling in human experience, and to experience it is to learn more about it. We will increase our capacity to share love that heals and transforms by loving, even as we become better athletes by practicing and playing the game. *Merriam-Webster*, in the definition of love, underlines the participatory character of love; that we learn how to love by doing it. This volume notes six dimensions of love: (1) strong affection for another arising out of kinship or personal ties; (2) warm attachment or devotion; to hold dear, even cherish; (3) admiration, desire to be in the presence of; (4) unselfish behavior, with loyal and benevolent concern for the good of another; (5) attraction to God as personification of love; (6) to like and desire, often associated with a sexual attraction and embrace.[7]

As we speak about God's love for us, we mean unconditional acceptance and unlimited love. Steven Post, drawing upon the classic work of Pitirim Sorokin, a Harvard sociologist of a previous generation, who wrote *The Ways and Powers of Love*, expands the meaning of self-giving love.[8] It has five essential qualities:

1. It takes the form of *intensive caring*; it must be strong, focused, and concentrated, moving beyond self-interest.

2. It must be *extensive*, extended to all in need, not just to those close by and loveable.

3. It has *duration* and does not end when it becomes difficult to express.

---

7. *Merriam-Webster*, s.v., "love." Note, I have used material in this section from my book, *Lovescapes: The Geography of Love*.

8. Post, *Unlimited Love: Altruism, Compassion and Service*, 133–55.

4. It is *pure*, free from ulterior motives and mixed with self-referencing and self-interest.
5. It is *adequate*, that is, it provides the appropriate response to the need.

Another interpreter of love, Daniel Day Williams, has a slightly different way of describing love, also using five descriptive categories:[9]

1. Individuality: Love gives a unique response in keeping with the particular needs of the one who is loved.
2. Freedom: The gift of love is given freely, not driven by other motivations such as the need to have love returned in kind.
3. Action: To love is to act for the welfare of the other, not just have vague feelings of attraction or the need to be loved in return.
4. Causality: The action of love will improve the conditions of the one who is loved.
5. Impartial Judgment: Love is given in the context and identity of the other person; it is appropriate for the person receiving the love.

We might use Stephen Post's definition of the essence of unlimited love as a summary. "The essence of love is to affectively affirm and to gratefully delight in the well-being of others; the essence of unlimited love is to extend this form of love to all others in an enduring, intense, effective, and pure manner."[10] I would add to Dr. Post's definition that it is essential that we accept ourselves and give to ourselves unconditional love; if we do not love our selves, it is very difficult to show love to others, in large part because we will be focused on our own needs. We too must fully accept that we are loved unconditionally by God, that we are worthy of love, and then to gratefully delight in our own well-being. With self-acceptance, we increase our capacity to love. We remind ourselves that of the counsel of Jesus: "to love our neighbor as ourselves" (Mark 12:31). As we love ourselves, we can move on and give true and life-giving love to others.

SETTINGS WHERE LOVE IS PRESENT

Love is one of those human emotions and actions which are both present in us as human beings and then cultivated by our experiences and the

9. Williams, *Spirit and Forms of Love*, 142–44.
10. Post, *Unlimited Love*, 19.

context of our lives. Love becomes central to our feelings and behavior if we have been present in a nurturing environment, have cultivated our endowment of love as we are created in image of God, and as we are empowered to love by the presence of the God, often called the presence of the Holy Spirit. We look first at the dimensions and character of a nurturing environment that empowers us to love.

We move toward a life filled with love and contentment when the environment in which we live has the presence of love. The first layer of our environment is one's immediate situation and where one lives. We achieve high levels of gratification and feelings of love if this setting is filled with love. We begin to understand love if we are loved and the setting around us respects and cares for all who are present. In this setting, we perceive what it means to love and respect others, although the message of our environment may be somewhat difficult to read; it will be mixed and complex, and how we grasp and manage it will shape our capacity to love and be a positive presence in it.[11]

Our environment will have a set of structures that hold it together, and they are intertwined, often one with another. In our early years, we experienced this setting, but it felt like just the way things are, and we were relatively unaware of how we were being shaped by it. There was the immediate environment of our family, and we were profoundly influenced by the way it functioned and how we were treated. The family, of course, was shaped by a whole range of other systems; it was nested in a vast complex of structures and systems, all the way to our global environment. Yet it was our immediate setting that was so important if we are to flourish in the evening of life, that is, to have had a life filled with love and a compassionate purpose.

In our maturity, we are helped if we understand how we have moved through the complex of systems and managed our developmental stages, describing the stairsteps of our growth. People such as Sigmund Freud, Carl Jung, Jean Piaget, Erik Erikson, Lawrence Kohlberg, Urie Bronfenbrenner and many other developmental psychologists gave us the gift of seeing the stages of life and how we needed a certain kind of environment at each stage for healthy growth toward maturity. Each of these people, in their respective points of view and domains, left us a marvelous legacy for self-understanding. We use this self-understanding to create

---

11. Ferguson, *Lovescapes*, 114.

environments in which we have the greatest potential to live wisely and well in the evening of life. It will have a mixture of the following features:[12]

1. The mature individual will thrive in a setting where there is a healthy measure of freedom and choice. Our mental health is sustained in a setting where we have a say in how we live. We have a sense of self-worth as we make good decisions about life.

2. Mature individuals will thrive as they use their ability to navigate wisely through a complex array of shaping influences in order to create and continue a life of meaning and contentment. There will be a sense of accomplishment; I have done well.

3. The environment in which the mature person seeks meaning and deep peace is layered, complex, and changing. Again, as one manages the complexities of the culture and the immediate settings of life, there is joy and gratification in being able to manage.

4. In the evening of life, there are some influences that an individual must manage and shape in order to increase the capacity to grow in a healthy way and love, and others that are simply present and at times negative, and must be dealt with carefully. The world is not always simple and safe.

5. This array of shaping influences on the mature person may have either a negative or positive impact, and in the evening of life, we need to be able to choose those settings which are positive. Once again, as we discover and learn about the character of these influences and make good choices, we are gratified.

6. It follows, of course, that these shaping influences may empower us and move us toward peace and contentment or they may be life-denying, removing our freedom of choice and our peace of mind. As they are harmful, we learn to change course and move in different directions. The years of experience of those in the evening of life will guide us.

In the evening of life, we will manage the challenges of aging best by an understanding of how we were shaped, at each stage of life, by our complex environment and having the freedom to select a pattern of life that enables us to make choices about how to live wisely and well. Self-understanding and making decisions about how we live are essential

12. Ferguson, *Lovescapes*, 130–31.

ingredients of the healthy and fulfilling life. I have been profoundly helped by self-understanding and having freedom of choice. However, while I reflect and am grateful for this understanding, I am finding a measure of discomfort and threat by the larger arena in which I live, my region and my nation. I am worried and sense that I must find the best ways to cope.

- My nation may not be a setting in which there is justice and security, and I am not sure that I will have adequate food, high quality health care, and equal rights under the law.
- My nation might not be a nation at peace and may not keep me secure and free from external threat.
- My nation may not maintain an economy in which I am assured of having adequate wealth to live out these final years in a way that gives me security and comfort.
- My nation may not provide my grandchildren with a promising future.

So, I long for a nation that lives by the values of honesty and integrity, an adherence to equal justice before the law, a way of managing violence, and a nation that secures and protects the freedom of all of its citizens.

ENDOWED AND EMPOWERED TO LOVE

Even in the evening of life, I know I must do my part and lend a hand to those who continue the quest to pursue a more just and humane society and world. Once again, my understanding of love, that is how we find the capacity to love and how we engage in a loving spirit, rise to the surface in shaping my way of life.

I have been influenced over the years by my Christian faith and its teaching, shared with my Jewish and Muslim cousins, that we are created in the image of God. We share with them as well the understanding of God as the personification of love and truth. The New Testament has the two "God statements." God is light (truth) as expressed in Jesus (John 1:4) and "is love" (1 John 4:7–8). If, indeed, we are created in the image of God, then truth and love are an integral part of our endowment. We are created with the capacity to understand truth and be truthful, and to understand love and be loving. These dimensions or endowments are somewhat embryonic, within us as potential, and must be drawn out and cultivated. We do have the capacity to be authentic and have integrity, as we learn how to reach inside and become people who are truthful in all aspects of our behavior. As God is one, the heartbeat of all that is, so we too, as those created in the image of God, can be one, that is, people with integrity who can be trusted. Does that mean that we have still have the capability to act out of fear and insecurity and hurt others or create settings that are harmful to others? Yes, but to act in these ways is to not be true to our endowment and to live inauthentically.

So it is with love; that is, we are created in the image of God, and God is love. Yet we must be in touch with our capacity to love and find the best ways to express it in accord with the two great commandments: to love God with all of our heart, and with all of our soul, and with all our mind, and with all of our strength; and to love our neighbor as we love ourselves (Mark 12:29-31). We become what we are intended to be by our endowment in the image God; we learn how to *be* truth, to have integrity, and to be authentic in all aspects of our lives. So, it is with our endowment of love, that as we grow and mature, we consciously seek to be those who love. There will be a period of growth and development, as we take our endowment of being created in the image of God and draw it out and cultivate it as a way of life.

As we engage in the growth toward being authentic and truthful, and learn more about the full meaning of love and how it becomes our center, we in the Christian tradition emulate the one who was full of truth and love. "The law indeed was given through Moses; grace and truth came through Jesus Christ. No one has ever seen God. It is God the only Son, who is close to the Father's heart, who has made him known" (John 1:17-18). It is in the evening of life that we often more clearly understand what it means to be true and loving and what it means to live wisely and well.

Once again, we ask how we can become authentic and loving. It is well and good to have these ideals and to acknowledge that Jesus was the best human example of one who achieved and expressed truth and love. Yes, these ideals are the best expression of being the person whom God wants us to be and the best expression of being a good person even if God is not a part of or the foundation of our outlook. But we know how difficult it is to live day-to-day and across the years of our lives into the evening as an authentic and compassionate person. The partial answer to this question is that it is part of the process of becoming, of growing, of moving in the direction of full maturity. It is certainly the goal of so many of us in the evening of our lives. We look back to our starting quote by St. John of the Cross, "that in the evening of life, we will be judged by love alone."

If we had been able to sit with St. John, he likely would have answered our question, even as his model in life, Jesus, might have answered the question. Both would say it was a process, involving three major components.

1. They would have said that you were created in the image of God and have the potential to be loving and truthful in all aspects of your life. You have the potential to live with integrity and compassion, especially in the evening of life. You were created in the image of God, the one who is Truth and Love. These qualities are within you, and you, with the empowerment of God's Spirit, need to draw them out and practice them.

2. It is also a process of growth, of learning, and of discipline to lure these inherent qualities out into the open. Even Jesus had to grow into his full personhood to become the one who could love those who crucified him and tell the one on the cross next to him, "Today, you will be with me in paradise" (Luke 23:43). Study the life of Jesus, and indeed others who have lived a saintly life, and you will discover that they had to start, grow, become, and then arrive as those filled with love and truth.

3. We need to remember and claim the reassurance of the biblical message, present in the Hebrew Bible as well as the New Testament, (and in the Qur'an as well), that God will come alongside of you, fill your life with love and truth, and be an endless resource of direction and empowerment to live authentically and compassionately. The New Testament in particular will speak about God's Spirit, the Holy Spirit, who is the power and presence of God that fills your life with wisdom and the capacity to be those who express love and truth in all aspects of their lives. "When they bring you before the synagogues, the rulers, and the authorities, do not worry about how you are to defend yourselves or what you are to say; for the Holy Spirit will teach you at the very hour what you are to say" (Luke 12:11–12). As Jesus spoke with the disciples toward the end of journey, he said to them: "I still have many things to say to you, but you cannot bear the now. When the Spirit of truth comes, he

(she) will guide you into all the truth; for he will not speak on his own, but will speak whatever he hears, and he will declare to you the things that are to come" (John 16:12–13). Jesus reassured his dearest friends, those whom he loved fully, that the Spirit of God would guide and empower them to be people of integrity and love. Chapter 16 in John's Gospel is the place where the disciple John speaks about the way that Jesus said good-bye. I leave, but the Spirit of God will inform and empower you to be truthful and loving.

The message to the few is now the message for the many. We are in the process of becoming; we have been endowed with the capacity to live authentically, and we are empowered to be those who make love the core of lives. Now, we are committed to be authentic and love those who come our way, especially those who are not very loveable. In the evening of life, as we seek to live wisely and well and desire to flourish, God is present to comfort, heal, forgive, guide, and empower. In deep gratitude, we serve with integrity and love.

The essence of the good life is to live with loyal love to all of those who have been with us across the years, never allowing bitterness, regret, and a sense of betrayal to get in the way.

Terms, Resources, and Discussion Questions

Terms

1. *Agape*: Unlimited and unconditional love.
2. Spirit: The inner character of movement or a person; in reference to God, it is the power and presence of God available to humans and at work in the world.
3. Endowment: What is present in or is given to a person or a cause, as in the case of being born with the capacity to love and be authentic.
4. Empower: To provide the energy, capability, and resources for a person to live in a particular way, often in reference to living wisely and well.
5. Integrity: The capacity to live in harmony with one's stated values.

SECTION THREE

Resources: Books to Read and Consult

1. Duncan S. Ferguson, *Lovescapes: Mapping the Geography of Love*
2. Anders Nygren, *Agape and Eros*
3. Stephen G. Post, *Unlimited Love: Altruism, Compassion, and Service*
4. Irving Singer, *The Nature of Love*, 3 volumes
5. Frank Rogers Jr., *Compassion in Practice: The Way of Jesus*
6. Denis De Rougemont, *Love in the Western World*

Discussion Questions

1. How would you define love?
2. How many kinds of love are there and what is their nature?
3. How do we find the energy and motivation to love?
4. How would you describe your ability to be a loving and compassionate person?
5. How would you describe your level of integrity and ability to be truthful?

CHAPTER TEN

The Love of Others and the Community of Faith

"No one has greater love than this: to lay down one's life for one's friends."
(JOHN 15:13)

"God is love; and they who abide in love, abide in God, and God in them."
(I JOHN 4:16B)

"But I say to you that listen, love your enemies, do good to those who hate you, bless those who curse you, pray for those who abuse you. If anyone strikes you on the check, offer the other also; and from anyone who takes away you coat do not withhold even your shirt. Give to everyone who begs from you; and if anyone takes away your goods, do not ask for them again. Do to others as you as you would have them do to you. If you love those who love you, what credit is that to you? For even sinners love those who love them. If you do good to those who do good to you, what credit is that to you? For even sinners do the same. If you lend to those from whom you hope to receive, what credit is that to you? Even sinners lend to sinners, to receives as much again. But love your enemies, do good, and lend, expecting nothing in return. Your reward will be great, and you will be children of the Most High; for he is kind to the ungrateful and the wicked. Be merciful, just as your Father is merciful" (Luke 6 :27–36).

SECTION THREE

THE NATURE OF TRUE LOVE

The teaching of Jesus offers us a way of understanding love that is filled with great expectations; it is comprehensive in scope and life-giving for all who engage in its practice. Those who heard him likely asked themselves if it was possible to love as Jesus taught and practiced. Those of us who read about his life and teaching are a bit overwhelmed by what he taught and then illustrated by his loving actions. It appears as we read the biblical stories that there was a good measure of awe by those who were with him and heard him speak and saw him love the unlovable. We, also, who read his teaching and trace his actions, are equally in awe. He taught a radical form of selfless love, demonstrated it by his actions, and then invited his followers to join him by living as he taught in word and deed. He caught the attention of many, and millions over the centuries have accepted his invitation to join him in a life of love.

The expression of love that Jesus taught and lived was more than just having a quality or characteristic in one's personality. For example, when we say that "she is friendly" or "he is an ambitious person," we describe a value and quality in the life of the person, but seldom say, "friendly is who she is." We may say of another person that they are loving in their behavior, but do not imply that love is integral to who they are. Jesus invited his followers both *to love* and, as far as possible, *be love*, to make unconditional acceptance of others as a foundational component of one's personhood and identity. He is asking his followers that love to be love, making it who and what they are, not just what they do, although loving actions are foundational to his teaching as well. This understanding of love is present in the biblical definition of God, using that quality to describe and define who God is; the Bible teaches that God *is* love, not just one who on occasionally expresses loving behavior.[1] It is an ontological statement about the nature of God, and it is carried over in the statement about the nature of Jesus and his teaching. Many were drawn to Jesus because he epitomized what he taught; he was a person who truly loved and had profound integrity and was consistently true to his identity.[2]

---

1. 1 John 4:13–21

2. There are occasions in the New Testament in which he shows irritation, even anger, but these descriptions may be understood as reactions to unloving behavior, perhaps a sort of "tough love."

There were those who met Jesus and may have been initially drawn to his radical teaching, but after some reflection decided that life had other options and demands and offered more practical ways of living. They had to take care of themselves and their families and earn a living. They were to live in a world in which the vast majority of people had to scramble day-to-day just to survive. They must have felt that they had to focus on immediate needs and work hard in order to stay ahead in a complex and demanding world; they knew it would be easy fall behind. In their hearts and minds was the realization that it is a competitive world, one in which not all will thrive, let alone survive. The idealistic teaching of Jesus may not work in such a world. People have too much to do, are stressed and worried, and would find loving others, especially those who are difficult to love, to be too much to expect.

They asked and now we ask: how is it possible to live a life of love like the one that Jesus encouraged in others and practiced? After all, if we practiced what Jesus appears to be asking and took literally what Jesus taught, we would get behind in our work and not be able to take care of all our responsibilities and live a normal life. If they followed his teaching in a literal way, they would simply be shoved aside by those who were more realistic and ambitious. Succeeding generations may have asked or thought that, after all, he ended up on a cross as he lived a life of love. Why would he invite his followers to live in the same way? A brief review of what he taught underlines why he said that love was the essence of life, even if being loving leads to some risk. What did he teach about love and what were the ways that he loved and encouraged us to love?

- Love your enemies.
- Do good to those who hate you.
- Pray for those who curse you.
- Offer the other cheek to those who strike you.
- Offer your shirt to the thief that steals your coat.
- Give to those who beg from you and don't expect to be repaid.
- Let the thief have what has been stolen from you.

   In short, do to others as you would have them do to you. By the way,

- If you love those who love you, what is special about that? Even sinners do it.

- If you do good for those who have done good to and for you is behavior practiced by nearly every person; what's the big deal?
- If you lend someone some money or goods, then to want to be repaid is only natural.

No doubt Jesus had to listen and respond to those who questioned why they should go beyond what is normal human behavior. His message created discomfort for many people. What is remarkable is that he stayed with his deepest values by clearly stating them and then practicing them. One can almost hear him saying in a loving spirit: love your enemies, do good to others who may not be loveable, and expect nothing in return. Do good for the sake of the good, not to be benefited in some way. Love for the sake of the other, not because you will be admired, but because it is the right thing to do. Be merciful, just as God is merciful to you. God's love for us does not wait until we are loveable.

THE HUMAN RESPONSES TO THE TEACHING OF JESUS

Jesus not only taught these values, rooted in unconditional love, but lived them, and it was very hard, even for the cynical, to call him a hypocrite and discredit him. In his time and across the centuries, people have responded in a variety of ways to the radical teaching of Jesus, not just the ethical teaching which he embodied, but also his guidance in spiritual formation and theological understanding. It is hard to capture and nuance all of these responses to the life and teaching of Jesus; they are vast, but let me suggest a few categories or types of response as illustrative, noting that each one has many subgroups. As we do, we will be able to gage our response and will likely learn that we have traces of more than one of these types of response.

There were in his time and across then centuries who have responded in a positive way, in terms of belief and in terms of practice. There are those today who have been profoundly moved by his teaching, have altered their way of life in response, and have attempted in a variety of ways to *incorporate the teaching of Jesus into their lives and the social settings in which they live and have some responsibility.* Many of these people became the Christian church and, now, in their response continue to be the church, one that teaches and encourages loving behavior. There are active participants in the contemporary church engaged in following Jesus in a life of love, although it is all too easy to say that love is not the central way of life for all those in the contemporary church. The first response, then, is a true commitment to the life of love.

The deep and profound value of love is nearly universal, one that goes well beyond the mission of the Christian church. What is clear, however, is that love is a true expression of those who have endorsed the Christian faith. We see this value present and taught by Christians in different historical eras, different locations, other cultures, and in using a variety of languages. Are people in the community of faith consistent in loving? No, but love is close to being a universal ethical norm, and it is in the Christian church where this value is honored and taught, a setting in which many come to learn how to love.

There were and continue to be those who have thought or continue to think that the ethic of love is present in other religions of the world and even present in more secular expressions of ethical norms.[3] As one might expect, given this reality, there is resistance to the beliefs and behavior of the Christian church that have an exclusive tone; that Christians have ultimate truth, not just in their theological orientation but also in affirming love as the foundation of their ethical teachings. This exclusive orientation has been challenged, and especially so within other faith traditions. People often ask why many Christians think their beliefs and ethical norms are unique to them. As a response, many other *communities of faith have reaffirmed their religious faith, noting that it too gives love a high priority*. Jewish people, for example, would say that love is central to their religious outlook, and it was natural for Jesus to teach about love; he was Jewish. This is a second type of response to the invitation to make love central to one's life, one growing out of the ethical norms of another religion. It is likely that Jesus would have said: "God is present to the human family in its diversity, and love is present within many cultures and traditions. Together, make love the center piece of your practice."

For example, some of his contemporaries accused Jesus of being heretical in challenging some of the practices of the Judaism of his time and setting. Others may have thought that he was uninformed, impractical, and too idealistic in his teaching. It was not uncommon for the religious leaders of his time to question Jesus, especially as people began to turn to Jesus for renewal and guidance. There are those in this category in the present, offering alternative ways of living in a spiritual way, perhaps respecting Jesus and his ethical teaching, but unable to accept the Christian

---

3. It is true that the ethical norm of love is present in many of the religions of the human family.

church's teaching that the Christian way is the only way to be related to God. A wide variety of religions affirm the historical Jesus who taught and practiced love, but say that love is also taught and practiced in other religious traditions.

There were those, then and now, who saw or see him as just another fanatical religious person whose teaching was unrealistic and irrelevant. A third type of response is that Christianity was and is now often *a social nuisance that should rejected*. His followers are almost cultic and lean toward being exclusive and judgmental. Those with this point of view wished then and continue to wish that Jesus and his followers would just go away. Again, it is more of a rejection of the Christian church and its theology that may be exclusive, even arrogant in its narrow belief system. There is a rejection of religious teaching that is tribal and judgmental, but not the rejection of the teachings on love of the first century teacher from Nazareth.

Some of the Roman leadership had been told that they might run across some strange and radical religious teaching in their assignment in the region of Palestine, but were told to just keep these groups in line with the legal requirements and maintain social order. *Tolerate* them, even though they may be a nuisance. They are not usually dangerous, although one of their number, Jesus of Nazareth, not unlike that other radical, John the Baptist, has quite a following. Comparable government authorities exist today that view religious groups as hypocritical and a social nuisance, yet they are generally tolerated because of the beliefs of so many people and a commitment to a free society.

Of course, there was the majority of people in the time of Jesus who had enough to deal with in the flow of their lives without adding one more concern and responsibility. They were and are *too busy to care about religious belief and ethical norms*. Many in the time of Jesus simply ignored him, a fifth response, and succeeding generations have continued to ignore his life and teaching in part because of other demands on their lives.

THE RESPONSE OF THOSE IN THE EVENING OF LIFE: BECOMING AND BELONGING IN COMMUNITY

These types of response to the life and teaching of Jesus are present today. There is a clear majority today that fit into one of these different categories.[4] It is relatively common for most of us, even in the evening of life, to say that it would not be wise to add one more regular meeting or activity to our lives. There is some credibility in this observation, although it may be the case that we need to do a little subtraction and addition in reference to our priorities. Some activities and experiences in life are more nurturing and gratifying than others, and to make some shifts in how we spend our time may give us a new lease on life.

I have been especially conscious of this possibility as I have associated with those in the evening of life, many of whom are living in retirement communities. I am at that stage in life and have chosen option one, attempting to shape my way of life around the life and teachings of Jesus. Foundational for me is to give special attention to how I might find loving ways to relate to those around me and then suggest and work toward cultivating patterns of creating a more just and humane world.

As I move around and talk with those who are seeking to live wisely and well in the evening of life, I discover that they are asking many of the same questions I have been asking regarding the nature and flow of human life. These questions are ones for which they, as I do, really want answers. Many are lonely and lack deep and fulfilling relationships. Others express that their lives have lost meaning and purpose, and that they are just existing as they wait for the end of life. It is not uncommon for them to let the questions about how to live the meaningful and joyful life just nag at them, and they do not seek to find good answers. A glass of wine to reduce stress and worry may be a better way.

In my reading, conversations, and interviews, and as I look within my own experience, I have discovered a range of deep existential questions that are being asked by those in the evening of life, ones that a glass of wine does not touch. I have found and maintained that many of them might at least partially be answered by a life of faith, not a narrow and exclusive frame of reference, but one that is open and spacious, living with questions, providing guidance, and has the support of a community. It is often in the support of a community of faith in which we feel safe, are enabled and empowered to face many of the questions of aging, and then find ways to move into a sense of well-being and to flourish.

In short, it is hard to be alone and find answers to life's questions, although many do try. It is easier to find answers in association with others; it is helpful to have a loving community (or communities) in the evening

---

4. (1) Have other religious beliefs, (2) see the church as a social nuisance, (3) just tolerate religious people, or (4) are too busy to even care.

of life. The evening of life can be and often is a lonely time, filled with worry, fear, and discontent. The scaffolding that has held life together has been dismantled. As I examine what I need as I age, even as a borderline introvert, I need to be with others and participate in a few groups in which I feel accepted and comfortable, ones in which there are programs and activities that offer valuable learning and foster good friendships.

What I have discovered in the search for a healthy community is that they are present if one has gumption to search for them and to join at least one of them. In my search, arriving at a new location in my early eighties, I have found a common sociological pattern of communities within communities, smaller communities encased within other larger communities. I discovered that there were several that seemed too large and diverse, but then learned that there were smaller communities within the larger ones, more likely to meet my needs. For example, I have often found community support and meaningful activity in a church community. In addition, I needed more than just a large worship service on Sunday mornings. I would go away from them just as lonely. I am glad that I made the effort to not only be in a church service, but attend some small groups with more specialized interests. One was a men's book group; I was welcomed, and found that new friendships have developed. I continue to attend the worship services which are nurturing, but it is in the small groups where I am able to find support and engage in learning and spiritual growth with others. I also learned that I needed to take the initiative, stay with it, and realized that it takes time to enter into a new association of people. By getting involved with this men's book study group, I was soon on a first name basis with several other men near my age and with comparable needs. As they learned about my background and experience, I was invited to engage in ways to provide adult education programs, in part because the church had placed more emphasis on youth groups and had focused their educational offerings for children and teenagers. Before long, I was invited to assist the church in developing adult education programs, classes, workshops, lectures, reading groups, and the occasional trip to a conference or retreat. I now belong in this community, and my concern now, given my age, is that I might easily become too involved. Yet I have found a home where I am accepted and have warm friendships.

I also discovered, moving to a new location, that I continued to need the support of my family; it is foundational and provides a setting of security in which there is understanding and ways of functioning that make life manageable, even joyful. The relationship with my wife of nearly fifty years is the heart of my safe and joyful world, and it would be hard to overstate its value for me. Together, we are finding ways to link with our extended families and friends, traveling on holidays for visits, and using the several electronic forms of connecting on a regular basis. I "zoom" regularly with a group of retired pastors. This way of connecting is not perfect, yet both my colleagues and I have a keen sense of belonging and sharing decades of common and rich experience and joyful activity.

I have also learned, although it was not as obvious as the value of the communities of family and friends, is that I need a community that *offers ways of learning and service*, ones in which I can be engaged in "doing good" and join with friends with whom I find support and inspiration. I also know how important it is to be living in town or city, one in which I am comfortable and feel that I belong because of some history and to some extent because of its quality of services and opportunities for social enrichment and responsibility. Place and space are important. Further, there is the larger circle of belonging related to location: city, state, region, and country, all of which gives me a sense of belonging to places where I have lived, have good memories, and which even partially suggest my identity. These larger circles of belonging, region, state, and nation help me to complete the quest of having a clear identity and sense of belonging. As I explore these components of community life and sense of belonging, I discover there are some gaps, but for the most part I fit in at each encasement or level, home and family, within a city, within a state, within a region, within a country, and now, more than ever, within a world that is threatened and in crisis. I am a dot on the map that is placed in the right place.

FINDING ANSWERS TO LIFE'S QUESTIONS

It is from this pattern of community life, one that has shaped and now supports my identity and values, that I face the more personal challenges and complex questions that come my way in the evening of life. It is in the search for answers to these questions that I have learned more about what has become the firm foundation of my life.[5] I want to share a sampling of the questions that have surfaced for me as I move into the evening of life, providing if not complete answers, at least directions for finding guidance.

5. In a review of these questions, I have discovered that many are oriented to personal questions, time-frames, and human need. I will be selective, knowing that each person will find the questions and answers that match their needs.

1. *Who am I and how have I become this person*? It is in the evening of life that we sense more keenly our identity and the kind of person we have become. We are able to answer these questions in a more confident way than we might have a few years earlier when we were "on the way." We have gone through a growth process, one that is filled with a complex history of people and events, and one in which we have responded to the world around us in healthy (or unhealthy) ways. There has been family, school, career, continuing experiences of learning, travel, vacations, hobbies, and patterns of personal reflection. Perhaps most important, we have been in relationship with a range of people with whom we have been closely associated, family, school mates, colleagues in work, neighbors, and people from other countries and cultures. These relationships have been varied and most of them healthy and life-giving, although there were others less so and perhaps creating a measure of self-doubt and insecurity.

Let me briefly illustrate from my experience. I am grateful to have had a family that stayed together in my early years, one that gave me opportunities for growth and development. I sense I have been privileged in many ways. But because of some childhood trauma, some alcohol abuse on the part of my parents, and even the feeling of being inadequate that is associated with being the youngest and always needing to learn what others had already learned, my childhood was not perfect. I was often reminded that I didn't know what others already knew. I nevertheless felt grateful for so much and have found that even partially healthy environment in which to grow up is exceedingly important; it has a lasting impact across the years. I do grant that my family held together, but it was not always a healthy environment.

Attractive locations and relatively good schools were important. But my well-being had more to do with whether I felt loved, supported, and encouraged. It was these factors that made the real difference. Even with some negative influences in my childhood, I found a way that worked for me. I found a lane; books were good friends, and the school work interesting, although I attended five different elementary schools. Gradually I became a fair student and loved to learn. I am still a good student and love to learn. It has been and is a comfort zone for me. I do essentially know who I now am, how I got here, and I am comfortable with this identity.

2. *Why am I here? Do I still have some value?* As we age and move into retirement, it is easy to feel that we no longer have a meaningful or professional role in life. We may help some with household chores or

volunteer in the community to help with a social cause. Yet these endeavors are modest and contribute only a little to our sense of value. Before we retired, our work contributed to our identity and feelings of self-worth. We may also sense that we were here because we are part of a family and have a clear role within the family.

I do have a wonderful marriage and we have a son, now with children. The family has given me a clear sense of my responsibilities and contributed to the answer of why I am here. In addition to the family, I also felt vitally important in my professional life, contributing to creating a better society and securing our financial future. In retirement and as I age, I have had to review whether I still have value. I engage in this review because my experiences in childhood of feeling lonely and inadequate remain with me in a low-level way. Gratefully, however, I am at a mature and comfortable stage in life, and in a setting that I know and have had positive experiences. It is the place where my parents retired and essentially finished their lives, and where my family often vacationed. The array of feelings associated in this setting has put me in a personal space where I want to help others feel secure and where they belong. I am in a place where I can help others learn, have a small part in healing their troubled souls, and encourage them to find ways to flourish. I feel at home and have a role, although some discomfort remains.

3. *Where am I going? What is my future?* As we age, the earlier feelings of advancing in one's career and creating a good setting for the family were vitally important, yet with the passing of time, these feeling may have slipped away. We sense that we have passed that stage, and that new challenges have emerged. We do have fulfilling experiences in the present, but we also know that night comes for all of us and that our days are numbered. Our task now is to create a meaningful and pleasant retirement, and this responsibility also has some challenges. We may find that we have less energy and are limited on what we do for recreation and how best to stay healthy. In addition, we may find that we have to make friends in new settings, and not depend on our work life where I was with others daily. We may find that some of the activities we dreamed of doing in retirement have not materialized. We may not play much golf or travel to exotic settings; both are expensive, and the last cruise was sort of boring. We read some, but an hour or two a day is plenty. We go out to eat in nice restaurants, but come back wondering if violating the restrictions of my diet was worth that expensive and calorie laden meal. Retirement, too, has a wide range of challenges.

Another personal response: I am pleased that I am not totally preoccupied with the challenges of aging, although some are present and I am very aware of others that are on the way. I am still very active in teaching and writing, regularly engage in physical fitness activity, and I am one who loves to visit new places in the world; we do travel. I continue to go in the direction of learning, reading stimulating literature and exploring new subjects. I am privileged to even do some teaching. Yet, in the background are the realities of aging, and I know I only have few years left. I will enjoy today!

4. *How do I want to change and grow?* In the evening of life, there is often the feeling that we have developed as a person and become mature, experienced the joys and challenges of family life, and have had a satisfying professional life. In essence, we have learned what we need to know in order to manage life and have felt fulfilled in our life work. The sense of continuing to develop, learn, and become more mature has less importance to us than it did when we just finished our formal education, then got married, became fully employed, and engaged in a fulfilling family life. Yet in the evening of life, there is still an important future for which we need to plan and we hope to find gratifying.

Let me share from my own life on how I began to answer questions about how to flourish in the evening of life, and how I continue to work on the answer. Initially, I am making progress on how to let the actions and memories of negative experiences of the past, especially ones that created fear and insecurity, and those in which I was unkind and hurtful to others, lose their power. I want to continue to move away from being preoccupied with past failures and become one who loves freely and naturally, one who has integrity, and one who regularly gains new insight that enriches my life. I want to continue to move toward being guilt free and have a clear conscience. I am seeking to be authentic in all ways, to explore new worlds that delight and challenge me to grow, and to advance in my capacity to be more loving, to truly care for the well-being and deep happiness of others.

5. *Does my current life really matter? Will I leave a legacy?* Yes, we in the evening of life still matter and are able to have a comfortable role in our setting with some responsibilities. However, it is likely that our role has changed and that we should not be passive about this change, but fully engaged using the changes to guide us in creating a way of life that is fulfilling and enables us to set goals that are appropriate for the time and context in which we live. Perhaps we have less responsibility

to fewer people now in evening of life than we did earlier, yet we are still able to contribute to improving the lives of others because of our experience. Once again, I want to share very briefly some of what I have thought about this question and the ways that I have tried to answer it. I begin with the recognition that I have learned a great deal about life, how to live more wisely, how to engage in meaningful work, how to keep healthy and fit, how to find activities that are meaningful and enjoyable, and how to be kind, even loving. I want my legacy to be that I lived well, was responsible, achieved a measure of success, and had the joys of a good family life. But most of all, I want my legacy to be that that I was loving and helped others to find relief from suffering and move toward finding a good and happy life.

6. *How do I go about living in the evening of live and what are the challenges I face?* As we attempt to answer these questions, we of course need to engage in a thoughtful assessment of the setting in which we find ourselves. Will I be surrounded by caring people, those who will help me stay healthy, and will I be in a comfortable setting and have access to what I need to continue to engage in satisfying work. We will want to be in a setting where there is the recognition of our changing needs, knowing that we will live differently that we did when younger. Our capacities are more limited, and yet we want to engage in activities that are enriching and that improve the lives of others.

We will need to assess carefully what we can do, given the changes in our physical strength and the recognition of the aging process. So, in order to go about living in the evening in life, we will want to consult with those whom we trust to help us assess our capabilities and find ways to engage in the activities that are the most satisfying. For me, I will want to continue to have opportunities to be better able to help improve the lives of others. I will want to find good opportunities for service, and perhaps continue writing and teaching in modest ways. I want also want to uproot the power of being controlled by the shadow of my childhood and the mistakes in midlife. I want then to use my modest gifts and talents and continue to be active in helping to educate others on how best to face the challenges of living a peaceful life in the senior years. I want to translate what I have learned across the years into ways of assisting others to heal emotionally, and then invite them to join with me in actions of selfless and unconditional love of others.

7. *Who else is involved as I try to live wisely and well in the evening of life?* At the heart of the answer of who else is involved in the evening of

life is those in the family who will continue to care for us as we age and have severe limitations. If there are very few family members who are able to help, then there may be lifelong friends who can assist us in having a safe and secure setting, one in which we are treated with respect and have a good measure of comfort. In addition to the assistance of care by family and friends, those of us in the evening of life will need a comfortable and secure setting in which to live, one that will enable easy access for medical treatment. As I move more fully into the evening of life, I find that it is my wife, younger than I am, who is best able to assist me to be safe, healthy, and happy. I want also, if our situations reverse, to be able to assist her to be safe, secure, and as contented as possible. Further, that together, we hope we can, even as we age and maybe because of it, be available to our son and his family and be able to make their lives filled with meaning and joy. For as long as possible, we want to be present for them as they need understanding, guidance, and savvy to manage life in a world in crisis.

8. *What social systems surround me and how do I belong?* As we age, we do hope for and have the need of a suitable and comfortable setting, preferably our home with access to the social systems we need to continue to engage in meaningful and enriching activity. Those of us in the evening of life do need a "social system" that works and cares for us; home may no longer be ideal, even if the intentions of those in the home are to be as helpful as possible. Professional services may be needed. Fortunately, the setting in which we live has several fine retirement communities that offer excellent services, and the wise strategy of shifting the service to the changing needs of those in declining health. As I ponder this reality, I would like to continue to be in a setting in which I can continue to do some writing, and on occasion, even some modest teaching. It is likely that the social system available to me with these continuing goals will be the church, although aging will steadily decrease my capacity to use the church as a social setting in which I can lend a hand.

It is not long before I will be the person in need, not the one who offers the service. I have made peace with this reality, knowing full well that my ability to provide service is diminishing. Increasingly, I will need some care. I have discovered that an integral part of service is to create a good context for seniors to continue some aspect of their professional work. The service of "the social system" should design and create infrastructure that enables seniors to engage in some form of meaningful work.

9. *What values will guide me in the process of moving into and through the evening of life?* Most of those in the evening of life want to be guided by untarnished *truth*, although some may want to pretend that the evening of life brings no changes. Yet in aging, we need to understand the changes to our body, mind, and spirit and then find ways to navigate the complex world around us. It is to everyone's advantage and satisfaction if there is not too much hidden or not shared with those who are moving toward the end of life. We do better when we know!

Yes, there are those whose condition may limit their understanding and whose needs are more for comfort than to know the details of our condition. But surprises are difficult, and full knowledge is the best way to help those who age. My hope is that I will be able to understand my condition and still be able to make wise decisions about care. Still another value, in addition to being honest and truthful, is to share the realities of aging and approaching death in ways *that are loving for all concerned*. My hope is that I will have wisdom to share the truth in love with those for whom I care, and that they will have love for me as my needs increase. I want all those in the evening of life to have this wisdom to find just the right resources, words, and settings where love and truth are not only possible, but where their presence might be received with gratitude and be healing and reconciling as the end nears.

10. *How do I truly flourish in the evening of life?* Our purpose in life, while deeply rooted in being truthful and loving, may take a particular form as situations emerge and we change with the passing of time. As we are able, we can continue many of the activities and sustain relationships that empowered us to flourish when we were younger. As we are able, we should continue in those activities that were healthy and nourishing. I understand my purpose in life, as long as I am healthy, to continue to find ways of helping others live wisely and well, be filled with joy and inner peace, and to stay healthy and not suffer. I will flourish in the evening of life if I can have a small part in participating in these goals. As I move beyond my capacity to be of help to others, then I will flourish when I am able to continue to engage in activities that were joyful at an earlier stage in life. At successive points along the path of aging, these activities will change as I change. Then I will engage in what I can do, be grateful, help those who suffer, and cultivate a sense of deep peace, knowing I am surrounded by Love and Truth.

SECTION THREE

Terms, Resources, and Discussion Questions

Terms

1. Unconditional love: Similar terms are self-giving love, or self-emptying love. It is the giving of oneself for the sake of another without conditions.
2. Community of faith: Belonging to and being with a group of people who have a deep belief in the divine and form a community support around this belief and engage in mutual love and service to those in need.
3. Forgiveness: Releasing the negative feelings you have about a person or group that have caused you to feel anger or grief, and then reassuring them that there are no longer any negative feelings.
4. Reconciliation: Making amends to restore a relationship, and being honest with another with the intention of having a relationship of peace with him or her.
5. Social settings/structures: The organization designs and governance structures that exist in and guide those in a particular population or organization.

Books and Resources

1. Greg Baer, *Real Love: The Truth about Finding Unconditional Love and Fulfilling Relationships*
2. Gary Chapman, *The Five Love Languages*
3. Denis De Rougemont, *Love in the Western World*
4. Karen McLaren, *The Art of Empathy: A Complete Guide to Life's Most Essential Skill*
5. Gerald G. May, *The Awakened Heart: Opening Yourself to the Love You Need*
6. Irving Singer, *The Nature of Love*, 3 volumes

Questions for Thought and Discussion

1. How would you describe your response to the invitation of placing love at the center of your life initiative even though you're vulnerable?
2. What support or lack of it have you experienced by the groups you have joined?
3. How do you think it is possible to become a more loving person? And is it important?
4. How important is your family background and experiences as a child in your capacity to build and sustain relationships of love?
5. What do you think is the best way both to receive love and to give love to another person?

CHAPTER ELEVEN

The Love that Seeks Justice and Healing for All Who Suffer

"Then the king will say to those at his right hand, 'Come, you that are blessed by my Father, inherit the kingdom prepared for you from the foundation of the world; for I was hungry and you gave me food, I was thirsty and you gave me something to drink, I was a stranger and you welcomed me, I was naked and you gave me clothing, I was sick and you took care of me, I was in prison and you visited me.' Then the righteous will answer him, 'Lord, when was it that we saw you hungry and gave you food, or thirsty and gave you something to drink? And when was it that we saw you as a stranger and welcomed you or naked and gave you clothing? And when was it that we saw you sick or in prison and visited you?' And the king will answer them, 'Truly I tell you, just as you did it to one of the least of these who are members of my family, you did it unto me.'"

(Matthew 25:34–40)

FOUNDATIONAL TEACHING

As I began my Christian journey as a teenager, I began to understand that receiving love from those in my circle of friends was a foundational component of my new faith. Several were active in their churches, and our shared faith was an essential part of our friendship. I was also fortunate enough to be able to see the presence of love in the leaders who guided the groups in which I was present. When I was sixteen and playing on the baseball team of my high school, I was surprised to see the pastor of the church that I frequently attended with my girlfriend had come to one of our practices. He was careful not to be intrusive, just interested in the activities that were important in my life. He said very little about it, but reassured me by his visit that he was *there* to guide and help as I might need it. A bit later, in another church setting where I went to the youth group, the busy pastor of the church invited me and two or three of my friends to go to the California beach, a few miles from Palo Alto over to Half Moon Bay. There were empty beaches there at that time, not just the city that now crowds them. It was great fun, but more than just fun; I felt cared for in a life-giving way, and I found myself asking whether I was that important.

I had similar experiences during my college years, and it was during this period of time that I discovered that there was another dimension of my faith journey that needed to be added to my personal faith and the mutual support of friends. It was one that I was aware of, yet an outlook that I had not yet fully grasped and was just beginning to understand. The university courses I was taking, both in history and sociology, were helping me to see this other aspect of caring and loving. Not only do we give attention and care to a single individual and close friends, assisting them in their growth toward maturity in life, but we also look at the context in which they live and many others live. I had to write the occasional paper for these courses and in doing the research for these papers, I soon began to realize that love extends beyond giving attention one on one to others, but it also expressed when we are concerned about the social conditions that cause people to suffer. The majority of the people in Menlo Park and Palo Alto were doing well in terms of being surrounded by wonderful education, stimulating programs and opportunities, and access to all that was needed in moving wisely through life. It was all there. Yet what I was studying at the university encouraged me to look at people who were marginalized and lacked the access to a truly good life. The social conditions, and as I later learned, the social structures in which they lived, were unjust and the corporate systems in place discriminated against them.

I was also learning in my university years with wise leaders and teachers about those who challenged these unjust social systems, and the names of Mahatma Gandhi, Martin Luther King, Jr. and Mother Teresa surfaced along with many others. I learned about the quest for political liberation in India, racism in America, and the discrimination against women in many parts of the world. I also began to understand that the message of the Bible, and indeed the life and teachings of Jesus, were not exclusively focused on individual renewal, but also on the social settings that were inhumane and which discriminated against and prevented people from realizing their full potential as human beings. I noted as well that the name of Jesus was often used as a model in the quest for justice. Gradually, my orientation to my faith shifted slightly. The profound changes that came in 1960s also informed and intensified this shift. My faith orientation dramatically expanded to caring deeply about human suffering.

As I read the New Testament, I discovered that Jesus addressed inhumane and unjust systems as much as he helped individuals. Later, during the courses for my master's degree, I wrote a paper on Reinhold Niebuhr, not Billy Graham, not that Dr. Graham's work wasn't important. I learned that to truly love others was to give them personal care and also to pay attention to the social conditions in which they lived. And sure enough, as I continued my studies, I learned that Jesus was not only one in whom you put your faith in order to be in a close relationship with God; he was also an ideal model of a prophet who spoke truth to power and addressed the injustice he saw in the life of marginalized people of the world. I also began to realize that the apostle Paul was more than just concerned about justification by faith; he also challenged the whole unjust and violent Roman system, as well as helping a sick person or inviting one to trust God.

THE PROPHET'S ROLE IN THE HEBREW BIBLE AND THE NEW TESTAMENT

The Hebrew Bible, the Bible of Jesus, in a big-picture way, is the story of God being present in human history through Abraham, Moses, and great prophets, and asking them to improve the social conditions of the Jewish people. The leaders of Jewish society were called to create a country that would be free from war and be governed within the context of a just, compassionate, and peaceful social context.

It is also important to note that when Jesus decided to shift his orientation from carpentry to teaching as a rabbi, he first went to his cousin, called John the Baptist, a powerful and gifted prophet. He learned from John how to care about individual believers with healing and life-giving insight, and then, if you really do care about them, you must help to change the unjust social systems in which they live. The task is to create a society and a nation that is compassionate, cares for those who are poor and sick, and works to create a social structure that provides justice for all. Take care of those who suffer with a helping hand *and by* improving their living conditions!

Jesus learned from John and remembered a great deal of what he had read and been taught about justice by the Hebrew prophets. I expect that frequently, as he went back to the Galilee to begin his public ministry, Jesus drew upon the conversation with John and with his lifelong exposure to the Hebrew Bible. He likely read in Isaiah: "What to me is the multitude of your sacrifices? I have had enough of burnt offerings of rams?" And he continued to read: "Zion shall be redeemed by justice, and those in her who repent, by righteousness . . . He shall judge between the nations, and shall arbitrate for many peoples; they shall beat their swords into plowshares, and their spears into pruning hooks, neither shall they learn war anymore" (Isa 1, 2). He would have read in Jeremiah: "Now the word of the Lord came to me saying, 'Before I formed you in the womb I knew you, and before you were born, I consecrated you; I appointed you a prophet to the nations.' . . . Then the Lord put out his hand and touched my mouth; and the Lord said to me, 'Now I have put my words in your mouth. See, today I appoint you over nations and kingdoms, to pluck up and to pull down, to destroy and overthrow, to build and to plant'" (Jer 1, 2) From his cousin, he would have heard that even the leaders in Jerusalem must repent and be ready to receive "the kingdom of God" coming in the form of one greater than he, the promised messiah of the covenants who would transform the nation.

Contemporary New Testament scholarship has not always had full agreement on the precise ways Jesus understood himself as a prophet, but seldom has there been any doubt that part of his self-understanding was to serve in the role of a prophet.[1] His prophetic role has often been integrated with his role as a rabbi or teacher and his role as one who heals. There is little disagreement that in these roles he was one who invited the individual into a new and transformed life and then spoke directly to Jewish leadership about the need for a social order that ensured care and justice for all. He is quoted as saying: "Do not think that I have come to

---

1. See, for example the book by Bart D. Ehrman, *Apocalyptic Prophet of the New Millennium*, Richard A. Horsely, *Jesus and the Politics of Roman Palestine*, and John Dominic Crossan, *Jesus: A Revolutionary Biography*.

abolish the Law or the prophets; I have come not to abolish but to fulfill" (Matt 5:17). His aim was not so much to overthrow the current structures but to transform them and charge the leaders to govern with fairness and compassion. He underlined that the people will be well served in a system that integrates the religious understanding that God is love and cares deeply about individual believers with the way that God's love also cares about and wants to eliminate all forms of human suffering. He called for social systems that were just and fair, especially for the poor, and political leadership that creates a living environment that is filled with peace, justice, and compassion.

JESUS AS HEALER AND PROPHET

We have spoken earlier about the remarkable healing ministry of Jesus, emphasizing his compassion for those suffering from a range of diseases and disabilities. I circle back to this emphasis at this point to call attention to what is obvious but perhaps not always in our consciousness, that Jesus lived in a time preceding the rise of modern medicine. This meant that families with children and with elderly members faced a variety of illnesses which they did not fully understand. They had no family physician who was trained adequately to treat common colds and no hospital to receive those who had been in accidents and had serious illnesses. They did what the prevailing wisdom advised: rest, have a good diet, and on occasion isolate some sick people if the diseased was judged to be contagious. Many suffered, and when the word got out that there was one who had the capacity to heal, the sick and those who cared for the sick went for help. Luke's Gospel records one of these events:

> One day, while he was teaching, Pharisees and teachers of the law were sitting nearby (they had come from every village of Galilee and Judea and from Jerusalem); and the power of the Lord was with him to heal. Just then some men came, carrying a paralyzed man on a bed bringing him before Jesus; but finding no way to bring him in because of the crowd, they went up on the roof and led him down with his bed through the tiles into the middle of the crowd in front of Jesus. When he saw their faith, he said, "Friend, your sins are forgiven you." Then the scribes and the Pharisees began to question, "Who is this who is speaking blasphemies? Who can forgive sins but God alone?" When Jesus perceived their questioning, he answered

them, "Why do you raise such questions in your heart? Which is easier, to say, 'Your sins are forgiven you', or to say 'Stand up and walk?' 'But so that you may know that the Son of Man has authority on earth to forgive sins' he said to the one who was paralyzed, "I say to you, stand up and take your bed and go to your home." Immediately he stood up before them, took what he had been lying on and went to his home, glorifying God. Amazement seized all of them, and they glorified God and were filled with awe, saying, "We have seen strange things today" (Luke 5:17–26).

This story illustrates a number important points about Jesus, the healing prophet, who seeks health and justice for all those who suffer and are marginalized:

1. One contextual point is that the story was told many times before it was recorded and that what we have is likely a good summary of what occurred. But some questions about its authenticity, especially in the details, may need to be considered in that the story did go through an oral tradition before it was written.
2. It illustrates the influence of Jesus when and where there was illness, and it points to the desperation of friends and family to find a way for a loved one to be healed.
3. It illustrates the remarkable capacity of Jesus to heal.
4. It reveals Jesus, not only in his healing capacity, but also in a pastoral role. Jesus sensed that in this case the healing of a paralyzed person was also an occasion to speak about the forgiving grace of God. It was wise for Jesus to say that his sins were forgiven, especially if the poor man thought his paralysis was punishment for sins. Jesus was the good pastor, reassuring a suffering person of God's unconditional love. He reminded the troubled man of the gracious and forgiving love of God.
5. Jesus not only reassured the sick person about God's love, "your sins are forgiven you," but also illustrated by his healing that the power of God, flowing through the healer and prophet, not only forgives, but heals as well.
6. Jesus, the prophet, spoke truth to power by saying that the Pharisees and scribes (scholars and interpreters of the Law) had misunderstood the best interpretation of the Law (Torah), that a loving,

forgiving, and healing action is the true will of the God. God heals the whole person. It was a correct interpretation of the Law of God for Jesus to say, "Your sins are forgiven." This incident illustrates that Jesus understood that the person needed a sense of being forgiven, but also desperately needed to be healed physically. The sick man knew he was included in God's love (his sins were forgiven) and was healed by God's love (I can now walk because God has empowered Jesus to heal).

There are other stories in the Gospels that illustrate that Jesus understood the Law as the expression of the will of a loving God. The Law was intended to be both humane and just, caring for people in terms of their individual needs while at the same time ensuring that they would live in a setting that was guided by laws that were just and humane. Jesus often found himself in settings and occasions when the one interpreting the Law reflected a narrow and traditional interpretation, although one that they held sincerely. This narrow interpretation may have developed as a result of the need to simplify the issue so that all could understand it. Yet it also may reflect the tendency of leaders to gain power and authority by referring to the Law in order to control the behavior of the people. Perhaps they truly believed their narrow view, but Jesus nevertheless boldly challenged it. He sensed that it met their need for a simple law, one that would give them power and control. It was a way to manage behavior that might get out of control. But in this misreading of the Law, it missed its primary purpose, facilitating humane, fair, and just conditions so that all could flourish.

I want to call attention to two other stories in the Gospels in which Jesus demonstrates his understanding of the place of the Law as a way to express justice and compassion for the people rather than as means for leaders to unnecessarily restrict and control actions and behavior. These incidents have to do with the understanding of what was acceptable to do on the Sabbath and what was forbidden because it was judged to be "work." Matthew 12:1–8 gives us the account of how Jesus and the disciples walked the dusty trails of Palestine as they carried out their mission and had to find food as they traveled. Restaurants were not common, and it is likely that they had to find food in their natural surroundings:

> At that time Jesus went through the grainfields on the Sabbath; his disciples were hungry and they began to pluck heads of grain and to eat. When the Pharisees saw it, they said to him "Look,

your disciples are doing what is not lawful to do on the Sabbath." He said to them, "Have you not read what David did when he and his companions were hungry? He entered the house of God and ate the bread of the Presence, which it was not lawful for him or his companions to eat, but only for the priests. Or have you not read in the law on the Sabbath the priests in the temple break the Sabbath yet are guiltless? I tell you, something greater than the temple is here. But if you had known what this means, 'I desire mercy and not sacrifice,' you would not have condemned the guiltless. For the Son of Man is lord of the Sabbath."

Once again, we are invited into a legal case that often was dealt with by the Sanhedrin, which was much like the Supreme Court for interpreting the Law. Jesus takes the lead in this conversation with the Pharisees and moves directly to the point of view that there are times when mercy should be shown to those who are disabled or who are ill and need to be cared for, even on the Sabbath; mercy should be given priority. If the conversation had continued, I imagine that Jesus would have further explained his point, that mercy, a profound expression of compassion, is really what the Law is all about, not a literalistic and narrow interpretation that advocates a position, perhaps to control, that is really in opposition to the intention of the Law. The Sabbath, an important part of the Law, had the clear intention of ensuring that the people get adequate rest and a day to relax and be free of the demands of work, whether hard labor or difficult decisions in the office. The purpose of the weekly Sabbath was a time to be refreshed and reenergized. Jesus points out in this conversation with the Pharisees that it was certainly possible in the time of David to provide for basic human need; the great King did it, and even the priests in the temple were allowed to do it. Jesus, understanding his responsibilities to care for those who sacrificed so much to follow him, felt justified in offering some grain to his disciples, even on the Sabbath. He wants for his critics to understand that the Sabbath was set aside as a day of rest, not as day to deprive people of care. He teaches them that "The Sabbath was made for humankind, and not humankind for the Sabbath" (Mark 2:27–28). The Gospel writer, Mark, adds: "The Son of Man is lord even of the Sabbath" as a way of noting that Jesus had the divine sanction to interpret the Sabbath law.

It is important to note about several of these passages that the authors understand the term, Son of Man, and call Jesus the Son of Man, one with authority. The title, Son of Man, did have a variety of meanings in the time of Jesus. Yet these different and subtle meanings all express the foundational truth that when Jesus is quoted as serving the needs of the people or described as the Son of Man, it is an expression of the deep belief that he had a divine calling and vocation. He is the one who was to come and is now here as a transcendental figure to represent and express the will of God. Some have argued that he may not have used the title, but that it was given to him by the Gospel writers as their interpretation of one with a special mission from God.[2]

There is another similar story about the commitment of Jesus to heal those who have a disease or disability. He gives healing a very high priority, even if it goes against some of the customs and traditions of his setting. On another occasion he speaks about one of the deeply held beliefs that on the Sabbath, that in order for it to be kept holy, one must rest and worship; it was a perspective he affirmed as well. But the challenge came when it was necessary to determine what one should or shouldn't do on this holy day. The underlying issue for the religious community was to identify what was meant by *basic work* that should not be undertaken on the Sabbath. Luke records the story in chapter 6, verses 6–11:

> On another Sabbath he entered the synagogue and taught, and there was a man there whose right hand was withered. The scribes and the Pharisees watch him to see whether he would cure on the Sabbath, so that they might find an accusation against him. Even though he knew what they were thinking, he said to the man who had the withered hand, "Come and stand here." He got up and stood there. The Jesus said to them, "I ask you, is it lawful to do good on the Sabbath, to save it or destroy it?" After looking around at all of them, he said to him, "Stretch out your hand." He did so and his hand was restored. But they were filled with fury and discussed with one another what they might do to Jesus.

Matthew records the same incident in his description and adds (Matt 12:9–14):

> He said to them, "Suppose one of you has only one sheep and it falls into a pit on the Sabbath; will you not lay hold of it and lift

---

2. Titles such as Son of Man and Son of God have been examined with great care, and not all scholars are in full agreement as to their meaning. For our purposes in quoting these passages, we understand the term as one who has a special linkage with and calling from God, giving him authority. See volume 4 of John P. Meier's comprehensive study of Jesus, *Marginal Jew: Law and Love*, 285–93.

it out? How much more valuable is a human being than a sheep! So, it is lawful to do good on the Sabbath." Then he said to the man, "Stretch out your hand." He stretched it out, and it was restored, as sound as the other. But the Pharisees went out and conspired against him, how to destroy him.

It is clear that Jesus had deep respect for Sabbath observance, but also is profoundly committed to relieving suffering. He would not accept the interpretation that the Sabbath commandment prohibits healing love on the Sabbath day. He was asserting that expressing love and relieving suffering do not violate the commandment, and, in fact, even expand the meaning of the commandment by demonstrating that it is given for the health and well-being of people. Its observance provides a time free from all the stresses of work and a time to worship and honor God whose very definition is Love. He is also observing what so easily happens when a religious community turns sectarian and narrow, that certain norms and behaviors of the culture become legalistic rather than providing guidance for a life that is healthy and flourishing. I have been in and served a number of churches in my lifetime, most of which have been nurturing for me, yet I have noticed how easy it is for a congregation, even a denomination, to begin making rules that are rooted in cultural norms rather than representing biblical guidance. Distorting religious commandments can turn somewhat dangerous and a means of control, and great care must be given to provide settings that empower its members to be nourished and become whole.

Those of us in the evening of life need a faith orientation that ensures us of God's love and care, not one that unnecessarily restricts our behavior and makes us feel guilty. Yes, there are behaviors that are harmful, but most of us who are in last years of our lives have learned to avoid harmful behavior. Even if we fail, we need mercy, not narrow and legalistic control. Further, we should draw upon our wisdom to lend a hand to those who suffer, as Jesus did, and cultivate a faith orientation that is filled with understanding, empathy, and intelligent care for those who suffer. One great gift that many of us have in the evening of life may be wisdom; we have experience that has taught us how to manage not just the major concerns of life, but many of the day-to-day concerns as well. In addition, there are many of us who have been set free from self-preoccupation, although at times difficult if we are troubled or ill. But the majority of us have been set free to reach out and care for others with deep empathy and intelligent compassion. Or because of our suffering, we may have cultivated deep empathy for others who suffer.

SECTION THREE

PAUL AS MISSIONARY AND MINISTER

The apostle Paul, a devout Jew, was a natural leader and drawn to important causes. He thought he was on the right road by persecuting Christians. But when he was converted to the Christian faith, he became one who felt called to be a missionary of his new faith. He was born into a Jewish family in Tarsus, an important Roman city on the northeastern coast of the Mediterranean Sea. He was likely guided by his father about how to deepen his faith and study the guiding beliefs of Judaism. Early in his life, perhaps because of his great potential, he went to Jerusalem to study Judaism with a reputable Jewish scholar, Gamaliel. It was there that he may have become a Pharisee, a group of Jewish leaders that were especially devout, concerned about ritual purity, and were dedicated to the observance of the Law. He thrived in this setting and may have even become a member of the Sanhedrin,[3] a governing body within local Judaism, based in Jerusalem. He soon became known as a leader, although still relatively young.

As a Pharisee, Paul was predictably opposed to the rise of a new sectarian group that had formed around the life and teachings of Jesus. He saw this movement as a threat to his form of Judaism and engaged in a course of action to prevent it from being accepted and becoming a new and influential sectarian movement within Judaism. In a strange twist of fate or, more likely, providential care, it was while he was traveling in the region to oppose the new movement that he was converted to it. He had been informed about a coming Messiah, and somewhat ironically or, again, providentially, he was converted in a quite dramatic way and began to understand Jesus as the Messiah. He was transformed. He soon realized that he needed an extended period of time for processing what had occurred. After this period of reflection and study, he then began his work as a Christian missionary. He travelled extensively in the region of Asia Minor and the Adriatic Sea, founding new churches and writing several letters describing his new found faith. They became an integral part of the New Testament and have guided the church across the centuries. It is from his life and teaching that we learn a great deal about the early development of the Christian church. In the letters of Paul, we learn

---

3. It is unlikely that he was a member of the Sanhedrin in that he was still a relatively young student in Jerusalem, yet there are scholars who believe that he may have become a member of the Sanhedrin, given his connection with Gamaliel and his persecution of Christians.

THE LOVE THAT SEEKS JUSTICE AND HEALING FOR ALL WHO SUFFER

about the early expression of Christian life, the commitment to justice, and ways to live wisely and well in the evening of life.

Paul, a remarkable mission worker, often expressed his calling as an understanding and loving pastor. His work had several dimensions, and we might summarize them in three categories:

1. Expanding the mission of God to include everyone, not just the Jewish people;
2. Clarifying the relationship between Jewish teaching about the Law and the new gospel of grace based on the life and teachings of Jesus, and;
3. Leading the opposition to Roman belief and law that deified the Roman emperor and encouraged the expansion of the empire in violent ways.

There are many guidelines for belief and practice in the teaching of Paul that have great relevance for our desire to flourish, reduce human suffering, and help to create a society and world that is just and humane. It is beyond our purpose to write the volumes required to describe all that he taught; our goal is rather to lift out of Paul's life and teaching a few themes that demonstrate how the Christian faith invites its followers to open their hearts to the reign of God, to become transformed by the grace of God, and to join with others in the expression of love that seeks to heal and reduce suffering by helping to create a more empathic and just social order. He speaks directly to those of us in the evening of life who care about the goals Paul described.

One part of Paul's deep belief that became central to his mission was to overcome the division that separated Jews and Gentiles. A partial strength of Judaism in the time of Paul was that it was distinctive and interpreted the history of the Jewish people as representing the clear intention and guidance of God. As with most religions, Judaism did have beliefs and practices that logically followed from their foundational belief that there was one God, Yahweh, who was the creator and sustainer of the universe. From this foundational belief, the Jewish people felt chosen and called to a particular way of life. Paul's own personal history was centered in this grand worldview; he was a devout Jew. Following his conversion to the new Christian Way, he began to understand it as the next dispensation of God's way in the world. Paul remained a Jew, but added the new belief that Jesus had come to demonstrate by his life, teachings, and his last days, that the God of love was available to all people. He saw that his own mission was to be to Gentiles and had to make a case for this direction in his ministry. In fact, he had some fairly direct conversations with the apostle Peter and the brother of Jesus, James, about being called to spread the news of God's love to all people.[4] He prevails in these conversations; he writes to the Galatian church: "There is no longer Jew or Greek, there is no longer slave or free, there is no longer male or female; for all of you are one in Christ" (Gal 3:28). With Paul's mission, and the somewhat reluctant approval of other Jewish Christian leaders, the Christian community becomes inclusive, welcoming all. We in the evening of life need to follow Paul's teaching that God welcomes all people and that this conviction should be central to our code of ethics. There is no room in our faith for racial prejudice or discrimination against others who may come from a different culture and historical origin.

A second major contribution of Paul was to sort out the relationship between the centrality of the Law in Judaism and the gospel of grace in the new Christian faith. As Jewish people became Christian, they asked how their new faith in Jesus was related to their Jewish faith. There were some strong differences in that the new Christian movement was still a sectarian branch of Judaism. Paul, quite carefully in his writing, argues that the Law has its place in terms of behavior for Jewish Christians, but that the new faith in Jesus, endorsed by Gentiles, is the realization that they are now reconciled with God by their faith in the teaching of Jesus and the saving events of the life and death of Jesus. He goes on to say that the presence of God's Spirit in their lives guides and empowers us to follow the will of God. This deep belief was especially important for Gentiles, whom Paul said did not need to engage in all of the distinctive practices of Judaism. His argument is quite extensive in the Roman letter, chapters 5–11, with a description of the new way of life in the remainder of the letter. Paul does acknowledge the value of the Law with its guidance regarding belief and practice. He then goes on to argue that this new way of life, especially for Gentiles, is to accept by faith the fullness of God's presence and gracious love; all are included in the teaching and life of Jesus. It is now available to all. We are transformed and maintain our belief in and practice by the very presence of the Holy Spirit in our lives. "There is now no condemnation for those who are in Christ Jesus.

---

4. See the account in Acts 1 and 2 about the formation of the new church made up of people from different backgrounds. See Acts 13:1–3 for the commissioning of Paul to serve as a mission worker.

For the law of the Spirit of life in Christ Jesus has set you free from the law of sin and death" (Rom 8:1–2). He goes on to say: "What then are we to say about these things? If God is for us, who is against us? . . . No, we are more than conquerors through him that who loved us?" (Rom 8:31, 37).

A third dimension of Paul's teaching addresses the question of how to live faithfully as a Christian in the Roman empire in which the emperor is understood as divine. The short answer of course is "carefully." While this answer is often meant to be a humorous comment, it does in fact point in the direction of Paul's answer. Paul does get arrested by the Roman government and spends his last days in a Roman jail. In the book of Acts, we read about his time in a Roman prison, his trial and the arguments to set him free, and his continuing hope to travel to Spain to complete his missionary calling. It is a fascinating account with Paul's appeal directly to Caesar (Acts 25–28), his appearance before other levels of the judicial system, and his final missionary work in Rome. The letter closes: "He lived there two whole years at his own expense and welcomed all who came to him, proclaiming the kingdom of God and teaching about the Lord Jesus Christ with all boldness and without hindrance." It is both a sad and inspiring account of Paul's final days.

Prior to his arrest, he did write some words of guidance about how those with their new faith should relate to governmental authority. This writing occurs incidentally in a few places in his writing, but more intentionally so in the letter to the Romans, chapter 13. He begins:

> Let every person be subject to the governing authorities; for there is no authority except from God, and those authorities that exist have been instituted by God. Therefore, whoever resists authority resists what God has appointed, and those who resist will incur judgment. For rulers are not a terror to good conduct, but to bad. Do you wish to have no fear of authority? Then do what is good, and you will receive its approval; for it is God's servant for your good, and you will receive its approval. But if you do what is wrong, you should be afraid, for the authority does not bear the sword in vain. It is the servant of God to execute wrath on the wrong doer. Therefore, one must be subject, not only because of wrath but also because of conscience. For the same reason you also pay taxes, for the authorities are God's servants, busy with this very thing. Pay to all what is due to them—taxes to whom taxes are due, respect to whom respect is due, revenue to whom revenue is due, honor to whom honor is due" (Rom 13:1–7).

Books have been written in the attempt to interpret this passage in a way that guides us in our contemporary discussion about how to understand and relate to our government. I will be content with the following observations as it relates to the theme of this chapter, noting that Paul is a Roman citizen:

1. It is a more general statement of Paul about how we should understand and relate to the government authorities, not an attempt to speak directly to an individual situation, problem, or case. Paul, in general, believes that we should respect our government in terms of its primary function, to keep order, ensure justice, and provide direction for the flow of our common life and social concerns. Paul is not addressing, although he could have, a situation in which the government may have been unjust or how the government should take on the responsibility to create a more just and humane society.

2. He does believe in "law and order," at least in theory, because we need to have carefully designed ways to live together in harmony in a state or country.

3. So, it is wise to respect the authority of the government as it calls into account those who break the law or refuse to pay their taxes. This respect for the law will help everyone. Authority has a clear place in the way we manage our city or state, and of course our country.

4. As he continues his argument in the subsequent paragraphs, he makes an appeal to citizens to respect the government and live in a moral way. He goes on to say that our responsibility is to love others, not judge them. He stresses that we should not engage in poor behavior because it may cause others to stumble. He urges us to live in a way that cares for others rather than seeking our own pleasures and quests for power.

As I read these words of Paul, I find I want to ask him some questions, likely starting with a comment such as: "What you say is wise counsel in an ideal setting, but what about those settings where the government tolerates injustice and where many people, especially the poor, suffer? It is not so much what you say, but what you don't say that suggests a sort passive stance in reference to government responsibility." I would continue with some energy: "Shouldn't the government insist on fair and equal treatment of all people and provide them equal opportunity and a just social order?" I expect he would say that he was speaking in a general way, and then suggest that I read his other letters to sort out specific cases. I would partially accept this answer, but wonder if he shouldn't have said more about the Roman government and what he saw as he was in prison. I think I would ask him, "Why is there not more attention given to the sick, poor, and yes, prisoners, and those who are marginalized?"

This section remains a bit too conservative and passive for me as it has been traditionally interpreted. One might add in the interpretation some guidance on how to resist the government if it fails in its primary responsibilities and does not address injustice, poverty, racial discrimination, and bring aid to those who are marginalized. Then it might be wise to underline the way in which the government might take positive action to create a better life for its citizens. There is some risk that the passage might be used as a way to justify a passive and uncaring government using the argument that "the Bible says" and therefore we need to obey what we think it says. My own response, as one in the evening of life, is to go ahead and argue some with Paul, granting some acceptance to his general statement and giving credit to all of his other writing that is more specific and addresses injustice and the need to provide aid to those who suffer. I do wish Paul had said in this letter that we should use what talent and resources we have to relieve suffering in all of its diabolical forms and create programs that improve the lives of the citizens. Alas, he does so in his other writing.

I sincerely believe that we in "the evening of life will be judged by love alone." Jesus on the cross cared for the one next to him, and had deep empathy even for those who were in the process of crucifying him: "Father, forgive them, for they know not what they are doing" (Luke 23:34). In our mature years, we have the education, experience, some resources, and the time to give a portion of our lives to helping those who suffer and to create a better society.

From time to time, we may need to express brash boldness, suggesting that we should not hide behind our fears, should face the harsh realities of life, and care for those who suffer. "And, Paul, we will talk about all of this in heaven, if I ever get there."

SECTION THREE

Terms, Resources, and Discussion Questions

Terms

1. Social justice: The ideal condition in a setting in which all people are treated fairly and have equal opportunity, in large measure because the laws provide for and protect this ideal condition.
2. Sabbath: A day set aside for rest and worship; in the Jewish setting it is Saturday and in a Christian setting, it is usually Sunday.
3. Rabbi: Jewish teacher who often takes responsibility for pastoral care and religious services.
4. Pharisees: A group of leaders and government officials in the time of Jesus who were dedicated to following religious practices and observances with guidance from Jewish Law (Torah).
5. Mercy: A term used in ancient times when another is treated with forbearance and compassion.

Resources: Books to Read and Consult

1. John Dominic Crossan, *Jesus, A Revolutionary Biography*
2. Bart D. Ehrman, *Jesus: Apocalyptic Prophet of the New Millennium*
3. Richard A. Horsley, *The Prophet Jesus and the Renewal of Israel*
4. Richard A. Horsley, *Jesus and the Politics of Roman Palestine*
5. John P. Meier, *A Marginal Jew: Law and Love*, volume 4

Discussion Questions

1. Do you think that God treats people with a different background and cultural heritage, such as Jewish, differently than others, or does God treat all people equally? Are there any special privileges?
2. What did Jesus mean when he said in reference to the Sabbath, "I want mercy and not sacrifice"?
3. What kind of government policy and practice should we resist or try to change?

4. Is it ever morally acceptable to break the law of state or country in which you live?

5. In what ways should we consult the Bible and bring its teaching forward to guide our lives? What are some guidelines if we do use an approach gaining direction?

CHAPTER TWELVE

Conclusion: A Still More Excellent Way

> "In everything, do to others as you would have them do to you, for this is the law and the prophets."
>
> (Matthew 7:13)

THE ETHICAL TEACHING OF JESUS

The apostle Matthew, in his account and summary of the primary teachings of Jesus in his Gospel (chapters 5–7), is drawing his account to a close with this verse, quoted above, called the Golden Rule. It has been pointed out that this statement is not unique to Jesus; a form of it exists in other religious and ethical systems. It may be that Jesus, as well as Matthew, did know about this ethical maxim from other sources, although both saw it as an integral expression of the Judaism of their faith orientation. Matthew wisely inserts it as one of his closing thoughts in his description of the ethical teaching of Jesus. It is important to note that Matthew, and most likely Jesus, thought it was a good summary of the ethical norms of the Judaism that was their religious heritage. The language used for the summary is: "for this is the law and the prophets." In the Jewish tradition, based on the Hebrew Bible, one finds ethical guidance and indeed wisdom for life in what has been taught in "the law and the prophets." It is a special phrase, one that would be clearly understood by the Jewish community; it was a summary of their heritage, rooted in biblical law for every Jewish believer and made germane by the prophets to create a just and peaceful corporate life. I can almost hear a rabbi, as s/he is saying goodbye to a member of the congregation, "Have a good week and do good in the community. Follow the Law and the teachings of the prophets."

It is also important to note that Jesus was acquainted with this summary statement, the Law and prophets. He is quoted by Matthew as saying: "Do not think that I have come to abolish the Law or the prophets; I have come not to abolish but to fulfill" (Matt 5:17). As this statement is interpreted, it has generally been acknowledged that Jesus fully understood the teaching of the Law and the prophets, yet wanted to add a slightly different method of interpretation, one not based exclusively on a legalistic understanding of these teachings, but one based more on the way that these teachings guide and empower one to live an ethical life and to be spiritually renewed. His emphasis is on the gracious transformation of the person. As one reads the Law and prophets, one would then be guided by the Spirit of God and transformed in order to live by the ideals of the Law and the prophets. In this way, Jesus fulfills the obligations of the command. He teaches us that God not only asks us "to do good" by obeying the teachings of the "Law and the prophets," but also informs, reforms, and transforms us so that doing good naturally flows from who we are. We might say that when Jesus teaches us to "love our enemy," he not only guides our behavior, but also empowers us to be able to love our enemy, love being the primary way for humans to truly "do good" in society. When all is said and done, it is love that has the capacity to transform us, enabling us to move away from self-serving behavior and the inclination to go our own way, and perhaps "get even." Rather, in being forgiven, we are able to overcome all the pain and hurt that may be inside of us because of history, culture, and personal conflict. We are transformed and empowered to love. Love is a universal value.

It was how Jesus dealt with those who resisted his teachings, offering profound insight and resisting long arguments that would only deepen the differences and divisions. He chose to demonstrate his love by ministering to the poor and the sick. He lived with them, taught them, cared for them, and healed them. It was also how he dealt with those in power, often speaking directly, which is a part of informed love, but not resorting to violent action that would do harm. He doesn't "fight back," using violence, but "loves back" and creates a new kind of life-giving community.

He breaks the power of hate, prejudice, retaliation, and violence and replaces it with empathy, understanding, patience, and healing.

When asked by a lawyer, "Which commandment in the Law is the greatest?" he replied: "'You shall love the Lord your God with all of you heart, and with all of your soul, and with all of your mind.' This is the greatest and first commandment. And a second is like it: 'You shall love your neighbor as yourself.' On these two commandments hang all the Law and the prophets" (Matt 22:36–40). It is clear in the teaching of Jesus that love is the fundamental foundation of living a good and truly spiritual life. He clearly emphasized that that the true spiritual pathway is to love God with one's whole being, a foundational commitment and the very ground of one's life. Following from this foundation and center, we are to love others with the same intensity and care we have for our own life and all of its many phases and dimensions. If I am cold, I get a coat for the one who is sitting next to me who is likely cold as well. If a child is crying, I go and sit beside her or him, be there, offer help in whatever form is most appropriate and relieve the suffering. We would love and care for the children of Gaza. It is how we go into the world, to sit beside those in need, be present, see and hear the struggle and pain, and offer whatever help we can to the one who suffers. Like Jesus, we are not afraid to touch the leper or heal the daughter of the suffering Roman soldier, or say "today you will be with me in paradise" to the one who is being executed next to me. I will even love the soldiers as they put me on the cross because "they know not what they do."

PAUL AND THE MORE EXCELLENT WAY

Paul endeavored, as he was converted to the way of Jesus, to live in keeping with the ethical teaching of Jesus. In many ways he succeeded, although some interpreters of the life and teaching of Paul occasionally point out what they consider to be a failure here and there. Yet few have tried harder, and his legacy is certainly one of the greatest gifts ever given to the Christian community and even to all the people of the earth. As Jesus was a person who belongs to the world, regardless of history, culture, and religious belief,[1] so Paul has traces of being a person who belongs to the world, and not just a first century missionary who spread the word about the life and mission of Jesus in an isolated corner of the world. His

---

1. See Pelikan, *Jesus Through the Centuriese*, 220–23.

teaching on love, for example, has all the marks of being applicable in all settings and all time.

We do want to note that his teaching and travels were not free of occasional controversy, but few would question his faith and commitment to be a voice for the new Christian movement. He was a person of great integrity and courage, even when speaking boldly and directly occasionally got him into trouble. There was a prophetic edge to his speaking and writing. As it is with all prophets who speak truth to power, he too faced some resistance from those in power; Paul ended his life as a prisoner of Rome, although it was there as well that he loved those in need and wrote with eloquence and conviction.

He wrote and spoke often on the theme of love; there is a trace of it in nearly all of his letters. In the letter called First Corinthians, he speaks quite profoundly about love and introduces what we have already mentioned, his view on the more excellent way. Chapter 13 in the letter is organized around three major components of love: the preeminence of love, the practice of love, and the permanence of love.

He begins his development of the more excellent way by saying that love is preeminent to and more important than oratory: "If I speak in the tongues or mortals and angels, but do not love, I am a noisy gong or a clanging cymbal." I have occasionally heard a noisy gong or a clanging symbol, and may have had first-hand experience in creating these clashing and annoying noises. In Paul's culture and time, given the high level of illiteracy, a very important form of communication for scholars, teachers, and political leaders was a speech. There was no internet, television, or even a great deal of literature that was accessible to common people. Paul says that to deliver a powerful and compelling speech (or we might say putting a message on Facebook) is just a "noisy gong" if love and empathy are not present. Love must be the motivation of our speeches and be present in all of our communication. As we speak, we enter the world of the other and, as we are able, become at home in it as an expression of our love for the other person. We become sensitive to the listener and use language that delivers the message of profound caring about their suffering, their way of life, their concerns, and their understanding of reality. As possible, what we say, in many cases, should lay aside one's own feelings and outlook and move into the world as the listener.

All too often our words are an attempt to persuade the other person to move into our world and understand important concerns as we understand them. It is so easy to fall into self-referencing and assume that our concerns are more important than those of others. It is so easy to respond to the other who has just spoken about their suffering with our own tales of suffering and at least indirectly asking them to shift the focus and care for you. When this happens, the person in front of us will generally not feel heard or cared for in any way. Some mutual sharing is wise and healing, yet to fully listen to the other person is to express compassion authentically and demonstrate empathy. It is to move into their world with the response of love.

He goes on to say that love is even superior to knowledge. This observation catches my attention as one who values knowledge! "And if I have prophetic powers, and understand all mysteries and all knowledge . . . but do not have love, I am nothing." Love must be the guiding motivation of those who speak in a way that makes the great mysteries about life understandable. It is also the case for those who act prophetically in order to address social injustice and to create a more humane world. The use of our accumulation of knowledge and wisdom should be used for the good of the other and be motivated by love. As love is filled with wisdom, it has the capacity to cut through distracting details and self-centeredness.[2] It goes to soul of the other person. As we move toward prophetic concerns, advocating for social justice and care for the poor, love must be our driving motivation, not the praise that comes from having done well. Nor should strong resistance to our effort to make changes in order to increase justice prevent us from expressing love by improving the conditions in which others live.

In the same sentence, he also speaks about faith: "and if I have all faith, so as to remove mountains, but do not have love, I am nothing." Even Paul, the great teacher and model of a faith-centered life, underscores that faith without love is incomplete. In fact, faith without love is often dangerous; false faith leads others astray, and we are currently surrounded by it. For example, there are those with right-wing political outlook who claim that they reflect the teaching of Jesus, and as they speak against those who have a different point of view, they claim a sort of divine authority for what they way, often discriminating against those who are different from them. There are those who distort religion and use its influence for power for their own gain. Love resists all forms of prejudice, especially when it is justified with religious rhetoric.

---

2. See Ostaseski, *Five Invitations: Discovering What Death Can Teach Us about Living Fully*, 252–53.

Love is certainly preeminent over possessions and even the willingness to sacrifice one's life, for, if I "do not have love, I gain nothing." Paul is clear that love must be the driving motivation. The wealthy and those who are collectors of all the signs of wealth must be motived by love and use their assets for the good of those in need. Even those who are willing to die for a cause or a great truth must be guided by the contours and commands of love.

And what are those contours and commands? Of what does love consist? How do we practice love? First, he says that love is patient, that is, it takes time and has endurance; healing kindness and focused attention must be present, endure, and be sustained in all of our relationships. We all know that those who need love often are not all that easy to love. The profoundly needy are usually difficult to love, and it may require perseverance and courage to give the best we have to give in order for true love to be present. It certainly doesn't help if and when we get "hooked" by the word or action of another; it is all too easy to become annoyed, even angry, by the inappropriate behavior of the other person. We may find ourselves filled with frustration and say "enough"! It is then so easy to leave the person or to turn the attention back to one's self as feelings of frustration fill the interaction. It may be that the one to whom we are offering love doesn't understand our way and blocks our loving initiative. We may even feel rejection and become the target of anger. Then, it is so easy in such a relationship to stop empathic listening; we begin to feel annoyed or judged by the other person. We walk away and do not easily return.

In addition, there is the continuing risk that a subject comes up in another person's description of their pain, one that matches the pain in one's own life. When this occurs, we often resort once again to constant self-referencing in an attention-getting "me too" mode. This practice of self-referencing is one of the most common practices of daily conversation, even acceptable at times, but it often does take the attention away from the one who needs to be heard in a healing and compassionate way.

Feelings of insecurity may also occur when we are around those who may be gifted and have lives filled with achievement, honor, meaning, and joy. We may find ourselves just a bit intimidated and unsure of how to really make contact. In these relationships we will need to be ready to set aside the possibility of feeling threatened, envious, or not worthy of equal status. There are many risks in these settings, one of which is to try to demonstrate that we are also important. There is the tendency to try to use the conversation or activity in order to get attention, be seen and appreciated, even to boast, saying "I too have a fine education, have traveled to many countries, and have had excellent work opportunities." Often, we want to be recognized and be thought of as worthy and important. Because of this need, we may resort to subtle, although boastful and arrogant comments about our history and background. Seldom a day goes by that I don't hear and see this kind of exchange between people, or observe it in myself. When the attention does not turn to them, they find ways of insisting the they be acknowledged. If we do not get the attention and affirmation we may need, we may become irritable or resentful, as Paul suggests. It is not the way of love.

Nor is it the way of love to always turn the conversation in a way that gets the affirmation we want. We may even begin a conversation with a slightly untruthful comment in the effort to be valued. But, as Paul says, love does not rejoice in wrongdoing, but rejoices in the truth. In fact, love patiently bears all things, while believing in the good, and continues to hope for the emergence of the good, the true, and the beautiful. Love has endurance through the long struggle of creating kind and insightful conversation that nourishes all those who are present.

This is the practice of love, and in that practice, love gradually becomes permanent; as Paul says, it never ends. Other human behavior and social realities will cease. Oratory is impermanent. Even our knowledge will change and cease because it is partial and limited by time and cultural assumptions. What we once believed to be the case changes as new knowledge emerges. In fact, as we look back across history, we begin to understand how the human grasp of the reality that surrounds them has dramatically changed. The earth is not flat nor did it and indeed the solar system come into being in just a few thousand years. Our beliefs, though sincere, may often be like a child's understanding. Even now as we look for truth, as Paul reminds us, it is often like looking in a dusty mirror, and we only see partially.

But in faith, we sense that there is a profound truth that is permanent and trustworthy. A time will come for us when we encounter Truth, the personal God of love. As we wait for that time, we do so in faith, believing that it will come; it is the foundation of our hope. In the meantime, we love those who journey with us and all those who need loving care, knowing that to love is the most profound and deeply gratifying way to live. Love, Paul reminds, is preeminent, practical, and permanent.

GO AND DO LIKEWISE[3]

As I have spoken about love on many occasions, I find that a very common statement and question from the audience is: "Yes, I have heard that to love should be the central core and behavior of my life, but I find it very difficult to love. How does one become a more loving person?" The first part of the answer I have often given, though with caution and what I hope is a good measure of humility, is: "It is easier to understand what love is than it is to practice it." With some reserve, I often begin with some observations about why loving others, especially those in need, is so difficult. I generally mention first, in a quite extensive way, that selfless love is difficult because we are not yet a fully mature person and have an abundance of needs ourselves; we need love and have difficulty, because of our needs, giving love to others.

As I speak about this condition in which we find ourselves, there is usually the mention of our childhood and the nature of human growth toward maturity and whether our early life was filled with a nurturing environment of love. All too often, we move into adulthood with many of our own needs yet unfilled, and almost always with a measure of pain, and therefore have difficulty loving others. My own needs may be too pronounced.

I also point out that our culture, current events, and conditions in the larger world in which we live are filled with false values, complex forces, negative cultural norms, and range of social problems that confuse us, limit our growth toward maturity, and invite many values and goals that have little or no love within them to guide us. Where we reside, from our home to the entire globe, there is a shortage of love. It is the nature of our world. We do not see love around us or experience it and find it very difficult to express genuine love in such a context.

As the questions and conversations continue, there is usually a trace of agreement that our living environment has not empowered us or influenced us to be a truly loving person. At this point, I frequently introduce these people to settings and conditions that have encouraged and guided people into a loving frame of reference. At times, even in settings that are not religious, I point to development psychology and the social sciences that explain our movement toward maturity and health and have

---

3. See the fine book by William C. Spahn, *Go and Do Likewise*, for a practical guide for finding the motivation and resources to become a more loving person. See as well the parable of the Good Samaritan (Luke 10:25–37).

the capacity to point us in a positive way to a life of care and concern. In a religious setting, I speak about the teaching of love and point to those who have been models of compassion. I mention the Buddha and the great saints of Hinduism. In the Christian setting, of course, I try to articulate how it is that we fill our lives with divine love, even as Jesus did. I have done some writing in this area of human behavior, treating Christian formation with great care and not inadvertently suggesting that love is all of a sudden easy because one becomes a Christian. I often turn to a few observations, including the following:

1. The New Testament tells the story of Jesus and how he is the finest expression of the life of love that our world has ever seen. I stress that Jesus put love first, even in the most trying of circumstances. When he was asked what was the greatest commandment, the answer was very clear, love God with your whole being and love your neighbor as you love yourself.

2. I note that he taught that the loving life involves opening one's heart and mind to presence of God, understanding that God is Love and the source of love.

3. I speak about how the New Testament describes the presence of God as the Holy Spirit, the very power and presence of God available to us. Love is really a gift to us from God or a natural fruit grown from the tree of love.

4. I then turn to nurturing this relationship with God. As we cultivate a relationship with God, we find that we are motivated to begin to engage in the many-sided character and actions of love. I stress that our linkage with God empowers us to move toward being one who truly loves. I note that it should shape our daily agenda; the practice of love must be present in all of my interactions with others.

5. I then help them find some settings in which to actually practice love, perhaps provide some counsel for those with particular problems and concerns, and invite these new disciples to share their feelings, their moments of love, and ways that were so difficult because love was not present. I help them find settings where love is genuinely present.

6. At the heart of these conversations is that love does have the dimension of feeling. Feeling love and the sensing the love, which another has for me, is life-giving. Yet it is more; it also action. Yes, it is

cultivated by prayer, meditation, study, and worship, *but it is a practice and an activity.* It is not just warm feelings for our family and friends; or going to church and other settings where love is present. We must learn how to love even when we don't feel very loveable or loving. Jesus did it for the person next to him on the cross.

COMPASSION IN PRACTICE[4]

I want to borrow from Frank Rogers's book and to paraphrase his practical suggestions for learning how to show authentic compassion. He begins with the model of Jesus and describes the love that Jesus offered to all whom he encountered; these descriptions become our invitation. I want to stress that it is a conscious decision to become a loving person, more than just behavior you sort of fall into with a good heart. We make a commitment; there is a radical shift from being ego-driven and self-oriented to becoming open to the presence of God and other-person oriented.

In addition, there is the very important insight that underlines that we must learn how to love ourselves if we expect to love others.[5] If we do not love ourselves, it will be difficult to not be preoccupied with our own needs and then unable to extend ourselves to others in authentic compassion. Our goal is to ease their suffering and promote their well-being, not to be focused on how to win their approval and affirmation. We must be free from preoccupation with our own needs and interests. It requires that we be empathetic (in their world of thoughts and feelings) in our exchanges with others. Frank Rogers uses the word *pulse* as starting point of love and suggests that each of the letter which spell the word points us in a loving direction. The word pulse suggests that love is an always a present attitude and spirit.

1. "P" stands for paying attention; we are there for the other, with deep feeling and full presence.
2. "U" is understanding empathically; we move to a full understanding of the other with compassion.

---

4. Frank Rogers, Jr. has written a fine and very practical book entitled *Compassion in Practice: The Way of Jesus* in which he suggests five practical steps to take in cultivating compassion, with a thoughtful introduction and an expression of hope that the miracle of compassion will become reality for us. He then has four suggested practices, getting the reader in tune with the flow of compassion.

5. Rogers, *Compassion in Practice*, 80–84.

3. "L" is loving with genuine connection; we are authentic, listen carefully, and speak the truth in love.
4. "S" is seeing the sacredness of loving encounter; we honor the person as one created in the image of God.
5. "E" is embodying new loving behavior.[6] We understand and have the appropriate response to the one who is suffering.

When all is said and done, the bottom line is that we are empowered by God's Spirit to love and demonstrate compassion as Jesus did, to heal, help, restore, and make whole those whom we encounter in a consistent and long-lasting way.

It is in the evening of life that we will be judged by love alone. It is in the evening of life that we have the maturity, the skills, the time, and the opportunities to love others. It will be the most rewarding experience of our lives as the darkness begins to fall. With deep gratitude and peace, we become loving and move toward Love.

Our final commandment is to repeat what Jesus said about Love. "This is my commandment, that you love one another as I have loved you" (John 15:10).

Terms, Resources, and Discussion Questions

Terms

1. Golden Rule: The statement of Jesus that reads: "In everything do to others as you would have them do to you."
2. Law and the Prophets: In the time of Jesus, this term essentially meant the Hebrew Bible in the form that his contemporaries understood it. We sometimes use the title, Old Testament, a term many understand, but not widely used by Jewish people in that it is prior to the New Testament, but not old in the sense of being replaced. It is their Bible.
3. More excellent way: A term used by the apostle Paul in his first letter to the Corinthians that points them to the life of love. It is Paul's way of saying not to get bogged down in petty conflicts or details of belief, but follow the way of Jesus which is love.

---

6. Rogers, *Compassion in Practice*, 37.

4. Preeminence: A word that describes how Paul says that love is greater than other values and gifts, even faith and hope (1 Cor 13:13).

5. Greatest Commandment: Jesus is asked by a well-meaning and sincere person the question: What is the greatest commandment? Jesus replies that it is to love God with one's whole being and one's neighbor as oneself.

Books to Read and Consult

1. Dale C. Allison, *Night Comes: Death, Imagination, and the Last Things*
2. Katy Butler, *The Art of Dying Well: A Practical Guide to a God End of Life*
3. Andrew M. Greely and Mary G. Durkin, *The Book of Love: A Treasury Inspired by the Greatest of Virtues*
4. Frank Rogers, Jr., *The Way of Jesus: Compassion in Practice*
5. William C. Spohn, *Go and Do Likewise: Jesus and Ethics*

Discussion Questions

1. The concepts of Love and Law are addressed in the Bible. Which one should take priority and how are they related?
2. Do you think that self-love is necessary to be a person who has the capacity to love others?
3. Do you agree with the apostle Paul that love is our greatest virtue and that it should have preeminence over great literature, superb teaching, prophetic actions, and should be the foundation of these other activities?
4. Does love ever involve anger and bold action to stop behavior that you don't approve of? Is it possible to be angry and loving at the same time?
5. There are several different kinds of love, and several different words that describe loving behavior. What are some of these words and concepts, and how to do they differ in tone or emphasis with the word love?

Bibliography

Achtemeier, Paul J., ed. *Harper's Bible Dictionary.* New York: Harper & Row, 1985.
Adyashanti. *Jesus: Embodying the Spirit of a Revolutionary Mystic.* Boulder, CO: Sounds True, 2014.
Allison Jr., Dale C. *Constructing Jesus: Memory, Imagination, and History.* Grand Rapids, MI: Baker Academic, 2010.
———. *Night Comes: Death, Imagination, and the Last Things.* Grand Rapids, MI: Eerdmans, 2016.
Anderson, Megory. *Sacred Dying: Creating Rituals for Embracing the End of Life.* Berkeley, CA: De Capo, 2003.
Bailey, Kenneth E. *Jesus Through Middle Eastern Eyes: Cultural Studies in the Gospels.* Downers Grove, IL: InterVarsity, 1971.
Baer, Greg. *Real Love: The Truth about Finding Unconditional Love and Fulfilling Relationships.* New York: Gotham, 2003.
Bass, Diana Butler. *Christianity After Religion.* New York: HarperOne, 2012.
Berry, Thomas. *The Dream of the Earth.* San Francisco: Sierra Club: 1988.
Borg, Marcus. *Jesus: Uncovering the Life, Teachings, and Relevance of a Religious Revolutionary.* San Francisco, CA: Harper, 2006.
———. *The God We Never Knew: Beyond Dogmatic Religions to a More Authentic Contemporary Faith.* New York: HarperCollins, 2007.
Borg, Marcus and Crossan, John Dominic. *The Last Week: A Day-by-Day Account of Jesus's Final Week in Jerusalem.* San Francisco, CA: HarperSanFrancisco, 2006.
Bornkamm, Günther. *Jesus of Nazareth.* New York: Harper & Row, 1956.
Bourgeault, Cynthia. *The Wisdom Jesus.* Boston: Shambhala, 2008.
Brown, Brené. *Daring Greatly: How the Courage to Be Vulnerable Transforms the Way We Live, Love, Parent, and Lead.* New York: Penguin Random House, 2012.
Butler, Katy. *The Art of Dying Well.* New York: Scribner, 2019.
Carmody, Denise Lardner, and John Tully. *Mysticism: Holiness East and West.* New York: Oxford University Press, 1996.
Chapman, Gary. *The Five Love Languages.* Chicago: Northfield Publishing, 2014.
Chittister, Joan. *The Gift of Years: Growing Older Gracefully.* Katonah, NY: BlueBridge, 2008.
Chödrön, Pema. *No Time to Lose: A Timely Guide to the Way of the Bodhisattva.* Boston, Shambhala, 2015
Christopher, David. *The Holy Universe: A New Story of Creation for the Heart, Soul, and Spirit.* Santa Rosa, CA: New Story, 1981.
Corn, David. *American Psychosis: A historical Investigation of How the Republican Party Went Crazy.* New York, NY: Twelve, 2022.

Crossan, John Dominic and Reed, Jonathan L. *In Search of Paul: How Jesus's Apostle Opposed Rome's Empire with God's Kingdom.* San Francisco, CA: HarperSanFrancisco, 2004.

———. *Jesus: A Revolutionary Biography.* San Francisco: CA: HarperSanFrancisco, 1994.

Cousins, Ewert H., ed. *Hope and the Future of Man (Humanity).* Fortress, Minneapolis, MN: 1972.

Delio, Ilia. *Making All Things New: Catholicity, Cosmology, Consciousness.* Maryknoll, NY: Orbis, 2015.

———. *The Unbearable Wholeness of Being: God, Evolution, and the Power of Love.* Maryknoll, NY: Orbis, 2013.

De Rougemont, Denis. *Love in the Western World.* Princeton, NJ: Princeton University Press, 1940.

Desmond, Matthew. *Evicted.* New York: Crown, 2016.

———. *Poverty by America,* New York: Crown, 2023.

Echegaray, Hugo, *The Practice of Jesus,* Maryknoll, New York: Orbis, 1984.

Ehrman, Bart D. *Jesus: Apocalyptic Prophet of the New Millennium.* New York, Oxford University Press, 1999.

Erickson, Erik H. *The Life Cycle Completed.* New York, W. W. Norton, 1997.

Ferguson, Duncan S. *Mindful Spirituality: The Intentional Cultivation of the Spiritual Life, A Book of Daily Readings.* Eugene, OR: Wipf & Stock, 2018.

———. *The Radical Teaching of Jesus: A Teacher Full of Grace and Truth.* Eugene, OR: Wipf & Stock, 2016.

———. *The Radical Invitation of Jesus: How Accepting the Invitation of Jesus Can Lead to a Living Faith and Fulfilling Life for Today.* Eugene, OR: Wipf & Stock, 2019.

———. *Lovescapes: Mapping the Geography of Love: An Invitation to the Love-Centered Life.* Eugene, OR: Cascade, 2012.

———. "How Then Shall We Live as a People of Faith in a World in Crisis?" *Theology Today* 80 (2023) 18–28.

Fowler, James W. *Stages of Faith: The Psychology of Human Development and the Quest for Meaning.* San Francisco, CA: Harper & Row, 1981.

———. *Becoming Adult, Becoming Christian: Adult Development and Christian Faith.* San Francisco, CA: Harper & Row, 1984.

Fox, Matthew. *One River, Many Wells.* New York: Penguin/Putman, 2000.

Goldstein, Joseph. *Mindfulness: A Practical Guide to Awakening.* Boulder, CO: Sounds True, 2013.

Greely, Andrew M. and Durkin, Mary G. *The Book of Love: A Treasury Inspired by the Greatest Virtues.* New York: Forge, 2002.

Hart, David Bentley. *The Experience of God: Being, Consciousness, Bliss.* New Haven: Yale University Press, 2013.

Horsely, Richard. *The Prophet Jesus and the Renewal of Israel.* Grand Rapids, MI: Eerdmans, 2012.

———. *Jesus and the Politics of Roman Palestine.* Columbia, SC: The University of South Carolina Press, 2014.

Johnson, Steven. *Emergence: The Connected Lives of Ants, Brains, Cities, and Software.* New York: Sobor, 2002.

Julian of Norwich. *Revelations of Divine Love.* Translated by Mirabai Starr. Charlottesville, VA: Hampton Roads, 2022.

Julian of Norwich. *Showings.* Translated and edited by Edmund Colledge and James Walsh. *The Classics of Western Spirituality.* New York: Paulist, 1978.
Keating, Thomas. *Open Mind, Open Heart.* 20th anniversary edition. New York: Continuum, 2006.
Kornfield, Jack. *The Wise Heart: A Guide to the Universal Teachings of Buddhist Psychology.* New York: Bantam, 2008.
Küng, Hans. translated by Edward Quinn. *On Being a Christian,* Garden City, New York: Doubleday & Company, 1976.
Levison, John R. *Filled with the Spirit.* Grand Rapids, MI: Eerdmans, 2009.
Lewis, Thomas, Cemeni, Fari, and Lannon, Dan. *A General Theory of Love.* New York: Random House, 2000.
Macquarrie, John. *Christian Hope.* New York: Seabury, 1978.
Macy, Joanna and Johnstone, Chris. *Active Hope: How to Face the Mess We're in with Unexpected Resilience & Creative Power.* Revised Edition. Navato, CA: New World Library, 2012.
Mafi, Maryam, trans. *Rumi Day by Day.* Charlottesville, VA: Hampton Roads, 2014.
May, Gerald G. *The Awakened Heart: Opening Yourself to the Love You Need.* San Francisco: HarperSanFrancisco, 1991.
McLaren, Brian D. *A New Kind of Christianity.* New York: HarperOne, 2010.
McLaren, Karla. *The Art of Empathy: A Complete Guide to Life's Most Essential Skill.* Boulder, Colorado: 2013.
Meier, John P. *A Marginal Jew: Rethinking the Historical Jesus.* 4 vols. New York: Doubleday, 1991–2001.
Merriam-Webster's Collegiate Dictionary. 11th ed. Springfield, MA: Merriam-Webster, 2003. Continually updated at https://www.merriam-webster.com/.
Miller, Jack. *God: A Biography.* New York: Vintage, 1995.
Moltmann, Jürgen. *The Way of Jesus Christ.* Minneapolis, MN: Fortress 1993.
——. *Theology of Hope.* New York: Harper & Row, 1967.
Moore, Thomas. *The Soul's Religion: Cultivating a Profoundly Spiritual Life.* New York: HarperCollins, 2002.
Murphy, Frederick J. *The Religious World of Jesus: An Introduction to Second Temple Judaism.* Nashville: Abingdon, 1991.
Nygren, Anders. *Agape and Eros.* London: S.P.C.K., 1953.
Oliver, Mary. *American Primitive.* Boston: Back Bay, 1953.
——. *Devotions: The Selected Poems oof Mary Oliver.* New York: Penguin, 2017.
Oswald, Roy M. and Jacobson, Arland. *The Emotional Intelligence of Jesus.* New York: Rowman & Littlefield, 2015.
Pelikan, Jaroslav. *Jesus Through the Centuries: His Place in the History of Culture.* New Haven: Yale University Press, 1985.
Post, Stephen G. *Unlimited Love: Altruism, Compassion, and Service.* Philadelphia, PA: Templeton Foundation, 2003.
Pui-Lan, Zwok. *Postcolonial Politics and Theology: Unraveling Empire for a Global Word.* Louisville, KY: Westminster John Knox, 2021.
Rogers, Frank, Jr. *Compassion in Practice: The Way of Jesus.* Nashville, TN: Upper Room, 2016.
Rohr, Richard. *Falling Upward.* San Francisco, CA: Jossey Bass, 2013.
Rolheiser, Ronald. *Sacred Fire: A Vision for a Deeper Human and Christian Maturity.* New York, NY: Image, 2014.

———. *The Holy Longing: The Search for Christian Spirituality*. New York: Doubleday, 1999.

Runzo, Joseph & Martin, Nancy M. *Ethics in the World Religions*. Oxford, UK: One World, 2001.

Sandel, Michael J. *Justice: What's The Right Thing To Do*. New York: Farrar, Straus and Giroux, 2009.

Sanders, E. P. *Jesus and Judaism*. Philadelphia: Fortress, 1985.

Satir, Virginia. *People Making*. Palo Alto, CA: Science and Behavior, 1972.

Schweitzer, Albert. *The Quest of the Historical Jesus*. New York: The MacMillan Company, 1948.

Singer, Irving. *The Nature of Love*, 3 vols. *Plato to Luther, Courtly and Romantic, The Modern World*. Chicago: University of Chicago Press, 1987.

Smith, Huston. *The Soul Of Christianity*. San Francisco, CA: HarperSanFrancisco, 2005.

Smith, Susan Marie. *Caring Liturgies: The Pastoral Power of Christian Ritual*. Minneapolis: Fortress, 1999.

Spahn, William C. *Go and Do Likewise: Jesus and Ethics*. New York: Continuum, 2000.

Swinburne, Richard. *The Coherence of Theism*. Second Edition. Oxford, UK: Oxford University Press, 1993.

Taylor, Joan, and Hay, David M. *Philo of Alexandria "On the Contemplative Life": Introduction, Translation, and Commentary*. Leiden: Brill, 2020.

Thich Nhat Hanh. *The Heart of Buddha's Teaching*. New York: Broadway, 1988.

———. *Creating True Peace: Ending Violence in Yourself, Your Family, Your Community, and the World*. New York: Atria, 2003.

Thurman, Howard. *Meditations of the Heart*. New York: Harper & Row, 1953.

Tillich, Paul. *The Courage to Be*. New Haven: Yale University Press, 1952.

Underhill, Evelyn. *A Study in the Nature and Development of Spiritual Consciousness*. New York: Noonday, 1955.

Watt, Tessa. *Mindfulness: A Practical Guide*. New York: MJF, 2012.

Wilbur, Ken. *The Religion of Tomorrow: A Vision for the Future of the Great Traditions*. Boulder, CO: Shambhala, 2017.

Wright, N. T. *Jesus and the Victory of God*. Minneapolis, MN: Fortress, 1996.

www.ingramcontent.com/pod-product-compliance
Lightning Source LLC
Chambersburg PA
CBHW070317230426
43663CB00011B/2167